DeRosa Research and Trading, Inc.

# Central Banking and Monetary Policy in Emerging-Markets Nations

RESEARCH FOUNDATION

OF CFA INSTITUTE

## Statement of Purpose

The Research Foundation of CFA Institute is a
not-for-profit organization established to promote
the development and dissemination of relevant
research for investment practitioners worldwide.

ISBN 978-1-934667-23-1

19 March 2009

### Editorial Staff

Maryann Dupes
Book Editor

Cathy Gentry                          Cindy Maisannes
Assistant Editor        Publishing Technology Specialist

Lois Carrier
Production Specialist

# Biography

**David DeRosa** is the president and founder of DeRosa Research and Trading, Inc., a firm that does consulting and research on international capital markets. Previously, he worked at a variety of New York financial institutions in the capacity of portfolio manager, foreign exchange trader, and hedge fund manager.

Dr. DeRosa is on the boards of several major hedge fund groups. He has taught graduate level courses in international capital markets, derivatives, and corporate finance at the Yale School of Management (since 1996). He has also taught at the University of Chicago and Columbia University.

He received his PhD in finance and economics from the Graduate School of Business of the University of Chicago and his AB in economics from the College of the University of Chicago.

# Contents

This publication qualifies for 5 CE credits under the guidelines
of the CFA Institute Continuing Education Program.

# Foreword

"If you don't believe in central banking, you should move to the moon," joked one of my professors, the distinguished University of Chicago economist Robert Aliber, 30 years ago.

As a student, I had come under the influence of radical free-marketers who thought that the market, not the government, should determine what money is. If the market thought that cowrie shells were money, then they were money, likewise with bank notes, gold coins, or anything else that people agreed to accept as a medium of exchange and store of value. And I had challenged Professor Aliber to explain why, in his view, governments, rather than private individuals, should make this determination. He did so, of course, with the panache and wit for which he was then, and still is, well known.

In the present volume, one of Aliber's students, David DeRosa, who received his PhD from the University of Chicago and is now an adjunct professor at the Yale School of Management as well as the proprietor of a firm that does research on currencies and global financial markets, builds exuberantly on this theme. Although all countries need sound central banking and an effective monetary policy, DeRosa sensibly argues that it is in emerging-markets nations that this problem is most sharply brought into focus. Emerging-markets nations have suffered the most from periodic financial crises, hyperinflations, and sharp currency devaluations and thus need the most help. But recent events have shown that developed countries are not immune to these diseases.

DeRosa defines emerging markets as countries that are less productive economically than developed countries but that are nonetheless on the path to significant and sustainable growth. They are also "investable," meaning they have open capital markets to a greater or lesser extent. He argues that, to achieve their economic ambitions, they need to learn how to properly operate a central bank. This book is DeRosa's primer on central banks and monetary policy, with special emphasis on the emerging-markets nations.

The book begins with a review of monetary theory and modern monetary policy regimes, including inflation targeting and the Taylor rule. Next, DeRosa describes emerging markets as natural "open" economies, ones upon which trade and capital flows have a profound influence. Here, he introduces Robert Mundell's concepts of perfect capital mobility and the much heralded impossible trinity theorem. He then turns to a practical description of the workings of the foreign exchange market and its odd practices and terminology. (Having worked as a bank foreign exchange trader, DeRosa knows this market closely.)

The core of the book addresses the interdependence of foreign exchange regimes and monetary policy. These topics occupy three successive chapters. The first in this group describes foreign exchange regimes and the many expedients—managed floats, crawling pegs, target zones, and so forth—used by countries to avoid the perceived disadvantages of either freely floating or completely fixed exchange rates; DeRosa notes that these expedients have mostly disappeared. Arguably, the most innovative chapter is the one titled "The Paradox of International Capital." International flows of capital are of constant concern to central banks. Some economists regard capital flows as an essential ingredient for economic development, whereas others regard them as dangerous nuisances. Using his neoclassical framework to analyze capital flows, DeRosa argues that they are economically motivated and as such are neither capricious nor undesirable. Furthermore, he believes that concerns about the danger of global imbalances are exaggerated. The subsequent chapter is a review of the fundamental central banking functions, including topics of foreign exchange intervention, sterilization, and capital controls.

DeRosa concludes with a policy recommendation, namely, that emerging-markets nations seek a "minimalist" central bank: They should not be afraid of floating exchange rates, and they should be circumspect in their monetary policy initiatives. One way to conduct monetary policy is to use inflation targeting; another is to apply the Taylor rule. As for exchange rates, DeRosa argues that they are prices and, like other prices, should not be fettered without serious thought to the potential consequences.

Although this is primarily a book about the economics of central banking, DeRosa has embedded his neoclassical conviction that markets generally "work"—that is, they arrive at close to optimal outcomes. And when markets appear not to work, the solution is not necessarily to regulate or impede markets but, instead, to ask what factors caused a given market to fail and to mitigate those factors.

An inquiry into optimal central banking and monetary arrangements is poignantly timely. Since DeRosa finished writing this book, a financial crisis of almost unprecedented proportions has threatened to send the world into recession or depression. In response, the United States has, for the first time in its history, adopted what amounts to a zero interest rate monetary policy in an attempt to increase the availability of credit, motivate investors to take risk, and stimulate the real economy. Its central bank, the Federal Reserve System, has also radically expanded its balance sheet by buying—with "good funds," that is, federal funds that are acceptable to everyone—privately held assets of questionable value. In conversations since the book was written, DeRosa has said he believes that preventing a domino-style collapse of the banking system was a highly desirable measure. But he thinks that is as far as the initiative should go. He questions whether massive, taxpayer-funded bailouts of economically distressed industries make sense.

Although the parallels between emerging-market and rich-country financial crises are not exact, this book will stimulate the reader to think about why the central bank's actions in the United States and other developed countries were undertaken and what they are likely to accomplish. If we listen to DeRosa, we will be concerned because, as he demonstrates, central bank "heroics" (one of his terms) are rarely successful. He has shown this for the emerging markets—hence his recommendation of a "minimalist" central bank in such markets. The current crisis will test the extent to which his ideas extend to the developed world's central banks as well.

We are exceptionally pleased to present this challenging and charming book.

Laurence B. Siegel
*Research Director*
*Research Foundation of CFA Institute*

# Preface

This book is an outgrowth of a series of courses I have taught at the Yale School of Management on international finance, foreign exchange, and central banking in emerging-markets nations. When the Research Foundation of CFA Institute approached me about writing a book, I at first saw an opportunity to turn an enhanced version of my teaching materials into a published manuscript. But as I got into the project, the book began to take on a life of its own. In the end, what I have to offer the reader is a blend of economic history (especially of the emerging-markets central banks), explanations of relevant economic and financial thought (theoretical and empirical), and normative issues on running a central bank in terms of goals and practices.

Over the years, I have had illuminating discussions about the topics in this book with many friends and teachers, including, but not limited to, Robert Aliber, Milton Friedman, Anna Schwartz, Arnold Harberger, and Alan Stockman. Also, I wish to thank Steve Hanke, Bernie Munk, John Greenwood, and Desmond Lachman for helpful discourse.

I thank the Research Foundation of CFA Institute for its support. I extend special thanks to Laurence Siegel, the very able research director of the foundation. He has done yeoman's work in serving as an intellectual and literary editor. I am responsible for any errors.

DFD 2008

# Dedication

For Sibylle.

# 1. Emerging Markets and Their Central Banks

Before beginning an examination of central banking and monetary policy in emerging-markets nations, it pays to ask what is meant by an emerging market. The distinguished University of Chicago political economist Marvin Zonis divides the world into 40 developed or "first world" countries, 80 emerging markets, and 80 failed states. These sum to 200 countries, so Zonis is obviously counting a large number of small states and microstates; for example, Iceland, Luxembourg, and Bermuda fall into the developed country category but are too small to have any capital markets to speak of. Zonis' categorization is useful, however, in getting the ratios right and in making a clear distinction between, on the one hand, truly emerging markets and, on the other hand, failed states that have little hope of emerging as players in the global economy any time soon.

For the purposes here, an emerging-markets nation is one that is poorer than those in the developed world but that has capital markets (stock and bond markets) accessible to international investors. I also define an emerging market as one that is not just a less developed country but one that has adopted the institutional, legal, and financial structures that put it on at least a potential path to becoming a more developed country over time.

A more formal definition of an emerging-markets nation follows:

- The country has become a platform for sustainable economic growth. And as described by the International Monetary Fund (IMF), it has "undertaken economic development and reform programs and [has] begun to 'emerge' as [a] significant player . . . in the global economy."[1]

- It is sufficiently open to the global economy that it can freely accommodate international trade and, at the same time, allow international investors to have access to its bond and stock markets as well as the ability to make foreign direct investment.[2]

From an investment standpoint, emerging markets are those included in one or more emerging-markets equity or bond benchmarks. Among the largest emerging equity markets are Brazil, Russia, India, and China (the BRICs) as well as Mexico, South Africa, South Korea, Taiwan, Thailand, and Indonesia. My definition of

---

[1]"Emerging Markets," International Monetary Fund, website dated 19 October 2007, www.imf.org/external/np/exr/key/emkts.htm.

[2]Foreign direct investment is the acquisition of real economic assets, such as factories and real estate, as contrasted to equities or bonds, by foreigners.

emerging markets includes the 58 developing countries that Standard & Poor's puts in its various emerging equity market benchmarks, as shown in **Table 1.1**. To this number, I add 10 countries that are in one or more of J.P. Morgan's emerging-markets debt benchmarks but that are not in any of the S&P equity benchmarks. The total number of emerging-markets nations for the purpose of this discussion is thus 68. Table 1.1 also shows the major developed countries for comparison and gives per capita GDP data for both developed and emerging markets.

Note that per capita income varies greatly across the group. Most of these countries are "low to middle per capita income" as defined by the IMF; a few, such as South Korea, Israel, and Taiwan, are high income but do not meet index providers' liquidity, transparency, or other criteria for inclusion in developed-markets indices. GDP per capita is measured two ways so that the numbers can be compared across countries. One way is to convert GDP to a base, such as the U.S. dollar, using market exchange rates. The second way is convert GDP per capita using a purchasing power parity (PPP) exchange rate; the argument here is that a dollar goes further in an emerging or developing country.[3] Both measures are important, but PPP exchange rates are preferred for comparing living standards among countries.

Inclusion in an index means a country's securities are investable components of the world's portfolio wealth. Being in such an index is much more than a trophy; a large fraction of institutional investment is indexed, and most of the remainder is managed by taking active bets relative to an index, so the countries fortunate enough to be included in well-known indices receive automatic attention from investors as a consequence.

A market is called "emerging" because it is believed to be on track to a brighter economic future. Part of preparing for that future is developing the expertise to run one's own central bank. I am not prepared to state that all developing countries ought to have central banks, just the ones that are truly worthy of the term "emerging."

Also, an emerging-markets country is one that is developed to the point of attracting international investment in its bonds and equity shares. An understanding of central banking in emerging-markets nations is essential to assessing the attractiveness of either bonds or equities in a given country. Because international investors need to be able to repatriate their funds (that is, get their money back) if they are going to invest in the first place, a key issue in emerging-markets central banking is the openness of a country to movements of foreign capital. A country may first achieve emerging-markets status when its government issues international bonds, meaning bonds that are denominated in one of the world currencies (the U.S. dollar, euro, yen, and a few others) and traded on world markets.

---

[3] See Callen (2007) for a comparison of the two methods.

**Table 1.1. Per Capita GDP Data for Emerging-Markets and Developed Nations**

(data as of 2007 in U.S. dollars)

| Country | GDP per Capita at Market Exchange Rate | GDP per Capita at PPP Exchange Rate |
|---|---|---|
| **Emerging-markets nations** | | |
| *Countries in the S&P/IFC investable index* | | |
| Argentina | 6,492 | 13,300 |
| Brazil | 6,776 | 9,700 |
| Chile | 10,047 | 13,900 |
| China | 2,459 | 5,300 |
| Czech Republic | 17,138 | 24,200 |
| Egypt | 1,592 | 5,500 |
| Hungary | 13,901 | 19,000 |
| India | 973 | 2,700 |
| Indonesia | 1,845 | 3,700 |
| Israel | 23,161 | 25,800 |
| Mexico | 8,219 | 12,800 |
| Morocco | 2,171 | 4,100 |
| Malaysia | 7,509 | 13,300 |
| Pakistan | 849 | 2,600 |
| Peru | 3,787 | 7,800 |
| Philippines | 1,530 | 3,400 |
| Poland | 10,912 | 16,300 |
| Russia | 9,096 | 14,700 |
| South Africa | 5,843 | 9,800 |
| South Korea | 19,836 | 24,800 |
| Taiwan | 16,768 | 30,100 |
| Thailand | 3,776 | 7,900 |
| Turkey | 9,323 | 12,900 |
| *Countries in the S&P/IFC global index but not in the S&P/IFC investable index* | | |
| Bahrain | 27,746 | 32,100 |
| Colombia | 3,867 | 6,700 |
| Jordan | 2,645 | 4,900 |
| Kuwait | 44,421 | 39,300 |
| Nigeria | 1,164 | 2,000 |
| Oman | 12,492 | 24,000 |
| Qatar | 83,152 | 80,900 |

*(continued)*

**Table 1.1. Per Capita GDP Data for Emerging-Markets and Developed Nations**

(data as of 2007 in U.S. dollars) (continued)

| Country | GDP per Capita at Market Exchange Rate | GDP per Capita at PPP Exchange Rate |
|---|---|---|
| Saudi Arabia | 13,630 | 23,200 |
| Sri Lanka | 1,434 | 4,100 |
| United Arab Emirates | 43,339 | 37,300 |
| Zimbabwe | 151 | 200 |
| *Countries in the S&P frontier–markets index* | | |
| Bangladesh | 481 | 1,300 |
| Botswana | 6,780 | 16,400 |
| Bulgaria | 5,409 | 11,300 |
| Cote d'Ivoire | 993 | 1,700 |
| Croatia | 11,430 | 15,500 |
| Ecuador | 3,212 | 7,200 |
| Estonia | 16,171 | 21,100 |
| Ghana | 648 | 1,400 |
| Jamaica | 4,029 | 7,700 |
| Kazakhstan | 6,791 | 11,100 |
| Kenya | 794 | 1,700 |
| Latvia | 12,098 | 17,400 |
| Lebanon | 6,277 | 11,300 |
| Lithuania | 10,726 | 17,700 |
| Mauritius | 5,506 | 11,200 |
| Namibia | 3,577 | 5,200 |
| Panama | 6,058 | 10,300 |
| Romania | 7,452 | 11,400 |
| Slovak Republic | 13,766 | 20,300 |
| Slovenia | 22,934 | 27,200 |
| Trinidad and Tobago | 19,591 | 18,300 |
| Tunisia | 3,405 | 7,500 |
| Ukraine | 3,035 | 6,900 |
| Vietnam | 821 | 2,600 |

(continued)

**Table 1.1. Per Capita GDP Data for Emerging-Markets and Developed Nations**

(data as of 2007 in U.S. dollars) (continued)

| Country | GDP per Capita at Market Exchange Rate | GDP per Capita at PPP Exchange Rate |
|---|---|---|
| *Countries in one or more J.P. Morgan emerging market debt index but not in any S&P equity index* | | |
| Belize | 4,324 | 7,900 |
| Dominican Republic | 3,886 | 7,000 |
| El Salvador | 2,932 | 5,800 |
| Gabon | 7,759 | 14,100 |
| Georgia | 2,215 | 4,700 |
| Iraq | 2,016 | 3,600 |
| Macau | na | 28,400 |
| Serbia | 4,106 | 10,400 |
| Uruguay | 6,632 | 11,600 |
| Venezuela | 9,084 | 12,200 |
| **Developed-Markets Nations** | | |
| Australia | 43,798 | 36,300 |
| Austria | 45,599 | 38,400 |
| Belgium | 43,648 | 35,300 |
| Canada | 43,478 | 38,400 |
| Denmark | 57,040 | 37,400 |
| Finland | 46,769 | 35,300 |
| France | 40,200 | 33,200 |
| Germany | 40,315 | 34,200 |
| Greece | 29,385 | 29,200 |
| Hong Kong | 29,611 | 42,000 |
| Ireland | 62,934 | 43,100 |
| Italy | 36,201 | 30,400 |
| Japan | 34,402 | 33,600 |
| Netherlands | 46,389 | 38,500 |
| New Zealand | 30,999 | 26,400 |
| Norway | 84,595 | 53,000 |
| Portugal | 20,981 | 21,700 |
| Singapore | 35,427 | 49,700 |
| Spain | 35,576 | 30,100 |

(continued)

**Table 1.1. Per Capita GDP Data for Emerging-Markets and Developed Nations**

(data as of 2007 in U.S dollars) (continued)

| Country | GDP per Capita at Market Exchange Rate | GDP per Capita at PPP Exchange Rate |
|---|---|---|
| Sweden | 50,415 | 36,500 |
| Switzerland | 56,111 | 41,100 |
| United Kingdom | 45,626 | 35,100 |
| United States | 45,959 | 45,800 |

*Notes*: Macau became a Special Administrative Region (SAR) of China on 20 December 1999 under a "one country, two systems" agreement resembling that which applies to Hong Kong. Macau's bonds still trade independently. Iraq and Venezuela are examples of countries that meet my technical definition of emerging markets (they are in one of the specified benchmarks) but that are not currently emerging in an economic sense. Of course, the circumstances in these countries may change in the future.

*Sources*: S&P equity index information: www2.standardandpoors.com/spf/pdf/index/SP_Emerging_Market_Indices_Factsheet.pdf, accessed on 25 August 2008. JP Morgan bond index information: *Emerging Markets Bond Index Monitor*, J.P. Morgan Securities Inc., 30 June 2008. Market GDP information: http://en.wikipedia.org/wiki/List_of_countries_by_GDP_(nominal)_per_capita, column titled "CIA," accessed on 25 August 2008. PPP GDP information: http://en.wikipedia.org/wiki/List_of_countries_by_GDP_(PPP)_per_capita, column titled "CIA," accessed on 25 August 2008.

---

Aside from the fact that the emerging markets are less rich, in terms of per capita income,[4] than the developed world, in what other ways are they different?[5] Consider some aspects of why running a central bank might be more difficult in an emerging-market country.

▪ *Many emerging markets are greatly dependent on commodity exports.* The job of the central bank does not extend to stabilization of commodity prices. Strictly speaking, a movement in a commodity price is a relative price change, not an absolute price (or price level) change. That being the case, commodity price changes are outside the normal purview of a central bank. Consider, however, the case of an emerging-markets country that is vitally dependent on a single commodity export.

---

[4]The emerging markets are doing well relative to the nonemerging, nondeveloped countries. Consider that the IMF World Economic Outlook database has per capita GDP data (current prices in U.S. dollars, converted at market exchange rates) for 181 countries; 54 of the countries in the sample have a per capita GDP less than $1,000 per year.

[5]Calvo and Mishkin (2003) listed three fundamental institutional differences that set apart emerging markets: (1) weak fiscal, financial, and monetary institutions; (2) currency substitution and liability dollarization; and (3) vulnerability to sudden stops (of capital inflows).

If the price of its export commodity were to fall substantially, income would be adversely affected. The price drop might also cause outward capital flows (because of diminished investment opportunities) plus possible depreciation in the currency. In these ways, a movement in a commodity price might rapidly become a central bank issue, and a complicated one at that.

▓ *Few emerging-markets countries are well-diversified industrial economies; indeed, many have two-tier economies, one a fully documented market segment that forms part of the world economy and the other a local segment that functions outside the documented and taxed economy (i.e., a large gray or black market), and in some countries, the latter constitutes a sizable portion of the population and income.* Unquestionably, the existence of an underground economy is an impediment to the effectiveness of monetary policy. Still, monetary policy would affect this segment, just at a slower rate and in a less precise manner. But the problems caused by a large underground economy go far deeper than anything a central bank can solve.

▓ *Many emerging-markets countries have—or have had—large, and possibly out-of-control, fiscal deficits.* Here I can make an important demarcation in authority: Central banks are supposed to manage monetary policy; treasuries tax, spend, and borrow in the name of the government. The two institutions and their functions ought to be kept strictly separate. The danger is that too cozy of a relationship will end with the central bank absorbing, meaning monetizing, the debts of the treasury, possibly on demand. This sort of situation can completely undermine public confidence in the central bank and the currency.

▓ *Many emerging-markets nations have experienced extreme macroeconomic dislocations in the past—such as hyperinflation, currency crises, and economic collapse.* I believe that a properly run central bank can preclude the reoccurrence of these economic disasters. Indeed, that is, in large part, the purpose of this book.

▓ *Many emerging-markets countries have immature financial sectors and fragile banking systems.* Immaturity of the financial sector makes transmission of monetary policy difficult. Fragility of the banking system could circumscribe the policy options open to a central bank.

▓ *Some emerging-markets countries do not have truly independent central banks.* If the entire logic of this book is correct, emerging markets benefit from having independently operated central banks. "Independent" means that the central bank is not susceptible to political pressure from other parts of the government.

▓ *Emerging-markets countries have a pronounced vulnerability to the ebb and flow of international capital.* This issue touches on one of the most controversial areas of this field. Many economists now believe that smaller countries are at risk from the flow of foreign capital, both into and out of their borders. Some individuals hold the view that capital flows are external economic forces relative to the emerging and developing worlds. Emerging-markets countries are seen alternatively as the beneficiaries and victims of capital flows. The concern is that these countries may be neither the cause nor the master of capital flows that can rock their economies. They may be what the economist Guillermo Calvo calls an "external shock." A related idea is that the emerging markets, and maybe all countries for that matter, are at risk from so-called global imbalances. Mainly, these discussions are about the stunningly large current U.S. account deficit. These topics are discussed at length in Chapter 6.

All these factors point to the idea that central banking and monetary policy in emerging-markets countries are even more challenging than they are in developed countries.

## Should Emerging-Markets Nations Have Central Banks?

The central bank is the country's principal monetary authority. Central banks are integral parts of every modern economy. They have enormous economic power; they can foster growth; but they can also create economic disasters. They are responsible for conducting monetary policy in a manner so as to achieve their country's established macroeconomic goals, which may include ensuring internal price stability, full employment, and exchange rate objectives.

Central banks have the unique power to create the monetary base (which directly affects the money supply), conduct other aspects of monetary policy, influence exchange rates, control inflation (i.e., stabilize the purchasing power of money), and act as the guardians of public trust in the financial system and faith in the national currency. Central banks may also regulate and police the banking sector, and they can act as the lender of last resort, but these activities are outside the scope of this book.

So much then for the positive—what about the negative? Central banks can create inflation and even hyperinflation (which destroys the value of the national currency). They can turn a recession into a depression, spark a currency crisis, ruin the stock market, destroy the banking system, and otherwise derail a perfectly good emerging-markets success story. Because many emerging-markets nations are economically fragile, there is little margin for central banking policy errors.

The number of new central banks increased greatly in the second half of the 20th century. By one count, the number of central banks exceeded 170 by the year 2000 (see **Box 1.1**). Is it really necessary to have so many central banks? Does every country need to have a central bank?

Critics say the evidence clearly shows that emerging-markets central banks have done relatively poor jobs for their countries. Indeed, the history of many emerging-markets countries is one of repeating boom-to-bust cycles completed with episodes of hyperinflation and currency crises. Certainly, there were periods of prosperity and economic expansion, but these seem to always have ended in economic disasters.

## Box 1.1.  How Many Central Banks Exist?

At the same time that the world was learning how to live with flexible exchange rates, the number of developing countries was exploding. Some of this increase is attributable to the dissolution of colonialism and the disintegration of the Soviet Union. Whatever the cause, the number of new nations is large, as is the number of new currencies and central banks because almost every new country has insisted on having its own money and its own monetary authority. Hanke (2000) stated:

> During the last century, there has been an explosion of central banks and new national monies. In 1900, there were only 18 central banks in the world. By 1940, that number had risen to 40. After World War II and with the growth of newly independent countries, the number of central banks grew rapidly, more than tripling to 136 in 1980. Today, there are 173 central banks. (p. 3)

A portion of these new central banks that Hanke referred to are in the emerging-markets nations. Schuler (1996) counted the number of developing countries with central banks as follows.

|      |     |
|------|-----|
| 1950 | 51  |
| 1970 | 85  |
| 1993 | 126 |

The question, then, is whether these countries would have been better off had they not had central banks. A small developing country could do without having its own central bank if it decided to give up its own currency in favor of using another country's currency (dollarizing) or joining a currency zone.

Schuler (1996) is a ferocious critic of central banking in developing countries (with no distinction between emerging and nonemerging countries within the class of developing countries). His study of 155 central banks from 1951 to 1993 compared developing countries that have central banks with developed countries and with developing countries that have adopted currency boards, dollarization, or some other alternative to having a central bank. Schuler studied economic growth rates and currency quality. His measure of currency quality is an aggregate of inflation, exchange rates, devaluations, and currency confiscations. His work "indicate[s] that central banking in developing countries has performed worse than other monetary systems and worse than central banking in developed countries" (pp. 39–41) and that "monetary policy in most developing countries . . . yields a low-quality product at unnecessarily high cost to consumers" (p. 9).

Why do developing countries prefer to have central banks? One reason is that the creation of a central bank is part of a coming-of-age story for newly independent countries. Their leaders, for better or worse, want the trappings of independence. Having a currency and a central bank are as much about nation building as is having a national airline or first-time government bond issuance.

Still, many nations would do well to simply adopt the currency of a larger nation as their own. If national vanity is a large issue, the country could adopt another country's currency in disguise through a currency board or simply through a convincing act of irrevocable convertibility. This indeed was Panama's solution (although note that the country still remains in the emerging category). It introduced, at the time of its independence in 1904, a currency called the "balboa" that was legally exchangeable one for one with the U.S. dollar. Panama also took the unusual step of making both the balboa and the dollar legal tender. What Panama gained from this arrangement was near-absolute trust in its balboa, a currency that some dubbed a "private-label dollar." It also gained seignorage on the balboa float. But what it gave up was the ability to conduct monetary policy on its own. In that sense, it did not really have a full-service central bank. It also did not have the cost of running a central bank and did not have to allow for the time and work of making monetary policy decisions. This arrangement seems to have served Panama well. And one like it would probably do the job for many developing countries.

But this would probably not be the right course of action for most countries that are in the emerging-markets group. The basic definition of this category means that the country in question is on its way to working itself up and out of the developing-nations class. To make this jump, it will need to successfully run its own central bank, although to do this well can prove to be an excessively difficult task.

## Goals for an Emerging-Markets Central Bank

The overall goal of an emerging-markets central bank ought to be the same as for the country itself—to establish economic policies conducive to sustainable economic growth. To be successful, the central bank will need to create a stable economic environment that features low and stable rates of inflation.

Why worry about high rates of inflation? Fischer, Sahay, and Vegh (2002) found:

> Periods of high inflation are associated with bad macroeconomic performance. In particular, high inflation is bad for growth. The evidence is based on a sample of eighteen countries that have experienced very high inflation episodes. During such periods real GDP per capita fell an average by 1.6 percent per annum (compared to positive growth of 1.4 percent in low inflation years); private consumption per capita fell by 1.3 percent (compared to 1.7 percent growth in low inflation years) and investment growth fell by 3.3 percent (compared to positive growth of 4.2 percent in low inflation years). (p. 877)

Take this a step further. I can frame the question in a different way: What are the worst economic disasters a central bank might be able to circumvent? Economics presents an ever-changing landscape, so some of the future problems that a central bank faces will have little resemblance to historical episodes. But a central bank can never be excused for repeating its own past errors or those of other central banks. The worst errors that should never be allowed to reoccur are as follows.

**Hyperinflation.** Cagan's (1956) famous study defined hyperinflation as when the rise in the price level exceeds 50 percent per month.[6] On many occasions, hyperinflation has exceeded his measure by a good deal. I believe that hyperinflation is the ultimate verification of Friedman's (1968a) dictum that "inflation is everywhere and always a monetary phenomenon" (p. 39). For this basic reason, I believe that hyperinflation is completely within the grasp of a central bank to prevent because it is always preceded by explosive growth in the money supply. Hyperinflation is usually explained by the central bank's actions to help close what would otherwise be an impossible budget deficit.

**Chronic Inflation.** Hyperinflation is a spectacular but thankfully rare occurrence. With some exceptions, hyperinflation has a life expectancy measured in months or a few years. But chronic inflation, another variety of monetary disturbance characterized by high (but not hyper) rates of inflation, can persist for years on end. This kind of inflation infiltrates every aspect of the economy of the affected country. For example, inflation-adjusted contracting becomes a part of everyday life. Economists believe that chronic inflation has real economic costs. Latin America has suffered greatly from this type of inflation (see Pazos 1972 and Fischer et al. 2002).

**Deflation.** Deflation is falling prices, or to be more precise, a falling general price level. Deflation is a problem because when prices fall, there are wealth transfers from debtors to creditors (the money that debtors must repay generally becomes worth more in terms of goods). Meanwhile, the interest rate that is quoted in the marketplace, the so-called nominal rate, cannot go below zero. Hence, if the nominal rate is zero or close to zero, and if there is a substantial downward drift in the price level, the real interest rate becomes a large positive number. In severe cases of deflation, the real interest rate becomes enormous. Economists believe that economic activity, especially new investment, is curtailed by high real interest rates. The solution to deflation is to raise the rate of growth in the money supply, as Friedman's dictum would suggest.

**Depression.** According to at least one group of economists, the Great Depression in the United States (which spread to other continents) was caused, at least in part, by errors in monetary policy by the U.S. Federal Reserve. Real economic factors also were to blame (such as the Dust Bowl weather pattern), but it took a central bank

---

[6]Cagan (1956) studied seven hyperinflations that took place between 1920 and 1946. He defined a hyperinflation as beginning in the month inflation first exceeds 50 percent (per month) and as ending in the month before the monthly inflation drops below 50 percent for at least one year. Hyperinflation annihilates money-based claims, such as bank accounts and bonds. It does not, however, typically destroy the value of equity shares. DeRosa (1978) studied share prices during the German hyperinflation of 1922–1923 and found that equities generally kept pace with the tremendous rise in the price level for goods.

to turn what might have been merely a recession into the Great Depression. This issue is still hotly debated 45 years after the seminal study by Friedman and Schwartz (1963) was published and almost 70 years after the Great Depression itself ended. Yet this analysis warrants the most careful review by central banks.[7]

**Currency crises.** The 1990s saw emerging markets crushed by a series of spectacular currency crises. One by one, fixed exchange rate regimes exploded with coincidental crashes in stock and bond prices. The real effects were devastating as income and employment plunged. The question that every central banker must answer is whether these countries brought the crises on themselves by installing intermediate soft-peg exchange rate regimes. I believe that these types of crises can be avoided by adopting the philosophy of the bipolar view—either float, peg hard (through currency boards or dollarization), or join a currency zone.

This discussion anticipates what will be covered in subsequent chapters. I believe that the correct approach is for emerging markets to adopt a minimalist approach—a term I will define in detail in Chapter 8, the concluding chapter.

## Best Practices

The discussions in this book presume that central banks are beyond reproach in terms of honesty, motives, and conduct. I do not discuss corruption at the monetary authority, implicitly assuming that it, like Caesar's wife, is above suspicion.

But a central bank could be compromised without being outright corrupt. I know of no authority who would not readily agree that central banks had best be independent of external political forces. This ideal is difficult to achieve. The problem is that the executives who run a central bank are appointed by incumbent politicians who run the country. Therefore, the process of selecting the governor of the central bank and the top lieutenants should be transparent and without political motives.

Yet, independence too must have its limits. How far should a central bank's independent authority extend? Politics does have a place; it would be unwise for the central bank, all on its own, to have the power to arbitrarily change the goals of monetary policy. "Goal independence," as it is known among economists, is not desirable. The goals of monetary policy—such as whether to give total preference to fighting inflation or to have a dual objective of keeping prices steady while fostering employment, for example—ought to be determined by the political process, preferably with the outcome being memorialized in law. And once established, they should be permanent, or nearly so. What a central bank does require is "instrument independence," meaning unencumbered power to conduct monetary policy with the aim to achieve externally established goals.

---

[7]Students of the Great Depression and monetary economics will be interested in Bernanke's (2002) remarks delivered at a conference to honor Milton Friedman on the occasion of his 90th birthday.

In a narrow sense, discussions of best practices are often focused on the degree of transparency in the central bank's communications with the general public concerning monetary policy decisions. Thinking on this matter has undergone a revolution over the past two decades.

Federal Reserve Chairman Bernanke (2007a) mentioned that Montagu Norman, governor of the Bank of England from 1921 to 1944, had the motto "Never explain, never excuse." Indeed, before the 1990s, central bankers prided themselves on being virtual fortresses of secrecy concerning monetary policy. Alan Greenspan, the former Federal Reserve chairman, during congressional testimony in 1987, prided himself on "mumbling with great incoherence."

A new view has emerged that is diametrically opposite: Central banks do best when they are completely open with the public so that their policy decisions are broadly understood. Bernanke's aforementioned speech addressed a set of new measures designed to enhance Federal Reserve transparency though communications. He said, "A considerable amount of evidence indicates that central bank transparency increases the effectiveness of monetary policy and enhances economic and financial performance in several ways" (Bernanke 2007a, p. 1). He argued that the general public can make more-informed economic decisions when they better understand what their central bank is doing. Moreover, transparency can serve to "anchor" the public's long-term inflation expectations. Blinder, Ehrmann, Fratzscher, De Haan, and Jansen (2008), in their comprehensive review of the economics literature on central bank communications, concluded:

> The evidence suggests that communication can be an important and powerful part of the central bank's toolkit since it has the ability to move financial markets, to enhance the predictability of monetary policy decisions, and potentially to help achieve central banks' macroeconomic objectives. (p. 1)

Part of the drift toward transparency is motivated by the popularity of inflation targeting as monetary policy. In an inflation-targeting regime, the central bank publishes its target, or target zone, for the intermediate-term rate of inflation. The operation of such a regime requires the central bank to engage in abundant communication with the general public. The topic of inflation targeting is discussed in the next chapter.

There is another sense of best practice. The task of the central banker goes far beyond knowing the pulse of his or her own economy or what is happening in his or her region and in the rest of the world. What is needed is a consistent and logical understanding of the nature of the economic processes he or she faces. For example, a central banker must be able to distinguish what is temporary from what is permanent, identify economic distortions and understand their consequences, and have knowledge that allows him or her to distinguish what is controllable from what cannot be controlled. Most importantly, the central banker must be able to distinguish true pernicious economic manifestations from temporary aberrations or from legitimate economic adjustment mechanisms. The devil is not in the details but in the analysis.

It is with these sorts of things in mind that central bankers turn to the field of economics. And they are not disappointed, at least on some basic level. But even the casual reader of the professional literature can see that beyond an elementary level, the field, especially on topics of monetary policy, capital flows, and exchange rate regimes, is deeply fractured.

That said, economists do have important ideas for the central banker, and profound insights are to be found in this great gaggle of ideas and hypotheses. But for a central banker or policy maker to get something truly useful from the economic literature, he or she must do some hard work to understand the relevant issues and to get them right. If nothing else, such an exercise might provide a foundation that can serve as a point of departure for the consideration of new ideas.

Indeed, that is the challenge of this book. I make no pretense that any of the major issues in this complex field can be resolved permanently. Rather, the purpose is to extract from the writing of professional economists and central bankers, with due consideration to economic history, a consistent and logical guide to the main questions facing a central banker in an emerging-markets country.

Along the way, the ideas and theories of many economists and central bankers will be presented. Not all of them are useful or even correct. I review these ideas and theories with a critical eye, and my writing expresses a point of view. I make no attempt to be neutral. What survives scrutiny will be far from perfect. Riddles and anomalies always crop up, and there are plenty of problems that cannot be resolved by this or any other simple, unified approach.

# 2. Money Basics

Monetary theory can be said to have begun with the discovery of the famous quantity theory of money in the 18th century by the British philosopher David Hume.

## Quantity Theory of Money

The following is the main idea behind quantity theory. Suppose a sensationally irresponsible monetary authority unexpectedly and immediately doubles the supply of money in circulation. Suppose further that the general public regards this action as a one-off experience, something not likely to occur again. What will happen? The public had been holding the amount of money it had desired before the doubling of the money supply. At the instant after the event, everyone is holding twice as much money if one assumes the distribution was proportional to existing money holdings across the population. Some people may think they are richer by virtue of their new money holdings. But logic dictates there will be an attempt to reduce the amount of money people hold, and this process will create a spending spree. Jumping ahead to the conclusion, the process of spending must come to rest when the price level, meaning the average of the prices of all goods, has doubled. Actually, I can be more precise. Given enough time, the price of each and every good will have to exactly double because the change in the money supply does nothing to alter the conditions of demand and supply.

Hume (1752) wrote about the relationship between prices and the quantity of money:

> Money is not, properly speaking, one of the subjects of commerce; but only the instrument which men have agreed upon to facilitate the exchange of one commodity for another. It is none of the wheels of trade: it is the oil which renders the motions of the wheels more smooth and easy. If we consider any one kingdom by itself, it is evident, that the greater or less plenty of money is of no consequence; since the prices of commodities are always proportioned to the plenty of money. (p. 115)

Hume arrived at these insights despite his having none of the tools of modern economics. Throughout his paper, he relied on common sense and broad episodes in history, sometimes ancient history, to support his conjectures.[8] For Hume, money is the oil that makes the big gears move with less friction. He tells us that money on the margin is worthless, meaning that adding more of it in circulation does not enhance the wealth of society. Whatever there is of money, it is enough. (Note the distinction

---

[8]Interesting discussions of Hume's work in monetary theory can be found in Friedman (1992) and Lucas (1996).

between money and wealth: The hunger for wealth, for real economic goods, is never satisfied.) Furthermore, he stated that the quantity of money is proportional to prices; this relationship is what is commonly known as the "quantity theory."

McCandless and Weber (1995) conducted a simple but convincing empirical test of the basic quantity theory using data over a 30-year period (1960–1990) for 110 countries (see **Figure 2.1**). They worked with three money aggregates: M0, M1, and M2. They summarized their findings as follows:

- Growth rates of money supply and the general price level are highly correlated for all three money definitions for the full sample of countries and for both subsamples.
- Growth rates of money and real output are not correlated.[9]
- The rate of inflation and the growth rate of real output are essentially uncorrelated.

Monetarists define the price level as the average of the prices of all goods and services. Inflation is a sustained rise in the price level. Similarly, deflation is a sustained fall in the price level. Disinflation is a fall in the rate of inflation.

Simon Newcomb (the astronomer) and Irving Fisher developed and quantified Hume's insight on money. Today, the quantity theory is expressed in one of two forms. In the transactions expression, it is

$$MV = PT,$$

where $M$ is the nominal quantity of money, $V$ is the velocity of circulation (the number of times each dollar is used, on average, to make a purchase during a specific period of time), and $P$ is the price level. $T$ stands for transactions; it is an index of the total quantity of goods and services purchased and sold.

Strictly speaking, this is an identity. Friedman (1992) wrote of the importance of this equation: "Fisher's equation plays the same foundation-stone role in monetary theory that Einstein's $E = mc^2$ does in physics" (p. 39). He explained the equation as follows:

> Nothing can affect $P$ except as it changes one or more of the other items in the equation. Will a boom in the stock market, for example, change how much you can buy with a five-dollar bill? It will reduce the amount you can buy (raise $P$) only if it leads the Fed to create more money (increase $M$), or induces people to hold lower real cash balances, perhaps because they think the alternatives have become more attractive (raises $V$), or reduces the quantity of goods and services available for purchase, perhaps because workers are paying less attention to their work and more to their stock ticker (lowers $T$). (p. 39)

[9]An exception was the subsample of countries in the Organisation for Economic Co-operation and Development, in which these growth rates are positively correlated.

## Figure 2.1.  Long-Run Money Supply, Prices, and Growth

**A. *Average Annual Rates of Growth in M2 and in Consumer Prices during 1960–1990 in 110 Countries***

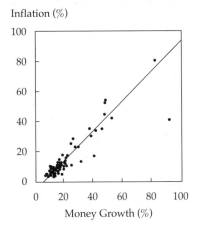

**B. *Average Annual Rates of Growth in M2 and in Nominal GDP, Deflated by Consumer Prices during 1960–1990 in 110 Countries***

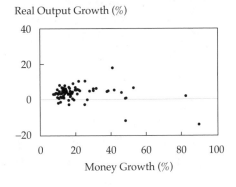

**C. *Average Annual Rates of Growth in M0 and in Nominal GDP, Deflated by Consumer Prices during 1960–1990 in 21 Countries***

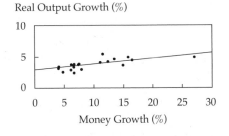

**D. *Average Annual Rates of Growth in Consumer Prices and in Nominal GDP, Deflated by Consumer Prices during 1960–1990 in 110 Countries***

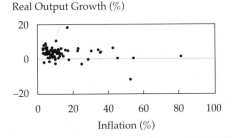

*Source*: Based on McCandless and Weber (1995).

In an alternative formulation, $y$, real income, replaces $T$:

$$MV = Py.$$

$V$ in this formulation is income velocity. It is the number of times the money stock must turn over to circulate nominal income. If velocity, $V$, were stable, there would be a short-run linkage between money supply and nominal income (price level, $P$, multiplied by real income, $y$). Alas, that is not the case.

# The Central Bank

A nation's central bank is its monetary authority. Its principal roles are to create money, in the form of both currency and reserve deposits of commercial banks, and to conduct monetary policy. Many central banks are also charged with regulating their country's banking system, but that is not a topic for this book.

The concept that central banks need to be independent of political control is never really in doubt in economic debates. But Mishkin (2004) made an important distinction between a central bank's "instrument independence" and "goal independence":

> Instrument independence is the ability for the central bank to set monetary policy instruments without government interference, while goal independence means the monetary authorities set the goals for monetary policy. The standard view in the literature is that central banks should have instrument but not goal independence. (p. 11)

**The Prototypical Central Bank.** Consider the balance sheet of what I will refer to as a "prototypical" central bank of a country other than the United States:

| Assets | Liabilities |
|--------|-------------|
| DA | C |
| FACB | R |

The assets of this central bank consist of
- Domestic assets (DA), usually government bonds issued by its country's treasury.
- Foreign assets of the central bank (FACB), usually government bonds issued by the United States or another large country.

The liabilities are
- Currency (C) in the hands of the public.
- Commercial bank reserves (R) held at the central bank.

Central banks usually pay no interest on commercial bank reserves held with them, which amounts to a tax on the banking system. Currency does not earn interest either. Through these means, the central bank is, in effect, financed at zero cost.

In fact, the balance sheets of central banks are cluttered with a slew of items. But these four items are the main categories needed to discuss monetary policy. I should note that some central banks issue debt, although I have not shown any on this balance sheet. This issue will be considered in Chapter 7. By convention, I do not need to be concerned with the concept of the owner's equity of the central bank, but I should note that a central bank almost always runs a profit (usually paid to the government's treasury). That said, China's central bank in recent times appears in need of a capital infusion to replace foreign-asset portfolio losses (also a topic for Chapter 7).

The sum of currency plus reserve deposits is called the "monetary base." It is sometimes also called "high-powered money" or simply "central bank money." Importantly, the central bank is the monopoly supplier of high-powered money. The monetary base is the platform for the broad-based aggregates, such as M2 (customarily defined as the sum of currency in the hands of the public, demand deposits, and savings account deposits). The broad aggregates, such as M1 and M2, are measures of the actual money supply in circulation. **Box 2.1** provides the Federal Reserve's definitions of the various measures of the money stock in the United States.

---

**Box 2.1.   Definitions of Monetary Aggregates in the United States**

M1: Measure of the U.S. money stock that consists of currency held by the public, traveler's checks, demand deposits, and other checkable deposits.

M2: Measure of the U.S. money stock that consists of M1, savings deposits (including money market deposit accounts), time deposits in amounts less than $100,000, and balances in retail money market mutual funds.

---

**Central Bank Objectives.** Each central bank has its own set of purposes and objectives (see **Box 2.2**). Many countries memorialize these in a law, usually called their "central bank law." But if there is one goal consistent across all central banks, it is to restrain inflation from being excessive. This goal may be approached directly, where there is a floating exchange rate, with monetary policy geared to limiting the rate of inflation. The approach called "inflation targeting" is one such example and one that I will discuss in this chapter. There are also indirect attempts to constrain inflation by maintaining a fixed exchange rate regime.

I do not know of any central bank that seeks to produce permanently a zero rate of inflation. Some inflation is acceptable, but that is usually no more than a few percent a year. A central bank that is able to maintain a low but stable rate of inflation without taking heroic policy measures is seen as a successful monetary authority.

In contrast, deflation, meaning a falling price level, is never acceptable. The asymmetry comes from the Fisher equation, under which the real interest rate is equal to the nominal (or money) interest rate plus the expected rate of inflation:

$$r = i + \pi^e,$$

where

$r$ = the nominal or market rate of interest on a fixed-income instrument

$i$ = the real rate of interest on that instrument

$\pi^e$ = the expected rate of inflation over the life of the instrument

## Box 2.2. Monetary Policy Objectives for Some of the Major Central Banks

Four of the major central banks have domestic price level stability as the primary focus for monetary policy.

### The European Central Bank

"To maintain price stability is the primary objective of the Eurosystem and of the single monetary policy for which it is responsible. This is laid down in the Treaty establishing the European Community, Article 105 (1)."[10]

### The Bank of Japan

"Currency and monetary control shall be aimed at, through the pursuit of price stability, contributing to the sound development of the national economy."[11]

### The Bank of England

"Monetary Stability: Monetary stability means stable prices and confidence in the currency. Stable prices are defined by the Government's inflation target, which the Bank seeks to meet through the decisions on interest rates taken by the Monetary Policy Committee, explaining those decisions transparently and implementing them effectively in the money markets."[12]

### Swiss National Bank

"The SNB's monetary policy strategy consists of three elements. Firstly, the SNB states how it defines price stability. Secondly, it bases its monetary policy decisions on a medium-term inflation forecast. Thirdly, it sets an operational target range for its chosen reference interest rate, the three-month LIBOR."[13]

In contrast, the U.S. central bank, called the Federal Reserve System, has a three-part objective.

### The U.S. Federal Reserve

"The Board of Governors of the Federal Reserve System and the Federal Open Market Committee shall maintain long run growth of the monetary and credit aggregates commensurate with the economy's long run potential to increase production, so as to promote effectively the goals of maximum employment, stable prices, and moderate long-term interest rates."[14]

---

[10]European Central Bank: Objective of Monetary Policy, www.ecb.int/mopo/intro/html/objective.en.html.

[11]Bank of Japan Act.

[12]Bank of England's statement on Monetary Policy, www.bankofengland.co.uk/monetarypolicy/index.htm.

[13]Swiss National Bank Statement on Monetary Policy Strategy, www.snb.ch/en/iabout/monpol.

[14]The Federal Reserve Act.

When an economy is in the throes of a recession, or depression, the central bank is apt to have set a very low interest rate. If prices are falling, the deflationary case, then the real interest rate will exceed the nominal rate. The faster prices fall, the higher the real interest rate, even though the nominal rate may be close to zero. Of course, a cure exists, one that is theoretically easy to apply: The central bank of a deflationary economy needs to inject high-powered money into the banking system. This case requires the central bank to become inflationary.

In addition to the primary goal of restraining inflation, central banks usually have more basic objectives, such as ensuring the stability of the banking system and preventing gross economic instability.

Some central banks, notably the Federal Reserve, have multiple macroeconomic objectives. The goals of the Federal Reserve are threefold. It must ensure acceptable rates of inflation, but it must also work to achieve maximum employment as well as moderate levels of long-term interest rates. Obviously, this is a much harder mandate than simply controlling the rate of inflation. At times, the various objectives contradict one another.

Other central banks have as their primary objective maintaining a fixed exchange rate, which as I mentioned earlier is a policy aimed, at least in part, at controlling inflation. The constancy of the exchange rate is accomplished by foreign exchange intervention, or at least by the threat of intervention, and by having macroeconomic policies that are consistent with the desired foreign exchange goals. Yet, clearly, this kind of central bank mandate is the most fertile ground for conflicts between the main objective—in this case, pegging the exchange rate—and achieving complementary or subsidiary domestic policy goals.

**Tools of Monetary Policy.** I now turn to a discussion of the various tools that central banks have at their disposal to direct monetary policy.

*Reserve requirements.* The reserve requirements regulate the multipliers by which the monetary base is adjusted to arrive at the broad-based money supply aggregates. Central banks have the power to set the size of the monetary base. Reserve requirements (or ratios) are the links between the size of the base and the monetary aggregates. Commercial banks are limited in their ability to convert deposits into assets by a requirement that they hold a fraction of the former in the form of reserves. A portion of this reserve can be vault cash. The remainder is in the form of deposits with the central bank (this is the R on the balance sheet shown previously).[15] The reserve ratio gives the fraction of deposits that must be reserved.

---

[15]"Required reserve ratio: The percentage of reservable liabilities that depository institutions must set aside in the form of reserves. Required reserves: Funds that a depository institution is required to maintain in the form of vault cash or, if vault cash is insufficient to meet the requirement, in the form of a balance maintained directly with a Reserve Bank or indirectly with a pass-through correspondent bank. The required amount varies according to the required reserve ratios set by the Board and the amount of reservable liabilities held by the institution" (Board of Governors of the Federal Reserve System 2005, p. 123).

It can vary by the size of the bank and by the nature of the deposit. Reserve ratios are monetary policy variables. The reserve ratio is a control variable on the money expansion process. A rise in the reserve ratio means the same sized monetary base translates to a smaller set of monetary aggregates. But this relationship among the monetary base, the required reserve ratio, and the broad-based aggregates is far from a precise linkage.

■ *Open market operations.* A more precise tool of monetary policy is the open market operation. This term refers to a central bank's purchase or sale of domestic assets (DA), with corresponding changes in the monetary base. For example, a central bank might elect to purchase bonds. It will conduct this transaction through a bond dealer, a financial institution with which it has established trading lines. When the central bank acquires the bonds, it pays for the transaction by crediting the reserve account of the dealer. As shown earlier, deposits with the central bank are part of the monetary base (the R on the central bank's balance sheet). This transaction leaves the dealer with a larger-than-necessary balance in its reserve account. These excess reserves are funds that can be withdrawn or lent to other institutions. The effect is that the central bank has added liquidity to the banking system, thus putting downward pressure on short-term interest rates. What is particularly interesting is the unique power of the central bank. Unlike anyone else, it has the power with a stroke of the pen to create money, literally, out of thin air. It also can destroy money, such as it does when it buys assets. The rule is that when a central bank buys domestic assets, the monetary base must rise; when it sells assets, the base must fall.

■ *Repurchase agreements.* Central banks are partial to doing what amounts to open market operations through transactions called "repurchase" and "reverse repurchase" agreements. The Federal Reserve defines these operations as follows:

- "Repurchase agreement (RP or repo): A transaction in which the Federal Reserve enters into an agreement with a primary dealer to acquire securities from the dealer for a specified principal amount at an agreed-upon interest rate and to return the securities on a specified future date. The maturity date may be the next day or many days later, with the maximum length set by the FOMC.[16] These transactions permit the Federal Reserve to increase the supply of Federal Reserve balances for the length of the agreement" (Board of Governors of the Federal Reserve System 2005, pp. 122–123).

- "Reverse repurchase agreement: A transaction—the opposite of a repurchase agreement—in which the Federal Reserve enters into an agreement with a primary dealer to sell securities from the System portfolio for a specified principal amount at an agreed-upon interest rate and to receive the securities back from the dealer on a specified future date. The maturity date may be the next day or many days later, with the maximum length set by the FOMC. These

---

[16]The FOMC, or Federal Open Market Committee, is the policy-making board of the Federal Reserve.

transactions permit the Federal Reserve to decrease the supply of Federal Reserve balances for the length of the agreement" (Board of Governors of the Federal Reserve System 2005, p. 123).

Repo and reverse repo operations are important instruments of monetary policy for many central banks. These transactions, which are shown on the central bank balance sheet, require regular maintenance because they have short maturity dates.

The mechanics are interesting. Suppose a central bank elects to use the one-week interest rate as its interest rate target. Furthermore, suppose it wishes to add liquidity by doing a one-week repo operation. In the course of this transaction, the central bank buys bonds from a dealer for immediate settlement (call this "leg one") and commits to sell the same bonds back to the same dealer in one week's time (call this "leg two"). The effect of leg one is to give an immediate increase in the monetary base because the central bank credits the dealer's reserve account for the cost of the bonds it has bought. But one week later, the monetary base will drop back down when leg two settles; the whole process reverses when the central bank, in leg two, sells the bonds back and takes the proceeds of the sale out of the dealer's reserve account. In practice, the central bank—unless it has altered its desired policy—will initiate a new repo operation just as the old one is coming to term. The new repo counteracts the effects of the second leg of the first repo. This process is called the central bank "rolling" its repo book. The large central banks use repo operations extensively and, therefore, accumulate very large repo positions. For this reason, one regularly sees them in the marketplace doing repo and reverse repo operations to maintain and sometimes adjust their repo transaction books.

In broad terms, monetary policy aimed at domestic conditions seeks to either modify interest rates or target numerical changes in the quantity of money. In the case of the former, the targeted interest rate is either an overnight rate, such as the federal funds rate, or a short-term (usually measured in weeks) interest rate. The central bank may post an explicit target, or target range, for the interest rate that it is prepared to back up by doing open market or repo/reverse repo operations. Similarly, quantitative targets, meaning the size of the money supply, can be achieved by doing open market operations and repo and reverse repo operations.

■ *Foreign exchange intervention.* Yet another central bank tool is foreign exchange intervention. This tool is very similar to an open market operation except that the assets bought or sold are foreign currency or foreign assets. In a basic intervention, the central bank buys or sells foreign currency in exchange for domestic currency. These operations also are done in two steps. In one transaction, the central bank must buy or sell foreign currency, and in the second, it buys or sells a foreign asset. Either way, the effect of the operation on the right-hand side of the balance sheet is the same as an open market operation because, by the basic accounting identity, when one side of the balance sheet (assets) changes, the other side (liabilities) must change in the same direction and by the same amount.

▓ *Sterilization.* Sometimes central banks conduct intervention but want the result to be no subsequent change in the monetary base, which leads them to conduct sterilization, or sterilized intervention (a topic that will be discussed at length in Chapter 7). The two basic forms of sterilized intervention are for the central bank to buy foreign assets and either (1) sell an equivalent amount of domestic assets (FACB rises and DA falls) or (2) issue liabilities on itself in equal amount to the foreign-asset transaction.

▓ *Discount window.* Another tool of central banking is called "discount rate policy." Central banks may allow their member commercial banks to borrow funds on a collateralized basis. The member commercial bank doing the borrowing places eligible collateral with the central bank and pays an interest rate called the "discount rate," which represents the cost of funds. A rise in the discount rate causes the demand for discount rate borrowing to drop, at least in theory, meaning that the cost of funds throughout the banking system should rise.

▓ *Direct instruments.* All the aforementioned tools of monetary policy are referred to as "market-based" or "indirect" instruments because they rely on the money and credit markets to achieve policy goals. A second group of tools is called "direct" instruments. They include such things as interest rate controls, credit ceilings, and directed lending (lending at the behest of the authorities, rather than for commercial reasons). These measures, by modern standards, are considered relatively ineffective and lacking in precision compared with indirect methods. Maino and Buzeneca (2007) correctly recommend against direct in favor of indirect instruments:

> During the last two decades, the IMF has explicitly advocated the use of market-based instruments to implement monetary policy, that is, to try to steer liquidity by influencing money markets through open market operations and auctions instead of relying on direct controls on credit and interest rates. (p. 3)

## Monetary Transmission Mechanism

The monetary transmission mechanism indicates how changes in the money supply translate into changes in macroeconomic aggregates, such as the price level, income, and interest rates.

**Demand for Money.** Modern quantity theory focuses on the demand for money. The classic work is Friedman (1956). The term "real balances" means the real value of the money supply when it is deflated by the price level. The proposition that the price level will double if the money supply doubles depends on the assumed behavior of the demand for money function. Economic agents demand greater levels of real balances at higher levels of real income. Hence, if real income is rising rapidly or if the demand for money is highly income sensitive, then a doubling of the money supply will result in a less than doubling of the price level.

The exact mathematical representation of the demand for real balances that is appropriate depends on the nature of the economy being analyzed. A simple form is

$$\frac{M^d}{P} = L\left(y, \pi^e, r, r^a\right),$$

where

$M^d$ = money demand
$P$  = price level
$L$  = demand for money function
$y$  = real income
$\pi^e$ = the expected rate of inflation
$r$  = the nominal interest rate
$r^a$ = the nominal rate of return on noncash assets

One would expect the demand for real balances to be greater at higher levels of real income and smaller for

- higher expected rates of inflation,
- higher interest rates, and
- higher rates of return on noncash assets.

The role of expected inflation comes about because inflation can be viewed as a tax on nominal assets, including money balances.

The framework is that the central bank determines the (nominal) money supply but economic agents determine the value of the money in real terms. As Harberger (2008) has stated:

> The first proposition of monetary theory is that people behave in regular and rational ways in determining their desired holdings of real monetary balances. These are usually defined as some concept of "broad money" (usually M2), deflated by either the CPI or the GDP deflater. Key variables in determining these holdings are the level of real income, the expected rate of inflation in the country, [and] real interest rates.

> The second proposition of monetary theory is that when people find themselves with monetary balances higher than they really want, they tend to spend more, thus bringing their balances closer to the desired level.

> . . .[A] corollary to the second proposition is that, yes, the monetary authorities determine the nominal money supply (M$^S$), but as people adjust their spending, the price level (P) changes so as to bring M$^S$/P into equality with the people's desired real monetary balances (M$^d$/P). (pp. 226–227)

So, although the central bank determines the nominal money supply, the people determine the real money supply, which brings us to the question of the monetary transmission mechanism. This rather formal term refers to the time sequence of how changes in the money supply affect income, interest rates, and the price level. As described by Friedman in a number of his writings (see, for example, Friedman 1968b), the traditional mechanism works as follows.

Suppose a monetary experiment, similar to the one outlined earlier, is conducted, but this time, the creation of money goes from zero to a constant rate of growth equal to 10 percent. One would expect that

- Prices would not respond immediately, and as such, all economic agents would be holding more real balances than they demand.
- The first visible effect would be a drop in the interest rate.
- Incomes would rise as economic agents mistakenly assumed their increase in real balances could be spent. This rise in demand would start to reverse the drop in the interest rate.
- Prices of goods would begin to rise only later, as the classical quantity theory predicts.
- A new equilibrium would be reached after some time, during which the price level would have risen faster than 10 percent. But eventually, it would settle down to a 10 percent growth path. The same would be true for nominal income. Nominal interest rates would reflect the new rate of price inflation.

The reason that the price level would have to rise faster than 10 percent at some time is that the revised expectation of inflation would cause the demand for real balances to drop—in effect, amplifying the result of the increase in the money supply.

Note that there is little or no effect on the real economy when all adjustments are made.[17] As Kamin, Turner, and Van 't dack (1998) have written:

> In recent years, many have argued that central banks should emphasize price stability as a single objective of monetary policy and eschew consideration of other goals such as growth or employment. The desire to limit the objective of monetary policy in this way is based on the near-unanimity among economists and policy-makers that monetary policy cannot affect the long-term growth of the economy. (p. 6)

**Monetary Policy Channels.** Today, economists prefer to look at the monetary transmission mechanism as a series of parallel processes operating through "channels."[18] Kamin et al. (1998) named four channels:

- The interest rate channel—monetary policy affecting the real economy through changes in the marginal cost of borrowing.
- The domestic asset price channel—monetary policy changing the prices of stocks, bonds, real estate, and other assets.
- The exchange rate channel—monetary policy altering the exchange rate, with implications for trade and foreign investment flows.
- The credit channel—monetary policy changing the availability of credit, especially in emerging-markets countries.

---

[17]Yet, there is some loss of economic efficiency because real balances are smaller, after the fact. There could also be a second-order effect that if inflation rates are unstable or unpredictable, various forms of investment and risk taking would be restrained.

[18]See Mishkin (1996).

Traditional monetary policy measures are aimed at the first channel. The usual paradigm today is that a central bank establishes a target level for a short-term interest rate. To make this policy effective, it must be prepared to enforce its target through open-market operations or through repo/reverse repo transactions. The other three channels—domestic asset, exchange rate, and credit—are usually lower-order considerations for a central bank.

Central banks are able to control interest rates of the very shortest maturities because they are monopoly suppliers of high-powered money. But that market power is limited to instruments with maturities that are exceedingly short. For example, the Federal Reserve targets the federal funds rate, an overnight market-clearing interest rate for reserve deposits of commercial banks. Other central banks target slightly longer (but still short-term) rates, such as one- or two-week money market rates. Transactions in these markets take place at or around the central bank's target rate. But if the market interest rate begins to move sufficiently far from the central bank's target, then something has to be done. Either the central bank can capitulate and change its target, meaning move closer to the market rate, or it can protest the market rate by conducting operations designed to bring the market rate back to the near vicinity of its target.

The question turns to how it could be that a central bank's forcing movements on only the short end of the yield curve—such as overnight or weekly interest rates—has a powerful influence on the economy. In the direct sense, changes in the official rate will be transmitted to short-term money market rates and to bank lending rates. Still, the impact on long-term interest rates is far from easily understood. One part of the answer must have to do with the fact that the response of the economy to a policy-driven change in the official (short-term) interest rate depends on the state of expectations at the time of the policy measure, and in particular on expectations about future policy measures. This point was made by Bernanke and Blinder (1992), who wrote that the interest rate on federal funds is "extremely informative" about future movements of real macroeconomic variables. They argued that innovations in the funds rate are a measure of changes in policy.

Still other channels exist, one of which is the quantity of money itself. This channel was the topic of a major international monetary debate when, in the 1990s and early 2000s, the Bank of Japan allowed its money supply growth to stagnate while domestic prices were falling. The Bank of Japan was convinced it had done all it could by driving the short-term interest rates to practically zero (the so-called ZIRP, or zero interest rate policy). Yet, monetarists everywhere were alarmed that prices were still falling and the money supply growth was stagnant. The Bank of Japan finally relented and introduced what it called "quantitative easing" as its new policy, which meant that the target of its policy was no longer the short-term interest rate but, rather, the size and growth of the monetary base. Actually what Japan focused on was commercial bank reserves held at the central bank, a component of the monetary base. The intent of the new policy was that if Japan created enough money, the quantity theory would halt the fall in consumer prices, meaning deflation would end and moderate inflation would begin.

## Limitations of Monetary Policy

There was a time, notably after World War II, when many economists believed that monetary policy could be used with such precision that central banks could "fine-tune" their economies.[19] Decades of disappointment taught otherwise. In retrospect, it is hard to believe this idea could have ever been taken seriously, especially when the two major monetary calamities of the 20th century, the Great Depression of the 1930s and the great inflation of the 1970s, both had deep roots in the failures of central bank policies.[20]

Five propositions from monetary economics are critically important for understanding monetary policy:

1.  Money has no direct effect on real activity in the long run.
2.  Inflation is a monetary phenomenon.
3.  The money supply can have a major impact on an economy in the short run.
4.  Monetary policy is at best an imprecise tool of stabilization.
5.  The nominal interest rate is a poor, and sometimes misleading, indicator of the tightness or ease of monetary policy.

The first and second propositions were borne out by McCandless and Weber (1995)—and by a great many other authors—as I noted earlier in this chapter. Points one and two are nicely summarized in the Bank of England's (1999) report "The Transmission Mechanism of Monetary Policy":

> In the long run, monetary policy in essence determines the value of money—movements in the general price level indicate how much the purchasing power of money has changed over time. Inflation, in this sense, is a monetary phenomenon. (pp. 3–4)

This statement should be no surprise because money does nothing to fundamentally alter the long-run productive capacity of the economy by way of technological improvements or by expanding the supply of the factors of production.

When Hume (1752) wrote that "the greater or less plenty of money is of no consequence" (p. 115), we can presume he spoke of the long run. In the short run, money can have a major impact in terms of both the real and nominal sides of the economy (point number three).

---

[19]Sometimes the term "fine-tuning" meant creating an optimal mixture of monetary and fiscal policy—arguably an even more difficult task.

[20]See Bordo and Schwartz (1997) for an excellent and thorough summary of monetary history of the 20th century. Friedman and Schwartz (1963) is a classic analysis of money and monetary policy. Bernanke (2002) is an interesting discussion of the Friedman and Schwartz contribution.

The fourth point, lack of precision of monetary policy, comes in large part from Friedman's (1961) famous generalization that "monetary actions affect economic conditions only after a lag that is long and variable" (p. 447).

In a later paper, Friedman (1972) concluded that money affects prices well after it affects output:[21]

> The highest correlation for industrial production is for money leading three months for M1 and six months for M2. What was a surprise was to find that the highest correlation for consumer prices was for money leading twenty months for M1 and twenty-three months for M2. Quarterly GNP data give similar results. Clearly, monetary policy changes take much longer to affect prices than to affect output. (p. 15)

More recently, the Bank of England (1999) reported that it takes "on average" up to one year in industrial countries for changes in the money supply to have its peak effect on demand and output. The timing of the impact of monetary policy is a function of such factors as the state of business and consumer confidence, the stage of the business cycle, events in the world economy, and expectations of future inflation. In summary, "The impact of monetary policy is subject to long, variable and uncertain lags" (p. 9).

There is at least one other reason why monetary policy is less than "textbook precise." The role that expectations play is inordinately tricky. Anyone who has been involved in the trading of foreign currency or interest rate–related markets knows that traders hang on every word and nuance of central bank policy announcements. Every action is studied, and forecasts are made of forthcoming policy actions. This phenomenon is more formally presented in a well-known paper by Lucas (1976) that has come to be known as the "Lucas critique." Bernanke, Laubach, Mishkin, and Posen (1999) provided an apt metaphor for Lucas's argument about the complexity of expectations and policy:

> There is an important difference between rockets and the people who make up the economy, which is that people try to understand and predict the actions of their "controllers" (the policy-makers), while rockets do not. (p. 12)

Bernanke et al. (1999), and Lucas by extension, use the rocket metaphor to distinguish economics from engineering; the latter might use principles of physics to control the trajectory of a rocket with great success. Such precision in control cannot be expected in economics, where economic agents are engaged in an elaborate exercise of predicting, and responding to predictions about, future economic policy.

The fifth point, the interest rate and the tightness or looseness of monetary policy, is commonly misunderstood. If the nominal interest rate is high by historical standards, people think monetary policy is tight; if it is low, they think policy is

---

[21]Batini and Nelson (2001) presented evidence that Friedman's lag structure is present and intact in the modern monetary experience in the United Kingdom and the United States.

loose. Yet, look at this situation more closely. Say that the nominal interest rate is relatively high. That could mean the central bank has recently tightened. Or it could mean the central bank has done nothing to prevent runaway inflation. According to the Fisher equation, nominal interest rates impound the expected rate of inflation. Hence, the high interest rate could be simply a reflection of inflationary expectations. Similarly, a low interest rate, speaking historically, could mean that recent policy has been loose or that there is almost no expectation of inflation (perhaps because of a successful prior tightening). Finally, a low nominal interest rate could simply mean that the level of economic activity is dismal, not that the monetary authority is being generous with credit.

**Limitations of Monetary Policy in Emerging Markets.** The effectiveness of monetary policy may be even more limited in emerging markets than in developed countries.

In Chapter 1, I discussed the principal differences between developed economies and emerging markets. These differences include the strength and depth of the local financial system and the fiscal integrity of the government. Factors such as these affect the ability of the central bank to execute monetary policy with success. But other, larger factors must be considered. Mishkin (2004) stressed that for anti-inflation policies to be effective in emerging markets, the first focus must be on institutional development. In particular, he concluded that two institutional requirements must be met if inflation is to be controlled. The first is a "public and institutional" commitment to price stability: "Many emerging market countries have had a history of poor support for the price stability goal and since laws are easily overturned in these countries, it is not clear that laws will be sufficient" (p. 11).

Mishkin's second institutional requirement is a public and institutional commitment to preserve the instrument independence of the central bank, which means that, although the central bank does not determine its own policy goals, it has freedom to choose the means of achieving these goals. The government tells the central bank to fight inflation, for example, but that said, it is the central bank and central bank alone that decides *how* to fight inflation (i.e., when to expand or contract the money supply or to raise or lower interest rates).

**Rules vs. Authorities.** One of the very old debates in monetary economics is whether it is better to have a central bank that operates under fixed rules or, conversely, with discretion and empowerment in making policy decisions. This debate is closely associated with the Chicago school of economics (the school of thought associated with the University of Chicago), and it goes back at least as far as the writings of Henry Simons (1899–1948).[22]

---

[22]See, for example, Simons (1948).

As Bernanke et al. (1999) stated, "Rules are monetary policies that are essentially automatic, requiring little or nothing in the way of macroeconomic analysis or value judgments by the monetary authorities" (p. 5). As examples of fixed rules, the authors cited (1) the gold standard and (2) Friedman's calling for central banks to allow the money supply to grow at a fixed percentage rate annually, independent of economic or financial conditions. In essence, the advocates of a rule-based system seek to remove from the central bank any discretion in conducting monetary policy. This view may come partly from a distrust of central banks and partly from the belief that the task of executing monetary policy is beyond the abilities of even the best central bankers.

The polar opposite is having a monetary authority with discretion for operating monetary policy however it sees fit. That much trust in a central bank, especially in the emerging markets, never seems to last for long.

Central banks do not always seek broad mandates for the conduct of monetary policy. In fact, many times they organize their affairs so as to limit their flexibility, which was evident in the Asian central banks' decisions to adopt fixed exchange rate regimes in the 1990s (pre-crises), a move that severely limited their ability to make policy. Market forces destroyed these fixed exchange rate regimes, in particular in the late 1990s. Thereupon, the Asian emerging-markets central banks were forced to float their currencies, and at that point, they had full monetary discretion. Yet, almost immediately, these same central banks went in search of an "anchor" for their monetary policy, many deciding, at least for now, on inflation targeting. Although Bernanke et al. (1999) classified inflation targeting as a monetary framework, instead of a monetary rule, it is still correct to say that these central banks moved away from full discretion.

## Monetary Policy Regimes

Another way to understand monetary policy is to classify the activities of central banks as belonging to different categories of monetary policy regimes. Bordo and Schwartz (1997) defined a monetary policy regime as "a set of monetary arrangements and institutions accompanied by a set of expectations—expectations by the public with respect to policy maker's reactions and expectations by policy makers about the public's reaction to their actions" (p. 4).

The International Monetary Fund (2006a) publication *Annual Report on Exchange Arrangements and Exchange Restrictions* (*AREAER*)—which I write about at length in Chapter 5—contains the following categories of monetary policy frameworks. Note that the descriptions are my own.

- **Exchange rate anchor:** Examples of this framework are fixed exchange rate arrangements, currency boards, and currency zones. In the first two, the monetary authority stands ready to buy or sell foreign currency at given quoted rates to maintain the exchange rate at its predetermined level or within a range. The broader implication for exchange rate anchors is that they circumscribe the central bank's powers to engage in monetary policy. As such, the central bank, in effect, has adopted the monetary policy of the reserve currency's central bank.

- **Monetary aggregate target:** The monetary authority uses its instruments to achieve a targeted growth rate in a monetary aggregate, such as reserve deposits, M1, or M2. Adherence to the money supply rule becomes the central bank's nominal anchor. The objective is to achieve control over inflation, with the intellectual foundation being the very quantity theory itself.

- **Inflation-targeting framework:** This framework involves the public announcement of medium-term numerical targets for inflation, with an institutional commitment by the monetary authority to achieve these targets. This topic is discussed in the next section of this chapter.

- **IMF-supported or other monetary program:** The IMF refers to these programs as those that involve implementation of monetary and exchange rate policies within the confines of a framework that establishes floors for international reserves and a ceiling for net domestic assets of the central bank.

- **Other:** The country has no explicitly stated nominal anchor but, rather, monitors various indicators in conducting monetary policy. This category is also used when no relevant information on the country is available.

**Exhibit 2.1** displays the 2006 *AREAER* classifications for selected emerging-markets nations; it shows the unmistakable popularity of inflation targeting, a topic that I will turn to next.

## Inflation Targeting

Many central banks are committed to containing the rate of inflation. But those that have become inflation targeters have three common characteristics:

- The central bank binds itself or is bound by law to maintaining a numerical target (or zone) for the rate of annual inflation.
- The central bank uses as its target a forecast of the intermediate-run rate of inflation.
- The central bank openly announces its medium-term inflation target.

Bernanke et al. (1999) defined inflation targeting as follows:

Inflation targeting is a framework for monetary policy characterized by the public announcement of official quantitative targets (or target ranges) for the inflation rate over one or more time horizons, and by explicit acknowledgement that low, stable inflation is monetary policy's primary long-run goal. Among other important features of inflation targeting are vigorous efforts to communicate with the public about the plans and objectives of the monetary authorities, and, in many cases, mechanisms that strengthen the central bank's accountability for attaining those objectives. (p. 4)

**Exhibit 2.1. Emerging-Markets Nations: Reported Monetary Policy Framework and Exchange Rate Arrangement**

| Country | Monetary Policy Framework | Exchange Rate Arrangement |
|---|---|---|
| Argentina | Monetary aggregate target | Managed float |
| Brazil | Inflation-targeting framework | Independent float |
| Chile | Inflation-targeting framework | Independent float |
| China | Monetary aggregate target | Conventional peg |
| Colombia | Inflation-targeting framework | Managed float |
| Czech Republic | Inflation-targeting framework | Managed float |
| Egypt | Exchange rate anchor | Conventional peg |
| Hungary | Inflation-targeting framework | Horizontal band |
| India | Other | Managed float |
| Indonesia | Monetary aggregate target | Managed float |
| Israel | Inflation-targeting framework | Independent float |
| Jordan | Exchange rate anchor | Conventional peg |
| Korea | Inflation-targeting framework | Independent float |
| Malaysia | Other | Managed float |
| Mexico | Inflation-targeting framework | Independent float |
| Morocco | Exchange rate anchor | Conventional peg |
| Pakistan | Exchange rate anchor | Conventional peg |
| Peru | Inflation-targeting framework | Managed float |
| Philippines | Inflation-targeting framework | Independent float |
| Poland | Inflation-targeting framework | Independent float |
| Russia | Other | Managed float |
| South Africa | Inflation-targeting framework | Independent float |
| Thailand | Inflation-targeting framework | Managed float |
| Turkey | Inflation-targeting framework | Independent float |

*Source*: Based on data from the International Monetary Fund (2006a).

Inflation targeting can rightly be regarded as a "minimalist approach" to central banking in that it focuses the monetary authority on the single goal of maintaining an acceptable intermediate-term rate of inflation. In part, the popularity of inflation targeting is a manifestation of the disappointment that central banks have had with more elaborate and compound goals, such as trying to create jobs while fighting inflation. In this sense, inflation targeting is a retrenchment from the activist central bank days of the 1970s and 1980s.[23] Its popularity also reflects what Bernanke et al. (1999) described as a new consensus: "One element of a new consensus is that low, stable inflation is important for market-driven growth, and that monetary policy is the most direct determinant of inflation" (p. 3).

---

[23] See Bernanke et al. (1999).

Students of central banking have applauded inflation targeting if for no other reason than it requires greater transparency with respect to the operations and policy of central banks.

**Exhibit 2.2** shows a list of central banks for developed and emerging-markets countries that have decided to adopt inflation targeting according to the International Monetary Fund (2005). Thirteen emerging-markets central banks and eight from industrialized nations have declared themselves inflation targeters. Note that the move to adopt inflation targeting began in the industrialized countries in the early 1990s, starting with New Zealand in 1990, and later spread to the emerging markets, starting with Israel in 1997.

**Exhibit 2.2.   Inflation Targeters**

| Country | Inflation-Targeting Adoption Date |
|---|---|
| *Emerging-markets countries* | |
| Israel | Q2:1997 |
| Czech Republic | Q1:1998 |
| South Korea | Q2:1998 |
| Poland | Q1:1999 |
| Brazil | Q2:1999 |
| Chile | Q3:1999 |
| Colombia | Q3:1999 |
| South Africa | Q1:2000 |
| Thailand | Q2:2000 |
| Mexico | Q1:2001 |
| Hungary | Q3:2001 |
| Peru | Q1:2002 |
| Philippines | Q1:2002 |
| *Industrialized countries* | |
| New Zealand | Q1:1990 |
| Canada | Q1:1991 |
| United Kingdom | Q4:1992 |
| Australia | Q1:1993 |
| Sweden | Q1:1993 |
| Switzerland | Q1:2000 |
| Iceland | Q1:2001 |
| Norway | Q1:2001 |

*Source*: Based on data from the International Monetary Fund (2005).

Why does a central bank adopt inflation targeting? Consider the case of Brazil. It was unable to maintain its fixed exchange rate for the real, its currency, in 1999. Fraga (2000), a former governor of Brazil's central bank, wrote about the January 1999 crisis:

> The first decision we faced was whether to go back to a managed peg or a fixed-rate regime, or whether to float. For standard optimum currency-area reasons, we felt it made sense to allow the real to continue to float. As a result, we needed to find a new nominal anchor. A policy based on a monetary aggregate did not seem feasible, particularly considering the uncertainties inherent in the crisis sweeping through the Brazilian economy. Another possibility was the adoption of a fully discretionary policy with an explicit anchor. However given the degree of instability expected, a stronger and more transparent commitment was essential. To address this need, we opted for a full-fledged inflation-targeting framework. (pp. 1–2)

One of the reasons for going to inflation targeting is to secure an "anchor" for monetary policy. Why the need for an anchor? In former times, when currencies were backed by commodities, such as gold, convertibility provided the basis for the value of money. When currencies became fiat money (meaning after 1971), a concern developed that there was no natural restraint on central banks. What was there to prevent an errant central bank from destroying the currency by issuing too much money? The answer may be inflation targeting; its promise is to be a framework sufficiently robust so as to keep a central bank on the straight and narrow path.

Proponents of inflation targeting argue that its use helps to build central bank credibility.[24] They also say it establishes an anchor for inflationary expectations. What is more, if it fails, the social and economic costs will be low—certainly lower than what emerging markets already had experienced when their fixed exchange rate pegs broke in the 1990s. Critics are concerned that inflation targeting leaves too little in the way of discretion for the central bank and, accordingly, allows too little room for growth-oriented policies.

Still, the proof of the pudding is in the eating, as Friedman was fond of saying. How well has inflation targeting performed? Preliminary results are encouraging. The International Monetary Fund (2005) reported an empirical investigation of the 13 emerging-markets inflation targeters compared with 29 other emerging-markets countries. They found that inflation targeting is associated with a significant 4.8 percentage point reduction in average inflation and a reduction in its standard deviation of 3.6 percent relative to other strategies. In summary:

> Inflation targeting leads to a reduction in the level and volatility of inflation expectations, along with inflation itself. This confirms the notion that inflation targeting has an advantage over other regimes at anchoring expectations and building credibility on a more durable basis, even if in emerging markets inflation targets are missed [by] more—and more often—than in industrialized countries. (p. 171)

---

[24] See Mishkin (2000a).

But the study warned, "Although the success of inflation targeting in emerging markets to date is encouraging, the time elapsed since they adopted inflation targeting is short" (p. 171).

A note of skepticism needs to be sounded. Geithner (2006) stated (but did not comment on inflation targeting):

> Over the past two decades, most of the world has experienced a substantial fall in inflation. During this period, the rate of inflation in the United States fell to levels broadly consistent with most definitions of price stability, and inflation expectations at longer horizons imply confidence that these gains will also prove durable. These gains were matched in many economies around the world, the result not just of the now widespread practice of having a central bank with instrument independence commit to an implicit or explicit goal of price stability, but also of course of the effects of global economic integration on competition and labor costs. (p. 1)

That inflation rates fell practically everywhere is a fact. But was inflation targeting the cause?

On a higher level, the implicit assumption with inflation targeting is that a central bank needs its powers to be corralled. Yet, a cynic could argue that no anchor is needed for an honest central bank and that for a rogue central bank, no anchor is strong enough. Moreover, there is no such thing as a policy that cannot be abandoned in times of adversity or stress. The anchor is only as good as the central bank or the government that stands behind it.

From another point of view, it could be said that inflation targeting might be an enormous benefit to emerging-markets central banks because it has given so many of them the courage to try flexible exchange rates. Absent this so-called anchor, they might have already retreated back to fixed exchange rates. There is another type of anchor, in the form of monetary policy rules, to which I now turn.

## The Taylor Rule

Taylor formulated his now famous monetary policy rule in 1992, which he proposed as a guideline for U.S. monetary policy. Taylor's original empirical relationship, known as the Taylor rule, states that

$$r = p + \frac{1}{2}y + \frac{1}{2}(p - 2) + 2,$$

where

    $r$ = the federal funds rate

    $p$ = the rate of inflation over the previous four quarters

    $y$ = the percent deviation of real GDP from trend

If the rate of inflation is "on target" (say 2 percent) and real GDP is on trend (say 2 percent, making $y = 0$), then the federal funds rate should be set at 4 percent.

Regrouping the terms demonstrates that the coefficient on $p$, the number by which $p$ is multiplied, is 1.5. That means a monetary authority using the Taylor rule would raise the nominal interest rate by more than the rise in the rate of inflation; thus, the real interest rate must rise. And this action is supposed to be the antidote to rising inflation. Also, the real interest rate would fall when the rate of inflation slowed. The Taylor rule also responds to the rise and fall of real income above or below trend. If inflation is held constant, it calls for a change in the interest rate, both nominal and real, by one-half and in the same direction as the change in real income from trend.

Taylor's rule became popular almost immediately with its first publication. Policy makers and central bank observers instantly saw the rule as charming in its simplicity. It is backed by empirical studies that show it being able to capture what were formally thought to be complex policy choices for the Federal Reserve.[25] Additionally, the Taylor rule, although derived empirically from historical data, provides a framework for conducting monetary policy on an ongoing basis. At a minimum, it serves as a benchmark for assessing the current state of monetary policy, and that alone is enough to make it extraordinarily useful to central banks.

In Taylor's (2000) words, a monetary policy rule is a "contingency plan that specifies as clearly as possible the circumstances under which a central bank should change the instruments of monetary policy" (p. 3). Taylor cited the example of a change in an instrument (such as the federal funds rate) that would accompany an increase in inflation or real GDP relative to potential GDP. The policy rule is expected to be a permanent, or nearly permanent, feature of central bank policy. In contrast, inflation targeting is not a monetary policy rule because it simply "gives a target for a variable." One of the chief criticisms of the Taylor rule is that it does not allow for policy measures to counteract conditions that are totally out of sample. Taylor might respond by saying that the central bank could still use his equation to measure how far it had deviated from its steady state framework in making exceptional monetary policy.

One question frequently asked about the Taylor rule is whether its author intends it to be used in a completely mechanical manner; in other words, does Taylor want to put his followers at central banks in a monetary policy straitjacket? Taylor (2000) made it clear that this was not his intention:

> Such criticism is misplaced: No one is saying—at least to my knowledge—that the proposed policy rules should be used mechanically. . . . Just because monetary policy rules can be written down as a mechanical-looking mathematical equation does not imply that central banks should follow them mechanically. (p. 5)

---

[25] Asso, Kahn, and Leeson (2007) wrote: "In addition to prescribing a method of reducing the swings of the business cycle, the Taylor Rule also apparently described the stabilization method unwittingly used by the Fed" (p. 2).

The question for my purpose here is whether the Taylor rule can be used for emerging markets as a guideline or general policy framework. The answer, according to Taylor (2000) himself, is in the affirmative. He went on to say that his monetary policy rules may require modification from the rules he developed for economies with "more developed" financial markets. Taylor discussed a potential modification to his original monetary policy rules for use in emerging markets. That modification is with respect to the choice of policy instrument.

Taylor's work with developed countries assumes that short-term overnight interest rates are the policy instrument. Yet it is possible to use monetary aggregates as the policy instrument. The reason has to do with the fact that in some emerging-markets countries, it is not yet possible to obtain a precise measure of the real interest rate, and knowing the real interest rate at its current and historical levels is essential for the calibration of the Taylor rule equation. Taylor has said it is possible to replace the interest rate with the money supply as the instrument of policy.

Once the mechanics and estimation issues are resolved, Taylor's discovery might provide a substitute for inflation targeting that can be used in the newly exchange rate–flexible emerging markets. Taylor (2000) stated:

> For those emerging market economies that do not choose a policy of "permanently" fixing the exchange rate—perhaps through a currency board or dollarization, the only sound monetary policy is one based on the *trinity of a flexible exchange rate, an inflation target, and a monetary policy rule*.[26] (p. 1)

---

[26] Taylor's use of the term "trinity" is not the same as the impossible trinity I discuss later in Chapter 3.

# 3. Emerging Markets as Open Economies

Almost by definition, emerging-markets nations are open economies, except where law and government policies erect obstacles to international trade and the circulation of investment capital. But in their natural state, openness derives from their relative small size within the world economy, from the importance of import and export markets to them, and from their interaction in global capital markets both as debtor and investor. The economic well-being of the emerging markets depends in no small part on trade and capital flows.

Economists generally hold that economic openness confers benefits with respect to access to new export and import markets as well as the ability to participate in world capital markets. But openness also means that the emerging markets have to deal with the consequences of external shocks from unwelcome or aberrant trade flows as well as from international financial crises. Furthermore, openness means that economic forces outside the emerging-markets nations' borders have large influences on their national income, interest rates, prices, and exchange rates. Indeed, being an open economy forces a country to sacrifice some of the effectiveness and the freedom that policy makers have in conducting monetary and fiscal policy compared with what policy might be able to achieve in a hypothetical closed economy. Still, despite whatever costs or disadvantages, the benefits from free and open markets are taken seriously by most nations.

## Balance of Payments

Any discussion of the open economy must begin with consideration of such concepts as the current account, capital account, and balance of payments. These concepts are important because, among other things, they relate to the sustainability of monetary policy and the permanence or fragility of the exchange rate regime. They also indicate whether a country is building up or running down external indebtedness.

Generally speaking, the balance of payments accounts refer to a framework for recording transactions between a country and all other countries during a particular period of time. These are transactions for the purchase and sale of goods, services, capital assets, and financial assets, and they also record the flow of investment income and monetary transfers. Transactions that cause money to flow into a country are credits to be posted to the balance of payments accounts, and transactions that represent money flowing out are recorded as debits.

The IMF collects and publishes extensive data on international transactions in its *Balance of Payments Statistics Yearbook*. It groups transactions into three main categories: the current account, the capital account, and the financial account.[27] In brief,

- The current account records transactions for goods and services, investment income, and unilateral transfers with foreigners.[28]
- The capital account (CAPAC) records capital asset transactions for capital goods (fixed assets) with foreigners.
- The financial account (FA) records purchases and sales of financial assets with foreigners.

Taken together, these three accounts balance in the sense that they sum to zero, conceptually. For example, a current account deficit must be accompanied by an equally large surplus in the sum of the capital account and financial account in order to finance the deficit. The distinction between the capital and financial accounts reflects a modern view. Often, when people speak of the "capital account," they mean the sum of what the IMF calls the capital and financial accounts. The measurement of international transactions is understandably imprecise. For this reason, the IMF's reporting includes an additional account called "net errors and omissions."

A subcategory of the financial account called the "changes in the official reserves account" measures the expansion or contraction in the central bank's holdings of foreign assets that could be used to satisfy the balance of payments—referred to here as foreign assets at the central bank (FACB). These items include monetary gold, special drawing rights (reserve positions in the IMF), foreign exchange assets (currency, deposits, and securities), and other claims. This category is important because the assets of the central bank, of which these are part, are the backing for the money supply. The size of the official reserves account is a policy variable for the central bank.

For purposes of analysis, it makes sense to segregate changes in the official reserves account from the rest of the financial account flows. The portion of the financial account not related to changes in central bank official reserves will be designated as FANCB (financial account non-central bank).[29] By definition,

$$FA = \Delta FACB + FANCB, \tag{3.1}$$

[27]See Hakkio (1995) for additional discussion of the current account.

[28]The term "balance of trade" refers to the net difference between exports and imports—that is, exports minus imports. The current account consists of the balance of trade plus net factor income from abroad (mostly dividends and interest on investments) plus net remittances. Of these components of the current account, the balance of trade is usually by far the largest. The balance of trade is sometimes confused with the balance of payments, discussed later in this chapter, but the two concepts are quite distinct.

[29]The current account, capital account, and financial account are all flow variables. The official reserves account is a stock variable, but the change in its level is a flow variable.

which leads to a well-known accounting identity:

$$-\Delta FACB = (\text{Current account}) + (\text{Capital account}) + (\text{FANCB})$$
$$+ (\text{Net errors and omissions}).$$
(3.2)

This expression can be simplified by ignoring the net errors and omissions and writing the current account as the difference between exports ($X$) and imports ($M$). Furthermore, in some contexts, the change in the official reserves account, $\Delta FACB$, is referred to as the balance of payments, BOP. The resulting "balance of payments accounting identity" may thus be written:

$$-\text{BOP} = X - M + \text{CAPAC} + \text{FANCB}.$$
(3.3)

**Box 3.1** shows the breakdown of China's balance of payments for the year 2005.

**Box 3.1. People's Republic of China, Balance of Payments: 2005 (US$ billions)**

| | | | |
|---|---|---|---|
| Current account | | | |
|    Exports | $762.5 | | |
|    Imports | 628.3 | | |
|   Trade balance | | $134.2 | |
|   Services | | (9.4) | |
|   Income | | 10.6 | |
|   Current transfers | | 25.4 | |
| **Current account balance** | | | $160.8 |
| Capital and financial accounts | | | |
|   Capital account | | $ 41.0 | |
|    Net foreign direct investment | $ 67.8 | | |
|    Portfolio investment | (4.9) | | |
|    Other investment | (4.0) | | |
|   Financial account | | $ 58.9 | |
| **Capital and financial account balance** | | | $ 63.0 |
| **Errors and omissions** | | | $ (16.7) |
| **Balance of payments** | | | $207.1 |

*Source*: Based on data from International Monetary Fund (2006b).

# Perfect Capital Mobility

Mundell's (1963) celebrated paper frames almost every discussion of foreign exchange regimes and monetary and fiscal policy.[30] He received the Nobel Prize in Economics in 1999 for his analysis of monetary and fiscal policy under different exchange rate regimes and for his theory of optimal currency areas. The key concept that Mundell introduced is "extreme capital mobility," elsewhere referred to as "perfect capital mobility." Mundell defined the concept as what would prevail "when a country cannot maintain an interest rate different from the general level prevailing abroad" (p. 475). He augmented this definition as follows:

> The assumption of perfect capital mobility can be taken to mean that all securities in the system are perfect substitutes. Since different countries are involved this implies that existing exchange rates are expected to persist indefinitely (even when the exchange rate is not pegged) and that spot and forward exchange rates are identical. All complications associated with speculation, the forward market, and exchange rate margins are thereby assumed not to exist. (pp. 475–476)

Perfect capital mobility is what fixes every country's interest rate to the single worldwide interest rate. Capital flows are infinitely elastic at the prevailing interest rate. Mundell further assumed that the prices of goods and nominal wages are fixed; thus, the analysis is the same in real and nominal terms (because there is no inflation anywhere). Two more elements of Mundell's model follow:

- The demand for money is a function of income and the interest rate.
- The balance of trade is a function of income and the exchange rate.

Expansionary fiscal policy in Mundell's model is the government's increasing spending that is financed with newly issued sovereign debt. His monetary policy is conducted with open market operations.

Mundell's analysis focuses on the broad implications of the differences between flexible and fixed exchange rate regimes. A series of theorems follows.

**Flexible Exchange Rates.** *Under flexible exchange rates, monetary policy is effective but fiscal policy is not.*

Under flexible exchange rates, the balance of payments cannot be anything other than zero because the central bank does not engage in transactions to fix or alter the exchange rate. Consider monetary policy first. Suppose the central bank conducts an open market operation to buy domestic assets. This operation increases the monetary base, and because of expansion by fractional reserves, it increases the broad-based monetary aggregates. Because the price level is fixed, the real quantity of money expands. This monetary expansion puts downward pressure on the interest rate, and accordingly, there is a large and probably sudden flow of capital out of the

---

[30]Credit for these ideas is shared by J. Marcus Fleming (1961, 1962, and 1978), and as such, parts of this analysis are often called "Mundell–Fleming."

country, which puts downward pressure on the exchange rate. This last effect causes the balance of trade to improve. Income, employment, and the demand for money then rise. In the end, the demand for money must rise by precisely enough to absorb all the new money created by the open market operation, and this must be the end result because of Mundell's concept of capital mobility.

To summarize, because of the open market operation, money supply rises, income and employment rise, and the exchange rate falls. The remarkable part is that monetary policy is effective despite the fact that interest rates and prices are fixed. In this model, monetary policy works through the channel of the exchange rate.

The second part of the theorem states that fiscal policy can have no effect on income and employment under Mundell's assumption of perfect capital mobility in the case of flexible exchange rates. Consider as fiscal policy an increase in government spending that is financed by the issuance of new debt.[31] New spending puts pressure on income and interest rates to rise. A massive inflow of capital ensues, leading to an increase in the exchange rate and a deterioration in the balance of trade. The latter is contractionary, and the process ends when the national income has returned to its original level from before the advent of the fiscal stimulus. The lesson is that fiscal policy in a flexible exchange rate environment can have no lasting effect on income and employment.

The same analysis for fiscal policy works for foreign trade shocks: An external trade shock cannot affect a country's income or employment, again because of perfect capital mobility in the case of flexible exchange rates. As Dornbusch, Fischer, and Startz (1997) wrote: "The important lesson here is that real disturbances to demand do not affect equilibrium output under flexible rates with perfect capital mobility" (p. 289).[32]

**Fixed Exchange Rates.** *Under fixed exchange rates, fiscal policy can be effective but monetary policy cannot.*

Under fixed exchange rates, the balance of payments is not zero because the central bank must add or subtract foreign reserves periodically to maintain the exchange rate peg. The picture thus has changed dramatically.

What is true about monetary and fiscal policy under flexible exchange rates is true in reverse for fixed exchange rates! Start with monetary policy. In the flexible exchange rate case, monetary policy works through the exchange rate; once the exchange rate is fixed, there is no channel for monetary policy.

---

[31]Some are skeptical as to whether an increase in government spending financed by the issuance of new bonds can stimulate the economy at all. Forward-looking economic agents would factor into their decision making the increased liability for future taxes created by the new bonds. This is known as the Ricardian equivalence theorem (see Barro 1974).

[32]Dornbusch et al. (1997) presented models similar in spirit to Mundell (1963).

## Box 3.2.   An Alternative Basic Macroeconomic Model

Many of the results that Mundell derived either change or become ambiguous when alterations are made to his assumptions. For example, Krugman and Obstfeld's (1997) best selling textbook on international economics contains an open economy model where fiscal policy has real effects when exchange rates are flexible. Their model does not have an assumption like Mundell's of a unique world interest rate. Instead, there is an asset market equilibrium brought about by interest rates and expectations of exchange rate movements. They posit that market participants believe there is a long-term equilibrium exchange rate, $E^e$, that is unalterable except in special circumstances. The exchange rate observed in the market is denoted as $E$ (quoted American—the number of units of domestic currency required to buy one unit of foreign currency). Equilibrium in the asset market demands that the domestic interest rate, $i$, be equal to the foreign interest rate, $i_f$, plus the rate of return on the currency that would be sufficient to move the current exchange rate to the long-term equilibrium:

$$i = i_f + \frac{E^e - E}{E}.$$

The second term is always zero in Mundell's model by his explicit assumption that the exchange rate is expected to never move.

Krugman and Obstfeld's idea is that movements in the exchange rate guarantee that their asset market equilibrium condition will be satisfied. For example, a temporary increase in the money supply would not affect $E^e$ (because the authors have assumed that $E^e$ cannot change). But the domestic interest rate would fall, income would rise, and the value of the local currency would have to fall. The reason why the exchange rate must fall is so that it is repositioned to rise, meaning it falls so it can then rise to compensate for the fact that the local interest rate has fallen. If the increase in the money supply is permanent, both the long-term value of the currency, $E^e$, and the current value of the currency must drop. This outcome is not dissimilar from Mundell except that the interest rate has changed.

More interesting is the case of fiscal policy. Fiscal stimulus that is temporary will raise output and raise the value of the currency. Here the logic is that the stimulus will raise income along with the demand for real balances. The latter will raise the local interest rate. To keep the asset market in equilibrium, the current exchange rate must rise to validate their equation (if the current exchange rate is below $E^e$ it must rise to absorb some of future exchange rate capital gains because the local interest rate is now higher than before). If the change in fiscal policy is permanent, it will cause both the long-term equilibrium exchange rate and the current exchange rate to rise. However, if the economy is at full employment, the permanent change in fiscal policy will cause crowding out of exports.

The subtle point is that fiscal policy was neutral in Mundell's flexible exchange rate world where interest rates were universally set to the world level. What Krugman and Obstfeld do is jettison the fixed world rate for a no-arbitrage condition (my term, not theirs) involving both interest rates and expected appreciation or depreciation in exchange rates. Their model allows for fiscal policy to influence the equilibrium in a world of flexible exchange rates. Also see Abel and Bernanke (2001).

For example, suppose the central bank conducts an open market operation to buy domestic assets. This action causes an expansion of the money supply (both of the monetary base as well as the broad-based aggregates). Pressure is on the interest rate to drop, which implies an outflow of capital. The exchange rate falls, or at least attempts to fall. Given the commitment to keep the exchange rate fixed, the central bank must begin buying its own currency and selling foreign assets. This maneuver will have to be continued until the pressure on the exchange rate vanishes, which means the money supply will have to go back to the level that prevailed before the open market operation.

Fiscal policy, in contrast, works like a charm, but it needs some help from monetary policy. A rise in government spending will raise income, which, in turn, pushes up the demand for real balances. That action puts pressure on the interest rate to rise. To maintain the fixed exchange rate, the central bank must counter the incipient inflow of capital by conducting open market operations to put downward pressure on the interest rate. If the central bank does not do so, the fixed exchange rate will be broken by capital flooding into the country.

Imbedded in the Mundell (1963) paper are two corollaries.

**Foreign Exchange Intervention.** *Open market operations and foreign exchange intervention are equivalent in impact on national income and employment.*

The two operations are virtually identical except that the foreign exchange intervention changes foreign reserves and the open market operation alters domestic assets. The impact on the money supply is identical.

**Sterilization.** *Sterilized intervention will have no effect on national income or employment.*

In sterilized intervention, the composition of the central bank's balance sheet changes but the size of the monetary base remains constant. Mundell showed that, under perfect capital mobility, open market operations combined with foreign exchange intervention (in the opposite direction) cancel out each other's effects on national income.

# The Impossible Trinity

One outgrowth of Mundell's work on capital mobility is a concept known as the "impossible trinity" (or the "inconsistent trinity" or simply the "trinity"). Mundell himself may not have used this catchy term, but he is widely credited for its intellectual foundation. The concept is that capital mobility constrains a central bank to having at most two of the following:

- a fixed exchange rate,
- an independent monetary policy, and
- openness to capital flows.

Perfect capital mobility à la Mundell is not required for the trinity to be impossible; a sufficient degree of openness to capital flows will do the job.

The trinity is a standard feature in discussions of international economics. For example, Obstfeld and Taylor (2002) stated:

> The macroeconomic policy trilemma for open economies (also known as the "inconsistent trinity" proposition) follows from a basic fact: An open capital market deprives a country's government of the ability simultaneously to target its exchange rate and to use monetary policy in pursuit of other economic objectives. (p. 7)

The trinity indicates that a country cannot have a fixed exchange rate if it wants to have both monetary independence and an open capital account.[33] Put differently, a country would have to freeze its capital account, meaning that it stops autonomous capital flows, if it wanted to have both a domestic-oriented monetary policy and a fixed exchange rate.

One economist whose work is associated with the trinity concept is Frankel (1999). Frankel's rendition of the trinity is depicted in **Figure 3.1**. Each of the three sides of his triangle has an "attraction," to use Frankel's term. These are monetary independence, exchange rate stability, and full financial integration. As with the previous definition, at most a pair of these attributes is attainable: A country can have at most two but never three of the attributes. Each vertex is adjoined by two attainable sides. The side opposite to any vertex is unattainable (i.e., "impossible"). At the vertex denoted "full capital controls," the country can have monetary independence and exchange rate stability but not full financial integration. At the "pure float" vertex, the country can have monetary independence and full financial integration but not exchange rate stability. At the "monetary union" vertex—for example, dollarization—the country can have full financial integration and exchange rate stability but not monetary independence with respect to the reserve currency.

The trinity is useful in understanding some recent historical episodes.

**European Exchange Rate Mechanism.** Before the launch of the euro (1 January 1999), the central banks of the European Monetary System (EMS) attempted to keep their exchange rates fixed within a target zone apparatus called the Exchange Rate Mechanism. Nonetheless, the individual central banks, notably the Bundesbank (German central bank), attempted to exercise their own independent monetary policies. In effect, it was an attempt to have all three sides of the triangle. Two major foreign exchange crises (1992 and 1993) plus dozens of realignments in exchange rates argued otherwise.

---

[33]Or to use the earlier classification, have open capital and financial accounts.

**Figure 3.1. Frankel's Impossible Trinity**

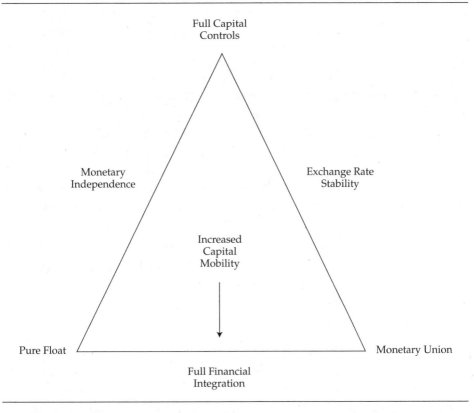

**Euro (since 1 January 1999).** Individually, the euro member countries are at the monetary union vertex of the triangle. They have financial integration and exchange rate stability, the latter because there are no legacy currencies, such as the French franc or German mark. Individually, they have no monetary independence. The euro zone, in contrast, is at the pure float vertex. The European Central Bank has monetary independence, and the zone is financially integrated, but there is no exchange rate stability (the euro moves freely against the U.S. dollar and Japanese yen, for example).

**Asian Emerging-Markets Crises of 1997–1998.** The precrisis history of Thailand, Indonesia, the Philippines, and South Korea led some observers to believe these countries had successfully defied the trinity: Each had open capital accounts, central banks that practiced independent monetary policy, and an exchange rate that was fixed. Once again, the impossible trinity seems to have had its way, because all these countries experienced ferocious currency crises leading them to abandon their fixed exchange rate regimes.

**China's Monetary Policy.** China managed to maintain its famous fixed exchange rate for the yuan throughout and after the Asian currency crises of 1997–1998. What made it possible is that China has never made its capital account convertible. China's *current* account, however, is convertible, and that arrangement has severely limited the central bank's ability to control the growth of money supply.

**Malaysian Capital Controls of 1998.** Malaysia upset financial markets in 1998 when it imposed capital controls more than one year after the Southeast Asian crisis erupted. This action allowed Malaysia to conduct independent monetary policy. At the same time as the installation of capital controls, Malaysia fixed its exchange rate. Over the course of the following year, Malaysia gradually abandoned its capital controls. Yet Malaysia kept the ringgit pegged to the U.S. dollar until the middle of 2005. In the end, this country found that it had more to gain than to lose from openness to financial markets.

Frankel's (1999) discussion of the trinity is interesting because of what he called "intermediate solutions," meaning the sides of the triangle as opposed to the vertices. He wrote, with respect to his triangle:

> The general trend of financial integration has pushed most countries toward the lower part of the graph. If one is at the bottom leg of the triangle, the choice is narrowed down to a simple decision regarding the degree of exchange rate flexibility. But even under perfect capital mobility there is nothing to prevent the country from choosing an intermediate solution in between floating and monetary union. (pp. 8–9).

I will return to this topic in Chapter 5 when I cover the topic of choice of exchange rate regime.

Other impossible combinations may exist—but not for Mundell's reasons—besides the ones called the impossible trinity. For example, a country that defaults on its sovereign debt may find it impossible to keep a fixed exchange rate regime, especially if there is some openness in capital movements. This appears to have been the case with Russia in 1998 and Argentina in 2001, when a declaration of default on maturing government debt occurred nearly simultaneously with the forced abandonment of the fixed exchange rate regime.

## Role of the Exchange Rate

Mundell's 1963 paper is a classic in the field and has framed debates on exchange rates ever since its publication. Nonetheless, I need to stress that Mundell's tidy results are highly dependent on his precise definition of perfect capital mobility and his assumption that prices and wages are fixed. For my purposes, the assumption of perfect mobility of capital may not put the analysis in the right focus, and neither may the construct of having a single, universal interest rate be realistic. Most economists believe that interest rates and price levels can be influenced by monetary policy. According to Abel and Bernanke (2001):

> In general, real interest rates in different countries need not be the same when countries produce different goods. The reason is that real interest rates in different countries measure different things. For example, the Japanese real interest rate measures the growth of an asset's purchasing power in terms of Japanese goods, whereas the German real interest rate measures the growth of the asset's purchasing power in terms of German goods. If the Japanese-German real exchange rate is changing, the two need not be the same. (p. 485)

I turn now to the role of the exchange rate, where I make some important distinctions. Macroeconomists tend to agree on two axioms with regard to the exchange rate. The first is that the long-run value for the exchange rate reflects the relative price levels in the two countries, which is basic purchasing power parity. If the same basket of goods costs $2 in the United States and £1 in the United Kingdom, the exchange rate ought to converge, in the long term, to £1 equaling $2. In the short run, this relationship is almost never exact, of course, meaning there are widespread obvious departures from the law of one price.

One way to measure such deviations is to calculate the real exchange rate, $R^{real}$, which is the product of the exchange rate ($E$) and the ratio of the local price level ($P$) to the foreign price level ($P_f$):

$$R^{real} = E\frac{P}{P_f}, \tag{3.4}$$

where $E$ is quoted American style (meaning in number of units of local, or domestic, currency per unit of foreign currency). I hasten to point out that foreign exchange conventions are confusing; a rise in $E$ means that the foreign currency has appreciated and that the local currency has depreciated. The latter is my focus. For example, if the exchange rate for the British pound goes from $1.50 to $1.60, $E$ will have risen but the value of the U.S. dollar will have dropped because it takes more U.S. currency to buy a specified amount of pounds. I would then say that the exchange rate (meaning the local currency, the dollar) has *depreciated*. Likewise, a rise in $R^{real}$ means the real value of the local currency has depreciated.

The second fundamental axiom of macroeconomics is that the current account is driven, at least in part, by the real exchange rate. Said another way, the current account depends on the joint product of the nominal exchange rate and the relative prices of domestic and foreign goods. An appreciation in the real exchange rate makes foreign goods less expensive for domestic residents and domestic goods more expensive for foreigners, which, all other things being equal, should lead to deterioration in the current account (meaning a smaller surplus or larger deficit). Additionally, the current account is a function of national income. A rise in domestic income ought to lead to an increase in the domestic demand for imported goods and, as a consequence, a deterioration (meaning a smaller surplus or larger deficit) in the current account.[34] Other factors influence the current account, such as foreign income, comparative advantages in trade, and taxes. Institutional factors, tariffs, quotas, development policies, taxes, and the like can materially affect the current account.

This economic logic is fine, at least as far as it goes. The trouble comes if one tries to reverse the causality—that is, if one wants to assert that the exchange rate is controlled by the current account position and, furthermore, that the primary role of the exchange rate is to cause a current account deficit or surplus to erode or completely disappear.

In the days of the gold standard, there was an automatic stabilizer of current account positions. It is called the "Hume price-specie flow mechanism." The international movement of specie would, in theory, crush current account balance deficits or surpluses. It worked through the quantity theory. The movement of physical gold represented changes in local and foreign money supplies, which, operating through the quantity equation, should have induced changes in domestic and foreign price levels. The country with the current account deficit exported gold; the country with the surplus imported gold. These, in turn, brought about changes in the price levels that ultimately reversed the flow of goods over time. The whole process should be as natural as the celestial clockwork that moves the planets around the sun.

But can it be presumed that there always exists such an automatic stabilizer and that even today a current account deficit or surplus is a self-liquidating phenomenon over time? If exchange rates are the vectors of such processes, then the existence of a deficit, for example, will bring about its own resolution by its forcing the domestic currency to depreciate. Likewise a surplus will cause the domestic currency to appreciate. This is all very elegant, terribly clever, but it unfortunately does not conform to what we observe in the modern world. In economics, what goes up does not have to come back down just because it went up in the first place. The world went off the gold standard in 1971. This shift ushered in the age of national currencies and floating exchange rates. But exchange rates, unlike gold specie movements before, have not assumed the role of moderator of current account positions. And indeed, there have been times when exchange rates have moved in exactly the opposite way as what current account positions would predict, as Greenspan (2003) stated: "Nonetheless, as the U.S. current account deficit rose from 1995 to early 2002, so did the dollar's effective exchange rate" (p. 2).

The critical element is the other side of the equation, namely, the capital account. Changes in the capital and financial accounts are driven by investor expectations about relative rates of return on capital invested around the world, with every consideration given to the present and future level of the exchange rate.

---

[34]See Houthakker and Magee (1969) for more on this topic.

Capital flows also respond to institutional factors, foreign income, foreign interest rates, taxes, capital controls, and the like. As was mentioned earlier, simple double-entry bookkeeping requires that a current account deficit (surplus) be matched by a capital account or financial account surplus (deficit). But what is the direction of causality in these relationships? Does the current account deficit, for example, create the capital or financial account surplus, or does the capital or financial account surplus cause the current account deficit? Again, Greenspan (2003) indicates:

> In as much as the balance of goods and services is brought into equality with the associated capital flows with adjustments in prices, interest rates, and exchange rates, how do we tell whether trade determines capital flows or whether capital flows determine trade? (p. 2)

Following Greenspan, note that in earlier times, when global capital was not nearly as mobile as it is now, it may have made sense to think more about the current account as the driver. But in modern times, a better understanding of the balance of payments comes from paying attention to the capital and financial accounts. Again, Greenspan (2003) wrote:

> Evidently, upward pressure on the dollar was spurred by rising expected rates of return that resulted in private capital investments from abroad that chronically exceeded the current account deficit. The pickup in U.S. productivity growth in the mid-1990s—the likely proximate cause of foreigners' perception of increased rates of return on capital in the United States—boosted investment spending, stock prices, wealth, and assessments of future income. (p. 2)

Note that Greenspan explained the movement in the dollar being directed from the capital and financial accounts, not the exchange rate moving to eradicate the current account.

This is the exchange rate phenomenon that has confounded central bankers in many emerging-markets nations: Net capital inflows are frequently associated with their exchange rate rising (not falling, as would be expected if one focused solely on the current account). Often, they see the need to protect their export industries from becoming less competitive internationally at the higher exchange rate, presumably because of the influx of foreign capital. This problem can be acute for the emerging- (and developing-) markets nations because many rely on expanding their export industries to jump-start economic growth. For this reason, some central banks have resorted to foreign exchange intervention (with and without sterilization) and even capital controls in attempts to tame the incipient rise in their currency. I will discuss these topics in Chapter 7.

## Emerging-Markets Capital and Financial Accounts

Two broad episodes in recent economic history illustrate the dynamics of the capital and financial accounts for emerging markets. The first is the case of Latin America and parts of Asia in the early 1990s, before the currency crises of the late 1990s.

Capital was flowing into these regions from the industrial countries, such as the United States and Japan. As Calvo, Leiderman, and Reinhart (1994) stated:

> After a decade in which little capital flowed to the developing nations, the 1990s appear to have launched a new era in which capital has started to move from industrial countries, like the United States and Japan, to developing regions, like Latin America, the Middle East, and parts of Asia. (p. 54)

They assigned the cause to a combination of domestic reforms:

> (i) successful price stabilization programs that may be accompanied by improved fiscal policy fundamentals and greater macroeconomic stability, (ii) institutional reforms, such as the liberalization of the domestic capital market, and (iii) policies that credibly increase the rate of return on domestic investment projects, such as tax credits and debt-equity swaps. (p. 55)

and external factors. The most important reasons among the latter are:

> Low short-term U.S. interest rates, decreasing returns in other investments, and a recession in the United States as well as in other industrial countries [that] converged to stimulate capital flows to regions where *ex-ante* returns are higher. (p. 56)

The second period follows the emerging-markets crises of the late 1990s, including the present time (2008), when capital flows are moving in the opposite direction from what was observed in the early 1990s. As will be discussed in Chapter 6, at the present, the United States is running what amounts to a truly massive current account deficit. That is, the United States is importing much more (in goods and services) than it is exporting. Accordingly, capital of the same size is flowing into the United States. One reason suggested by economists for the extent of the capital flows into the United States is that the country experienced significant rises in productivity beginning in the mid-1990s, as noted by Greenspan (2003). Productivity gains are thought to signal enhanced rates of return on capital, at least in the United States. Nothing like this was happening in the emerging-markets nations. As a consequence, emerging-markets countries, the same ones that were capital importers before 1997, have turned into capital exporters. That so much capital would be leaving the emerging markets is thought to be evidence of their being tainted by the sour experiences from the crises of the 1990s.

This is an example of how the capital account and financial account calculus can be affected, even distorted, by such things as taxes, restrictions on investments, abandonment of existing capital controls or threats of imposing new ones, and the degree to which the exchange rate is close to or far from being a free float. Choosing an exchange rate regime is obviously a complex question because fixed exchange rate regimes, in some incarnations, attract investment and in other incarnations, repel investors. Indeed, all the spectacular emerging-markets financial crises of the 1990s involved the dismantling of some form of fixed exchange rate system. This observation can be added to the factors explaining capital flows that are discussed in Calvo et al. (1994). Some part of the capital inflows to the emerging markets in the early 1990s were created by distortions arising from the fixed exchange rate regimes. Moreover, practically all the cash flows that subsequently flooded out from the emerging markets were prompted by expectations of imminent collapses of the fixed exchange rates (see DeRosa 2001a).

## Are Current Account Deficits Dangerous?

The question that naturally arises from these discussions is whether a large current account deficit in and of itself is a harbinger of economic disaster. Some economists blame the emerging-markets crises of the late 1990s on the fact that every one of the stricken countries was running a substantial current account deficit before it crashed. The extreme view is now sometimes heard that a country running large and persistent current account deficits will at best see its currency depreciate and at worst be visited by economic catastrophe. Is there something dangerous, if not odious, about current account deficits?

For example, Fischer (2006), in summing up the beliefs of attendees at an IMF conference on global imbalances, asked: "Why is almost everyone happy to have a current account surplus?" (p. 3). One key reason, according to him, was:

> The mercantilist instinct is very deep. In addition, the experience of the 1990s has persuaded policymakers that it is not good to run a large current account deficit, which in most countries is translated into the view that a current account surplus is better than a deficit. (p. 3)

This statement is remarkable. Fischer, a pre-eminent economist and former high official of the IMF, was telling the seminar of economists that their understanding of the current account is rooted in mercantilism. That doctrine professes that a country's wealth derives from its exports, more precisely from its exports exceeding imports, thereby creating a hoped-for current account surplus. Mercantilism was important in the history of economic thought only because it was wrong. It was the very concept that the great classical economists like Adam Smith, David Hume, and David Ricardo rejected in its entirety, and in so doing, they founded the field of economics.

But let me step back for a moment to consider what is bogus about mercantilism. The idea that a country grows richer by arranging to have a positive balance of trade is very seductive. A country could impose tariffs or subsidize industrial development of newly formed export industries. What could be wrong with preferring that money flow into, as opposed to out of, the country? On an individual level, if someone is earning more in dollars than he or she is spending, the result is a positive cash flow, which is good, right? Yes. The more an individual can earn by selling goods and services to other individuals in exchange for money, the better off the individual is. The subtle flaw is that what works for one individual in isolation does not work for an entire nation. There is a fallacy of composition.

Adam Smith tells us that the "wealth of nations" is not the balance of trade. The foreign sector is only one piece of any total economy. What about the nonforeign sector? More to the point, what about the country as a whole? Countries that engage in international trade will produce a different, better, and more valuable constellation of goods and services than they otherwise might if they did not have access to foreign trade. That is what one learns from the classical economist David Ricardo and his theory of comparative advantage (why it made sense for Portugal to produce wine and England to produce wool but for neither country to produce both).

---

**Box 3.3. Ricardo's Theory of Comparative Advantage**

Ricardo's theory of comparative advantage focuses on the opportunity cost of production of goods rather than the absolute cost advantage. Even though almost everything was cheaper in Portugal than in England in his time (to use his famous example)—meaning Portugal had an absolute price advantage in both of his two goods, wool and wine—the two countries garnered gains from trade. These gains came from the differentials in the opportunity costs of production in the two countries.

On the margin, England could make more wool than Portugal by giving up production of some wine; Portugal could make more wine than England by giving up the production of some wool. It simply makes sense for England to produce wool for export to Portugal and for Portugal to make wine for export to England. In this way, Ricardo shifts from absolute costs to comparative or opportunity costs.

Obviously trade theory has advanced tremendously since Ricardo's time; this discussion is highly simplified and is only meant to show that the classical economists succeeded in producing potent counterexamples to mercantilism.

---

In other words, the existence of foreign trade allows industries to play to their relative economic advantages. Alternatively, when consumers have the benefit of buying foreign-produced goods, their welfare is improved because the foreign-made goods may cost less than homemade items. Trade also introduces a greater variety of goods to local markets. Schuler (1996), who was writing in a slightly different context, had an excellent anecdote of the benefits of trade to consumers:

> Iceland has a terrible climate for growing bananas. Yet for years Iceland grew all of its own bananas, in hothouses, because the government imposed trade restrictions on imported bananas. Eventually the government removed the restrictions and Icelanders now eat bananas grown in the tropics. In a hothouse in southwestern Iceland, a lone banana tree remains as a minor tourist attraction. (p. 9)

Iceland may have a comparative advantage in fishing but not in tropical fruit agriculture. Schuler could have written that the lone remaining banana plant was a monument to the advantages of international trade or the folly of governments for obstructing it.

But one encounters the enemies of international trade everywhere—not just at seminars attended by economists who have fallen back into the trap of mercantilist thinking. Another old saying is that a country with a large current account deficit must be losing its competitive edge in manufacturing and services. For example, one hears repeatedly that the U.S. current account deficit stems from U.S. industry losing its competitive edge with Asia. The evidence presented includes the flood of imports of inexpensive goods from China and other relatively low-wage countries. Alternatively, these imports are seen as proof of the damage that trade can do to the United States.

The flaw in both sides of the argument is that a current account deficit requires a capital account surplus; if a country imports more than it exports, then its trading partners must become its investors. To say the current account deficit is caused by an uncompetitive home industry is to question the sanity of the foreign investors who are sending their capital to that very country. Why would anyone invest in an economy that is experiencing a marked deterioration in its industrial competitiveness? This logic suggests that a current account deficit is not, in and of itself, harmful. And that conclusion can be added to many other arguments that can be made by those economists who attended the seminar where they were gently reproached by Fischer for thinking like mercantilists.

In fact, there is nothing economically superior to having a current account surplus, nor is there anything inferior or even dangerous to having a deficit. A surplus in and of itself achieves nothing more than a positive balance of trade and the export of capital. Celebrating a current account surplus is genuflecting to mercantilist doctrine. But in truth, a surplus is not any safer than a deficit is dangerous.

Stein (2008), writing in the *Concise Encyclopedia of Economics,* said:

> Because the current account and the capital account add up to the total account, which is necessarily balanced, a deficit in the current account is always accompanied by an equal surplus in the capital account, and vice versa. A deficit or surplus in the current account cannot be explained or evaluated without simultaneous explanation and evaluation of an equal surplus or deficit in the capital account.

and

> Contrary to the general perception, the existence of a current account deficit is not, in itself, a sign of bad economic policy or of bad economic conditions. If the United States has a current account deficit, all this means is that the United States is importing capital. And importing capital is no more unnatural or dangerous than importing coffee.

A prominent exception is when a small country that is running large current account deficits attempts to peg its exchange rate. This was the situation in many of the emerging-markets countries in the late 1990s, when a manifold of currency crises erupted. Gross imperfections in state-planned development, extensive borrowing in foreign currencies (both private and government), and a host of domestic policy errors created the popularly termed "witches' brew" that ended in devastating macroeconomic meltdowns (see DeRosa 2001a).[35] That said, current account deficits in and of themselves did not cause these crises. These emerging-markets crises are more correctly seen as evidence of the impossible trinity theorem than of the toxicity of current account deficits.

But there is a plausible explanation for the views of the economists that I have been criticizing, perhaps rather harshly, as being mercantilists. They may well have been worrying not so much about trade flows per se but, rather, about the attending flows of capital. The argument might simply be stated that whenever capital flows uninhibitedly into a small country, meaning that the country has a current account deficit, there is the risk that it will suffer from either a sudden stop or a reversal in capital flows. I devote a considerable portion of Chapter 6 to this issue.

---

[35] Frankel (1999) disagreed with this assessment of the causes of these crises, which will be discussed in Chapter 5.

# 4. Foreign Exchange

The 20th century was witness to a series of radical exchange rate regime experiments, each, in turn, designed to create monetary stability. Most failed to bring about their intended purpose. What follows is a brief outline of the monetary history of the 20th century.[36]

## Some Foreign Exchange History

The classic gold standard (1821–1914) ended with the outbreak of World War I.[37] After the war, the economically developed European countries plus the United States, Japan, and a number of other countries embarked on a newly designed commodity-based exchange rate system called the "gold exchange standard" (1925–1931).[38] This system was anything but a success. As Bernanke (2004) wrote:

> Unlike the gold standard before World War I, however, the gold standard as reconstituted in the 1920s proved to be both unstable and destabilizing. (p. 8)

One outcome was deflation. Worse yet, according to some economists (Bernanke and others), the mechanics of the gold exchange standard had a pivotal role in the spread internationally of the Great Depression through the transmission of unwarranted monetary tightening. The gold exchange standard broke down in 1931 following the departure of the United Kingdom.

No centralized international monetary system was in place again until after World War II. The planning for such a system commenced at a famous meeting in Bretton Woods, New Hampshire, in 1944. With the end of the war in sight, the leaders of the Allied powers met to design a new, and hopefully improved, foreign exchange system for the world. The concept of the Bretton Woods system was that (1) the central banks of all member countries would keep their central bank foreign reserves in U.S. dollars, pounds sterling, or gold; (2) all members would maintain their exchange rate pegged to the U.S. dollar within a narrow ±1 percent tolerance band; (3) the United States would maintain its already substantial gold reserves,[39]

[36]See Bordo and Schwartz (1997) for an excellent summary of monetary policy regimes.

[37]See Bordo (1981).

[38]In a gold exchange standard, all member countries fix their currencies to a reserve currency. The reserve currency country, in turn, fixes its currency to a weight in gold. The reserve country agrees to freely exchange its currency for gold but only with member country central banks (specifically not with the general public).

[39]The United States emerged from World War II owning a very large portion of the world's gold supply, a fact that partially explains this unusual apparatus of Bretton Woods. See Bordo (1993) for an excellent account of Bretton Woods and the earlier gold-related international monetary systems.

settle its external accounts with gold bullion payments, and keep the dollar pegged to gold at the rate of $35 per ounce. Central banks could resort to using market intervention when needed to keep their currencies pegged to the dollar at the agreed-upon exchange rate.

The Bretton Woods declaration was signed in December 1946. Several large and unexpected devaluations, notably for sterling, occurred in 1949. Bordo (1993) stated that it was not until 1958 that the major currencies achieved full convertibility, although the system was functioning normally by 1955 (p. 166). Bordo (1995) called the 1959–67 period the "heyday of Bretton Woods" and added that Bretton Woods was a de facto "fixed exchange rate gold-dollar system" (i.e., one in which the price at which dollars could be exchanged for gold was fixed at $35) (p. 317). During this time, the dollar replaced sterling as the key currency.

The Bretton Woods system collapsed in the summer of 1971. Bordo (1993) described the collapse of Bretton Woods as having three basic causes:

> First, two major flaws undermined the system. One flaw was the gold exchange standard, which placed the United States under threat of a convertibility crisis. In reaction it pursued policies that in the end made adjustment more difficult. The second flaw was the adjustable peg. Because the costs of discrete changes in parity were deemed high, in the face of growing capital mobility, the system evolved into a reluctant fixed exchange rate system without an effective adjustment mechanism. Finally, U.S. monetary policy was inappropriate for a key currency. . . . Once the regime has evolved into a de facto dollar standard, the obligation of the United States was to maintain price stability. Instead, it conducted an inflationary policy, which ultimately destroyed the system. (pp. 177–178)

Bordo also compared the collapses of Bretton Woods and the interwar system: "The fundamental difference, however, was that the [Bretton Woods] system was not likely to collapse into deflation as in 1931 but rather explode into inflation" (p. 175).

In August 1971, the United States closed the gold window; in one stroke, this action removed the major currencies of the world from any linkage to gold. This was a monumental change, as Friedman (1992) wrote:

> Before 1971, every major currency from time immemorial had been linked directly or indirectly to a commodity. Occasional departures from a fixed link did occur but, generally, only at times of crisis. (p. 15)

And:

> For the first time in the history of the world, so far as I know, all major currencies are pure fiat currencies—not as a temporary response to a crisis, as often occurred in the past in individual countries, but as a permanent system expected to last. The countries of the world have been sailing uncharted seas. (p. 245)

In prior times, the presumption had always been that money not backed by gold, silver, or some other commodity would rapidly lose its credibility, if not its value in entirety. As Fisher (2006) wrote: "Irredeemable paper money has almost always invariably proved a curse to the country employing it" (p. 131).[40]

Yet, in 1971, the most economically powerful nations turned their backs on gold—a "barbarous relic," in the words of John Maynard Keynes (1924, p. 187) from half a century earlier—as a monetary anchor for the international system. Strangely enough, though, they apparently thought they could abandon the gold peg for the U.S. dollar but keep fixed exchange rates for all participating currencies against the dollar. In December 1973, the members of the G–10 countries signed the Smithsonian Agreement. The two important features were that it became acceptable for currencies to fluctuate with a wider bandwidth against the dollar (±2.25 percent) and that the dollar was devalued slightly by raising the price of gold to $38 per ounce. The gold window remained shut. When the Smithsonian system collapsed in March 1973, President Richard Nixon scrapped fixed exchange rates entirely and floated the dollar. The last vestiges of Bretton Woods were now gone, and since that time, the dollar has been floating[41] against all major currencies.

Floating exchange rates had arrived, but they came into existence only because there was no other alternative at that time, at least for the major currencies. Few governments ever truly trust the foreign exchange market. Practically every one of them has at one time or other felt the need to meddle in this market.

Europe, although content to let its currencies more or less freely float against the dollar and the yen—with some episodes of foreign exchange intervention from time to time—has displayed a tremendous aversion to letting markets determine exchange rates within its borders. From the end of the Bretton Woods period, the intra-European exchange rates have been manipulated, fixed, and finally, in the case of the legacy currencies that were folded into the euro, eliminated.

Then there are the emerging-markets currencies. Their governments, by and large, have spent upwards of three decades, since the end of Bretton Woods, experimenting with every conceivable form of fixed exchange rate regime. Many of these projects came to a crashing end in 1997 and 1998. I will review the varieties of exchange rate regimes later, in Chapter 5, but for now, I turn to some preliminary remarks about the foreign exchange market.

## Interbank Foreign Exchange Market

The foreign exchange market is the largest of the financial and capital markets. Most of the volume of trading in foreign currencies is done interbank, where wholesale buying and selling of foreign currencies and derivative instruments on

---

[40]Note that the original date of publication was 1912.

[41]Note that it is correct to say either a "flexible" exchange rate arrangement or a "floating" exchange rate arrangement.

foreign currencies takes place.[42] Interbank foreign currency trading is over the counter and, as such, consists of private transactions between counterparties.[43] The interbank market has no centralized physical trading floor (like the New York Stock Exchange has). Rather, trading is conducted through a network of dealers. London, New York, and Tokyo are the largest centers for foreign currency trading, yet trading also takes place in dozens of smaller financial centers. Large money-center banks and a handful of investment banks constitute the core of the foreign exchange market, but central banks can at times be the dominant influence, especially in the case of emerging-markets currencies. Dealing banks conduct transactions on behalf of investment funds, hedge funds, corporations, central banks, and private individuals, although they themselves can be the source of a foreign currency transaction.

The overall market functions 24 hours a day during the trading week, which starts on Monday morning at 6 a.m. in Sidney and New Zealand and ends at 5:00 p.m. Friday in New York. Estimates of the size of the foreign exchange market can be found in triennial surveys conducted by central banks under the direction of the Bank for International Settlements in Basel, Switzerland. The most current survey was done in April 2007, and it estimated that the daily turnover in that month for all foreign currency trading was US$3.2 trillion notional dollars. The foreign exchange market has always been huge, but its growth in recent times is nothing short of remarkable; daily turnover grew by US$1.2 trillion between 2004 and 2007.

More than 80 percent of foreign currency trading is buying and selling U.S. dollars against other currencies. Trading is extremely concentrated in a handful of top currencies: The largest volume of foreign currency trading in April 2007 was the euro against the dollar (27 percent), followed by the dollar against the yen (13 percent) and sterling against the dollar (12 percent).[44]

The share of emerging-markets currencies of total turnover expanded over the past three years, having risen from less than 15 percent in April 2004 to almost 20 percent in April 2007.[45] Emerging-markets currencies trade overwhelmingly against the U.S. dollar, according to the 2007 survey (exceptions being the currencies of Bulgaria, Estonia, Latvia, Lithuania, and Romania—all of which are predominantly traded against the euro).

---

[42] A very small fraction of foreign currency trading is done on organized exchanges, such as the Chicago Mercantile Exchange.

[43] The terms for these transactions are governed by agreements between the parties—typically in the form of an International Swaps and Derivatives Association (ISDA) Master Trading Agreement or a Foreign Exchange and Options Master Agreement (FEOMA).

[44] Bank for International Settlements (2007).

[45] According to the Bank for International Settlements (2007), the category "emerging-markets currencies" for this breakdown includes only the Hong Kong dollar, Mexican peso, Singapore dollar, South Korean won, South African rand, Russian ruble, Polish zloty, Indian rupee, Chinese yuan, New Taiwan dollar, and Brazilian real. The most actively traded of this group is the Hong Kong dollar, which, according to the report, "has benefited from being associated with the economic expansion of China" (p. 1).

## Box 4.1.   Market Conventions

The convention of the foreign exchange market is to quote the euro, the pound sterling, the New Zealand dollar, and the Australian dollar when any of these currencies are traded against the U.S. dollar in terms of the dollar price of a foreign currency unit (this is called "American" quotation). These exchange rates are written as EUR/USD, GBP/USD, NZD/USD, and AUD/USD, respectively, for the euro, pound, New Zealand dollar, and Australian dollar all against the U.S. dollar. For example, a quotation for the euro (EUR/USD) of 1.0500 means that €1 euro is worth $1.05. Some other currencies are quoted against the U.S. dollar in units of foreign currency (called "European" quotation). Examples are the Japanese yen (USD/JPY) and the Swiss franc (USD/CHF). A quotation for the yen of 105.05 means $1 is worth ¥105.05.[46] Most emerging-markets currencies are quoted European when traded against the U.S. dollar.

## Spot and Forward Transactions

The most basic transaction done in the foreign exchange market is called a "spot deal." Some of the conventions of the market are described in **Box 4.1**. Spot deals in foreign currencies are done for a multitude of purposes, some commercial, some financial, and some pure speculation on the future direction of exchange rates. In a spot deal, counterparties agree to exchange sums of different currencies at a time in the future called the "value date."[47] Market convention is that the spot value date is two bank business days after the trade date. Local holidays do not count as valid value dates. Suppose a U.S.-based company sells computers to a company in Germany for payment in euros. The U.S. company would want to convert the euro proceeds of the sale to dollars at some point. This transaction could be done by doing a spot deal. Euros could be sold for dollars for settlement in two bank business days. The euro part of the transaction would settle locally in Germany or at another European banking center with local euro settlement facilities (including London, even though the United Kingdom itself does not use the euro). The dollar side would be settled at any banking center in the United States.

---

[46]Currency market participants use the term "pip" to mean the smallest unit of quotation in the foreign exchange market. Dollar/yen (USD/JPY) is quoted to two decimal places. EUR/USD, GBP/USD, and USD/CHF are all quoted to four decimal places. For these latter exchange rates, one pip is 1/100th of one U.S. cent.

[47]In foreign exchange jargon, a delivery date is called a "value date," transactions are called "deals," and traders are called "dealers." A forward contract is a transaction for value beyond the spot value date. This jargon sounds stilted, but it is the vocabulary of the marketplace. DeRosa (1996) has provided details of the mechanics of foreign exchange trading.

Forward transactions are central to the foreign exchange market. The general idea of a forward transaction is to agree now on the price at which goods or services will be purchased or sold later.[48] A forward foreign currency deal is done for extended settlement beyond the spot value day. A forward foreign currency deal is routinely quoted for delivery in 1 week or 1, 2, 3, 6, or 12 months, and sometimes even longer than 12 months.

Forwards are used by hedgers to manage foreign exchange risk. An example of a hedger would be a U.S.-based manufacturer that makes a deal to sell oil-drilling equipment to a company in England. Suppose the British company agrees to pay the manufacturer £100 million in one month's time. If the manufacturer wanted to "lock in" the dollar value of the proceeds of the sale—so as to avoid the risk of the pound falling in value—it could sell pounds forward for value in one month. This transaction would immunize the manufacturer against fluctuations in the pound against the dollar over that one-month waiting period. At settlement, in one month's time, the forward deal would require the manufacturer to deliver pounds and receive dollars at the previously agreed-upon price. Presumably, the manufacturer would use the pounds it receives from the sale of the drilling equipment to satisfy the pound side of the forward transaction.

Forward deals are also done to hedge the foreign exchange risk associated with portfolios of foreign securities. They are also used to take speculative positions in foreign currencies, which will be discussed later.

Forward exchange rates, called "outrights," are quoted for virtually every future delivery date for major currencies, such as the pound sterling, yen, Swiss franc, and euro. Forward outrights necessarily differ from spot exchange rates because of differences in time and in the interest rates between the buying and selling currencies. In actual practice, foreign exchange dealers quote what are known as "forward points," which are meant to be added to or subtracted from the spot exchange rate to arrive at the forward outright.

By way of illustration, suppose the three-month deposit rate on U.S. dollars is greater than the same-term deposit rate on euros. The forward exchange rate for euros could not be equal to the spot exchange rate because that would create a riskless but profitable arbitrage: Traders could borrow in euros (the currency with the lower interest rate), sell the euros for dollars, invest at dollar interest rates, and complete the transaction by selling dollars for euros forward to a date coinciding with the expiration of the euro loan. The use of the forward in the last step would hedge the currency risk associated with movements in the exchange rate during the period of

---

[48]Note that this is slightly different from a futures transaction. The futures price is usually very similar to the forward outright with the same expiration date. The critical difference between futures contracts and forwards is that with the former, variation margin—based on the daily price fluctuations—is paid and collected every day. Forwards pay only at expiration. DeRosa (2000) has an extensive discussion of the difference between futures and forwards.

the outstanding euro loan. These kinds of arbitrage opportunities do not exist in the highly efficient foreign exchange market. Indeed, the market sets the forward outright away from the spot by just enough to remove the riskless profit opportunity; in the example, the forward outright for the three-month euro would be above spot.

## Interest Parity

The relationship between spot and forward foreign exchange is called the "covered interest parity theorem." It can be expressed in a simple equation:

$$F = Se^{(R_d - R_f)\tau},$$

where $F$ is the forward outright to a date $\tau$ years (or fractions of years) in the future (quoted American), $S$ is the spot exchange rate (quoted American), $e$ is the base of the natural logarithm, and $R_d$ and $R_f$ are the domestic and foreign interest rates, respectively (expressed with continuous compounding).

Suppose, to continue with my example, the spot exchange rate for the euro is 1.2500 and the six-month dollar and euro deposit rates are 7 percent and 4 percent, respectively. The forward outright for six months would be equal to

$$F = 1.2500e^{(7\%-4\%)\frac{1}{2}} = 1.2689.$$

For European quotation, the relationship is written

$$F' = S'e^{(R_f - R_d)\tau},$$

where the primes denote currencies quoted European.

## Forward Swaps

The greatest turnover in the foreign exchange market is in forward swaps. A forward swap is a combination of a spot transaction plus a forward outright transaction in the opposite direction. Forward swaps are used to extend the value date of an existing spot or forward transaction.

Spot/next swaps and tomorrow/next (tom/next) swaps, two specialized forward swaps, are the workhorses of the foreign exchange market. Consider the case of a trader who has taken a long spot position in the euro against the U.S. dollar (i.e., long euros and short dollars). The deal calls for him or her to receive euros and deliver dollars in two bank business days. If the trader wanted to extend the value date to three bank business days, he or she could do a spot/next swap. For a spot/next swap, the first leg would be a spot deal to sell euros against dollars (as always, for value in two bank business days). The second leg would be to buy euros against dollars for value in three bank business days. In effect, this second leg is a forward outright for value in three bank business days.

Suppose, instead, the trader waited until the next day, meaning the next day after the original spot trade. He or she could then roll the position by doing a tom/next swap.[49]

·These two trades are an important part of the architecture of the foreign exchange market. They represent the position of the market rolling forward on a day-by-day basis. There are also forward swaps that push the value date out further on the calendar to any legitimate forward value date.

## Nondeliverable Forwards

Physical settlement of spot and forward contracts consists of delivery and receipt of each of the two component currencies. Banks in each currency's country are needed to facilitate the transfer of funds.[50] But in some situations, a central bank has actively attempted to suppress trading the foreign currency by making it illegal or difficult to settle spot and forward contracts in its jurisdiction. Certain emerging-markets countries have had an unfortunate history of installing such capital controls.

The foreign exchange market will have its way, nevertheless. As long as there are counterparties who wish to trade a currency forward, some of them wanting to buy and some of them wanting to sell, there will be trading in nondeliverable forwards (NDFs). Money-center banks manufacture NDFs to meet the needs of their clients. NDFs are cash settled, which means that at expiration, an NDF pays the profit or loss on the contract instead of delivering sums of foreign currency. The party who is out of the money pays the party who is in the money. The amount paid at settlement is usually denominated in U.S. dollars.

Market disruptions and persistent capital account restrictions give rise to offshore NDF markets.[51] Some examples of NDF markets are Russia after the August 1998 default, Malaysia during the period of capital controls in 1998–1999, and Argentina after its debt default in 2001.

A common way to negotiate NDFs is to use, as the initial forward outright, an estimate obtained by applying the interest parity formula to the observed spot exchange rate and the interest rates for the two currencies.[52] That said, Ma, Ho, and McCauley (2004) reported evidence that capital controls can segment onshore from offshore markets, at least in some of the Asian markets they studied.

---

[49]The first leg of the tom/next would be to sell euros for dollars for settlement on the very next bank business day. In effect, this is an "anti-forward" trade in that it settles in front of the spot value day. The second part of the trade would be an ordinary spot trade for value in two bank business days.

[50]Exceptions exist to this rule. For example, banks in London settle both sides of a trade in euro/sterling because London banks can receive and deliver euros for settlement despite the fact that the United Kingdom has not adopted the euro.

[51]There are also on-shore NDF markets. Australia had such a market in the 1980s, when residents were restricted in conducting foreign currency transactions. See Debelle, Gyntelberg, and Plumb (2006).

[52]Debelle et al. (2006) wrote that "when international investors have little access to a country's onshore interest rate markets or deposits in the local currency, NDF prices are based primarily on the expected future level of the spot exchange rate" (p. 59).

Lipscomb (2005, p. 4) cited EMTA, an emerging market debt trade group, which undertook a survey in 2003 to estimate the volume in NDF trading.[53] The top five NDF contracts were as follows:

| Currency | Amount (billions of US$) |
|---|---|
| Korean won | 307 |
| Chilean peso | 180 |
| Brazilian real | 179 |
| Taiwanese dollar | 163 |
| Chinese yuan | 68 |

Despite this large volume, NDFs do not always function as they are intended to. For example, Lipscomb (2005) described what happened with NDF contracts in Argentine pesos in 2001:

> Following the end of the Argentine peso's peg against the U.S. dollar in late 2001, Argentine authorities called an unscheduled market holiday for three weeks. This led to a disruption in determining the settlement rate of outstanding peso NDF contracts. As a result, even after foreign exchange trading resumed, the NDF market in pesos was stymied by continued uncertainty over fixing rates to be used for settlement. (p. 5)

NDFs, by definition, live in tough foreign exchange neighborhoods. They spontaneously come to life in reaction to central bank policies designed to limit or stop the functioning of the foreign exchange market. In that sense, they are the next-best thing to real currency trading, which means, especially given the environment in which they operate, that they are sometimes imperfect.

## Risk in Speculating and Hedging

If foreign exchange were a murder mystery novel, the missing evidence would be found buried in the forward market. The interest rate parity theorem reveals some of the market's secrets regarding what happens when a currency comes under speculative attack. This process is important for central bankers to understand.

A speculator, or hedger, who sells an emerging-markets currency short most likely has no interest in actually delivering and receiving the underlying currencies. Still, normal settlement requires sums of currencies to be delivered from seller to buyer in two bank business days. This two-day window makes it preferable to trade for a value date further in the future than the spot value day. The complication is

---

[53] Formerly known as the Emerging Markets Traders Association, the group is now known simply as EMTA. EMTA's 2003 *NDF Annual Volume Survey*, cited in Lipscomb (2005), is its most recent NDF survey at the time of this writing.

that the interest rate rises, sometimes skyrockets, in the course of a currency crisis. A higher interest rate is needed to compensate lenders for putting out money denominated in a currency that could be the subject of rapid depreciation in value. In other words, the interest rate rises to provide investors with a risk premium so that the risky currency is held and markets clear. Some central banks validate this proposition by raising their interest rate in an attempt to defend the currency by making short sales of currency costlier—and riskier—to initiate.

The reason that a higher interest rate is evidence that a currency is risky to short is apparent from the interest parity equation, but it is easier to comprehend with an example from the recent history of the Thai baht. The baht was managed under a basket peg regime before the July 1997 crisis. Although the Bank of Thailand fixed the spot exchange rate, it had no control over the forward baht market. By May 1997, as pressure mounted to eliminate the peg, the Bank of Thailand implemented capital controls. The controls effectively shut down onshore trading in the baht, although the offshore nondeliverable market continued to function in a fashion. This state of affairs lasted until the beginning of July 1997, when the bank relaxed the capital controls and unpegged the baht. After the fact, it looks like shorting the baht ought to have been a trader's bonanza. But the truth is that many elected to stay on the sidelines, and they did so with good reason.

The Thai baht is quoted using European convention. Given the peg, if the Thai baht interest rate $(R_f)$ rises, the forward $(F')$ will also rise. A speculator who wants to wager that the baht will drop can buy dollar/baht (go long U.S. dollars and short baht—or in the lingo of the market, "buy dollars"). This transaction is best done in the forward market, not the spot market, because a spot transaction requires delivery and receipt of currencies in two bank business days. Given the proclivity of central banks to suddenly install capital controls when their currencies appear to be under attack, rolling a baht position or even making prompt delivery may become impossible or at least inordinately expensive. Indeed, this is what happened in late May 1997 when capital controls were introduced. In contrast, the speculator with a forward position (with sufficient remaining time to expiration) would face no such immediate uncertainty.

But the forward has its problems too. The higher the level of $F'$, the more the dollar costs in terms of the baht. The risk to a speculator who is short the baht once a crisis is under way is more than what may come from the spot baht exchange rate rising. There is also risk that the baht interest rate will drop after the speculator sells baht forward. For example, the crisis could have subsided without the spot exchange rate changing but with the baht interest rate dropping back to a more normal level, which would have caused the forward rate to collapse back to its base level. And I stress that this could have happened with no change in the spot exchange rate. I will now illustrate this scenario, continuing to work with the case of the baht in 1997.

Suppose that before the crisis, meaning in early 1997, the baht was trading at a spot exchange rate of 26.00 to the U.S. dollar, the dollar interest rate was 5.5 percent, and the baht interest rate was 8.00 percent. Because these were realistic levels at the time, I will refer to them as the base case. The six-month forward was 26.3270 according to the interest parity formula. Timing is everything in trading. A trader lucky or skilled enough to have sold baht forward at this level probably made a profit.

But once the crisis began, the situation looked very different because the short-term baht interest rate rose dramatically. Suppose it went up to 12 percent, although, in fact, the baht interest rate eventually went much higher. This increase would have made the six-month forward 26.8589. A speculator or trader who sold baht forward at this rate faced a very different risk–return trade-off from the one faced by a trader who sold baht before the crisis got into full swing. Because the baht was under pressure, it would have been highly unlikely that its spot value would have risen in value against the dollar. At this point, the risk came from the possibility that the crisis would fade, whereupon the baht interest rate would go back down to what I have called the base case level. A trader who bought $10 million of dollar/baht forward—a relatively small amount in foreign exchange—when the interest rate was 12 percent would have lost $202,013 if the crisis had faded and the interest rate had returned to 8 percent.[54] If the baht interest rate had been 20 percent when the dollars were bought forward, the loss would have been $618,365 with a return to the base case. These are not inconsequential prospective losses, especially considering that a good deal of foreign currency trading is done on a highly leveraged basis. The general lesson is that there are no "one-way bets" in currency trading, no sure ways to make money.

The more specific lesson is that the chief risk in speculating in fixed exchange rate currencies is not necessarily from an adverse movement in the spot but from a movement in forward prices. This fact explains the motive of a central bank defending a fixed exchange rate regime by raising the interest rate. The best outcome from such a policy gambit is that that it will work quickly—meaning that it will squeeze speculators out of the market—before too much damage is done to the economy by the otherwise unnecessarily higher interest rate.

---

[54]Worse yet, if Thailand had dollarized, the loss might have been as much as $330,339, based on the 12 percent baht interest rate and under the assumption that U.S. and Thai interest rates would have been made equal.

# 5. Foreign Exchange Regimes

Dr. Franz Pick (1981), the world currency expert, once quipped, "Every country gets the currency it deserves" (p. 11).[55] Whatever these countries deserve, they certainly have had a practice of choosing variety. The choice of an exchange rate regime is one of the most important issues that concerns an emerging-markets central bank.

## Exchange Rate Regimes

The spectrum of foreign exchange regimes known in modern times runs from independently floating to hard pegs to currency zones. The variety of regimes is shown in **Exhibit 5.1**.

Each year, the IMF publishes an extensive review of all of the world's known exchange rate regimes and exchange restrictions under the title *Annual Report on Exchange Arrangements and Exchange Restrictions* (*AREAER*). The 2006 edition of the publication surveyed 187 countries. I will adopt the classification of exchange rates used in the 2006 *AREAER* but will at times group them into broad categories of my own making (i.e., floaters, intermediate, hard pegs, and currency zones).

**Floaters.** The *independently floating* countries (26) include the United States, Japan, and Switzerland. In theory, an independently floating exchange rate should be determined entirely by private market forces of supply and demand. An independently floating regime is one in which:

> The exchange rate is market determined, with any official foreign exchange market intervention aimed at moderating the rate of change and preventing undue fluctuations in the exchange rate, rather than establishing a level for it. (International Monetary Fund 2006a, p. 25)

The independently floating category, therefore, allows intervention as long as it is not specifically aimed at fixing the level.

---

[55] Dr. Franz Pick (1898–1985) was the arch foe of fiat money and an eloquent champion of gold as a monetary reserve and personal asset. His *New York Times* obituary credited him with having published more than 50 books plus regular newsletters. Pick's research on the history of paper currencies, including his biannual currency yearbooks, constitutes an important history of exchange rate regimes. He is also remembered for having expressed an ardent belief that all forms of paper money are destined to collapse in value. Unlike many gold advocates of today, Pick distinguished himself by conducting and publishing massive research on the history of currencies, many of which met their demise at the hands of nefarious governments. Although the overarching conclusions that gold is the supreme asset and that all currencies not backed by gold are doomed are hard to support, Pick's anecdotes do resonate.

**Exhibit 5.1. Exchange Rate Regimes for Emerging-Markets Countries, 1991 and 2006**

| | Floaters | | Intermediate (soft pegs) | | | | Hard Pegs | | |
|---|---|---|---|---|---|---|---|---|---|
| | Independently Floating | Managed Float | Crawling Band | Crawling Peg | Peg with Horizontal Bands | Conventional Pegs | Currency Board | Dollarization | Currency Zone |
| *Exchange rate regimes as of 1991* | | | | | | | | | |
| | Peru | South Korea | Chile | Brazil | India | China | Argentina | | |
| | | Pakistan | Colombia | Indonesia | Israel | Czech | | | |
| | | Philippines | Mexico | Poland | Malaysia | Egypt | | | |
| | | South Africa | | | | Hungary | | | |
| | | Turkey | | | | Jordan | | | |
| | | | | | | Morocco | | | |
| | | | | | | Russia | | | |
| | | | | | | Thailand | | | |
| *Exchange rate regimes as of 2006* | | | | | | | | | |
| | Brazil | Argentina | | | Hungary | China | | | |
| | Chile | Colombia | | | | Egypt | | | |
| | Israel | Czech | | | | Jordan | | | |
| | South Korea | India | | | | Morocco | | | |
| | Mexico | Indonesia | | | | Pakistan | | | |
| | Philippines | Malaysia | | | | | | | |
| | Poland | Peru | | | | | | | |
| | South Africa | Russia | | | | | | | |
| | | Thailand | | | | | | | |

*Sources:* Based on data from Fischer (2001) and the International Monetary Fund (2006a).

The euro does not appear in the survey as a floating currency because the *AREAER* classifies countries, not currencies. The member countries of the euro zone are reported as having "exchange arrangements with no separate legal tender" (International Monetary Fund 2006a, p. 25). The euro itself is independently floating against the U.S. dollar, the yen, and other currencies.

Under *managed float* (53 countries), there is no predetermined path for the exchange rate. The level of intervention is expected to be greater than in an independently floating regime. The IMF describes this regime as one in which the monetary authority attempts to influence the exchange rate without having a specific exchange rate path or target. The authorities operate in a manner that is "broadly judgmental." The guideposts could be macroeconomic indicators, such as inflation, the balance of payments, foreign reserves, or developments in capital markets.

In an extreme case, management of the exchange rate is so intensive that the term "dirty float" might be appropriate—although the *AREAER* does not use that term.[56]

**Intermediate (Soft Pegs).** The intermediate zone is where the soft pegs live, at the center of the spectrum between floating rates and hard pegs. The subcategories are crawling pegs, pegged exchange rates within horizontal bands, and other conventional fixed-peg arrangements.[57]

Under *crawling pegs* (five countries), the exchange rate is adjusted periodically in small increments at a fixed rate or in response to economic indicators. In this way, the pressure to devalue suddenly or by a large amount is gradually released by allowing the currency to gradually depreciate.

For *pegged exchange rates within horizontal bands* (four countries), the exchange rate value is confined within certain margins around a fixed central rate. Horizontal banded pegged exchange rates have historical precedent in the Bretton Woods and Smithsonian agreements as well as the Exchange Rate Mechanisms I and II. The width of the band is obviously critical to the sustainability of the system.[58] The tighter the band, the more the arrangement functions like a peg. The compromise is that looser-banded arrangements may be more durable.

---

[56]Calvo and Reinhart (2000) have stated, "Economic theory provides us with well-defined distinctions between fixed and flexible exchange rate regimes, but we are not aware of any criteria that allows us to discriminate as to when a managed float starts to look like a soft peg" (p. 28).

[57]The International Monetary Fund (2006a) has one other form of soft peg, the crawling band. This regime attempts to keep the exchange rate within certain limits of at least ±1 percent around a central rate. The central rate is adjusted periodically at a fixed rate or in response to changes in economic indicators.

[58]The Bretton Woods arrangement allowed 1 percent plus or minus deviation from the central parity rates. In retrospect, this was an amazingly tight tolerance. The bandwidths were widened in the Smithsonian period to ±2.25 percent. During the Smithsonian period, various European central banks fixed their exchange rates to each other within a narrow bandwidth of ±1 percent. This was known as the "snake" or the "snake in the tunnel." The Exchange Rate Mechanism I period featured two bandwidths, 2.25 percent for established currency members and 6 percent for newcomers. After the August 1993 Exchange Rate Mechanism crisis, the bandwidths were widened to ±15 percent.

In a *conventional fixed-peg* regime (44 countries), the central bank fixes its exchange rate to another country's currency or a basket of currencies. There is no commitment to irrevocably keep the parity. Usually, the currency is allowed to fluctuate narrowly around the peg (less than ±1 percent). According to the International Monetary Fund (2006a):

> The monetary authority stands ready to maintain the fixed parity through direct interventions (i.e., via sale or purchase of foreign exchange in the market) or indirect interventions (e.g., via aggressive use of interest rate policy, imposition of foreign exchange regulations, exercise of moral suasion that constrains foreign exchange activity, or through intervention by other public institutions). (p. 24)

**Hard Pegs.** The soft pegs are soft because they are more prone to adjustment and outright failure than hard pegs. The International Monetary Fund (2006a) has two varieties of hard pegs: currency boards and dollarization.

*Currency boards* (seven countries) are artifacts of the colonial era.[59] The basic idea is that the currency board issues currency with a pledge (which could be backed by a law) to do two things: (1) hold a sufficient quantity of another country's currency (the reserve currency) so as to be able to retire the entire domestic currency supply in the hands of the general public and (2) exchange domestic currency for the reserve currency at the fixed exchange rate upon demand (which is the reason that currency boards are sometimes called "currency vending machines"). The currency board, it is hoped, is a bullet-proof fixed exchange rate foreign exchange regime, qualifying it as a hard peg.

The term "dollarize" has come to mean a circumstance where a country adopts another country's currency, such as the U.S. dollar. The concept of dollarization is talked about more than it is practiced. The International Monetary Fund (2006a) lists nine countries that use another country's currency as their own. Seven use the U.S. dollar (Ecuador, El Salvador, the Marshall Islands, Micronesia, Palau, Panama, and Timor-Leste), Kiribati uses the Australian dollar, and San Marino uses the euro.

**Currency Zones.** The remaining *AREAER* countries are participants in currency zones. Examples are the euro zone, the members of the central African franc zones, and the various island nation members of the Eastern Caribbean Currency Union (ECCU).

**De Jure and De Facto Regimes.** *AREAER* is the standard reference for the classification of exchange rate regimes. How well does it report what actually exists? There are differences between de jure and de facto exchange rate regimes. Calvo and Reinhart (2000) analyzed the

> . . .behavior of exchange rates, reserves, the monetary aggregates, interest rates, and commodity prices across 154 exchange rate arrangements to assess whether "official labels" provide an adequate representation of actual country practice. We find that, countries that say they allow their exchange rate to float mostly do not—there seems to be an epidemic case of "fear of floating." (p. 1)

---

[59] See Schwartz (1993) for a comprehensive history of currency boards.

Reinhart and Rogoff (2003a) conducted considerable research into empirical taxonomy of exchange rate regimes.[60] One of their innovations was to distinguish countries that have single "unified rate systems," which they defined as "one official exchange rate and no significant 'black' or parallel market" (p. 2), from "dual/parallel" rates, which they described as often (roughly half the time for official pegs) functioning as "back door" floating regimes "albeit one usually accompanied by exchange controls" (p. 2). They also devised new categories of exchange rate regimes—15 in all—designed to capture the differences between official de jure regimes and actual de facto practices. One new class is "freely falling," which they defined as "cases with 12-month inflation over 40 percent per annum" (p. 4). This turns out to be a "crowded" category. They chose to use the term "freely floating" to mean the same thing as the *AREAER*'s "independently floating." They concluded:

> When one uses market-determined rates in place of official rates, the history of exchange rate policy begins to look very different. For example, it becomes obvious that *de facto* floating was common during the early years of the Bretton Woods era of "pegged" exchange rates. Conversely, many floats of the post-1980s turn out to be (de facto) pegs, crawling pegs, or very narrow bands. Of the countries listed in the official IMF classification as managed floating, 53 percent turn out to have *de facto* pegs, crawls or narrow bands to some other anchor currency. (pp. 3–4)

In retrospect, what Reinhart and Rogoff (2003a) have said ought not be a surprise. The *AREAER*'s categories of exchange rate regimes are essentially what governments report as their de jure currency regimes regardless of what is the true market reality. Ghosh, Gulde, Ostry, and Wolf (1997), Bubula and Ötker-Robe (2002), and Eichengreen and Leblang (2003) also have done work on categorizing de facto regimes. Empirical taxonomy of exchange rate regimes is not a complete solution, however, as Frankel (2007) has noted:

> That *de facto* schemes to classify exchange rate regimes differ from the IMF's previous *de jure* classifications is now well-known. It is less well-known that the *de facto* schemes also do not agree with each other!

**Exhibit 5.2** provides a short history of foreign exchange arrangements for the emerging markets. It reports official, or de jure, exchange rates with, in some cases, contrasting classifications by Reinhart and Rogoff (2003a).[61] **Figure 5.1** displays sample emerging-markets exchange rates against the U.S. dollar over the last two decades.[62]

---

[60]See also Reinhart and Rogoff (2003b).

[61]Note that the Reinhart and Rogoff (2003a) data end on 31 December 2001.

[62]More sample exchange rates can be found in the online supplemental materials at www.cfapubs.org.

**Exhibit 5.2. Emerging-Markets Nations: Reported and De Facto Exchange Rate Arrangements**

| Country (2006 *AREAER* classification) | De Facto Regime |
|---|---|
| Argentina (managed float) | Argentina introduced its "convertibility law" on 1 April 1991. The Argentine peso was convertible to the U.S. dollar at 1:1 under an arrangement that resembled a currency board. The peg was abandoned in January 2002 coincident with the government's default on certain international debts. RR characterized the peso as being freely falling/freely floating prior to the introduction of the convertibility law. They marked the end of convertibility on 1 December 2001, whereupon the peso became a de facto dual market with capital controls. |
| Brazil (independent float) | Brazil introduced the real on 1 July 1994 under the auspices of a preannounced crawling band with reference to the U.S. dollar. On 1 February 1999, market conditions had so thoroughly deteriorated that the Banco Central do Brasil was forced to float the unit. RR classified the real as freely falling/managed float. RR categorized it as a managed float starting on 1 September 1999. |
| Chile (independent float) | Chile operated the peso under a crawling band that commenced in January 1988. The center of the band was periodically adjusted, and the width of the band mostly increased over time. The crawling peg was abandoned in September 1999. RR noted that there was a dual market throughout the crawling band period. RR classified the peso as a managed float with unified markets as of 2 September 1999. |
| China (conventional peg) | RR noted that China operated the renminbi as a de facto crawling band around the U.S. dollar with multiple rates prior to 1 January 1994. At that time, China devalued the renminbi and then pegged it to the U.S. dollar at the rate of 8.25 until 21 July 2005. Small upwards revisions in the unit are tolerated from time to time. |
| Colombia (managed float) | Colombia operated the peso in a crawling band from January 1994 until September 1999. The band width was ±7 percent, and the slope was 11 percent with annual reset of center. RR noted that the peso became a managed float on 25 September 1999. |
| Czech Republic (managed float) | The Czech Republic instituted a crawling band around the German mark in September 1990. It transitioned to a managed float in May 1997. |
| Egypt (conventional peg) | Egypt pegged the pound to the U.S. dollar in October 1991. This regime lasted until December 2000, whereupon a horizontal band system was introduced. In January 2003, the pound was floated. In February 2005, the pound became a de facto peg to the U.S. dollar, although it is still sometimes described as a managed float. |
| Hungary (horizontal band) | Hungary installed a horizontal banded exchange rate pegged to the euro in May 2001. There was one devaluation in June 2003. The bandwidth is ±15 percent. In contrast, RR referred to the Hungarian forint as a preannounced crawling band around the euro with a ±2.25 percent band. |
| India (managed float) | India moved from a fixed exchange rate regime to a managed float in March 1993, whereupon the rupee became fully convertible. In contrast, RR listed the rupee as having been a de facto peg to the U.S. dollar from August 1989 to July 1991 and a de facto crawling peg since. |

*(continued)*

**Exhibit 5.2. Emerging-Markets Nations: Reported and De Facto Exchange Rate Arrangements** (continued)

| Country (2006 *AREAER* classification) | De Facto Regime |
|---|---|
| Indonesia (managed float) | Indonesia operated a crawling band regime pegged to the U.S. dollar until August 1997. Thereafter the rupiah has been a managed float. RR called it freely falling/freely floating from August 1997 to March 1999. They classified it as freely floating beginning in 1999. |
| Israel (independent float) | Israel became an independent float in June 2005. RR reported that in prior times, the currency was a crawling band around the U.S. dollar. |
| Jordan (conventional peg) | Jordan installed a crawling band to the dollar in February 1990. It switched to a peg to the U.S. dollar in September 1995. |
| Korea (independent float) | Korea operated a crawling band around the U.S. dollar commencing in March 1990. This became a crawling peg to the dollar in November 1994. In December 1997, the won became independently floating. RR classified the won as freely falling from 17 December 1997 until June 1998. They classified it as freely floating since July 1998. |
| Malaysia (managed float) | Malaysia operated its currency in a tightly managed float until September 1998, when it transited to a conventional peg. In July 2005, it made the ringgit into a managed float with reference to a currency basket. RR classified the ringgit as a de facto moving band around the U.S dollar from 5 September 1975 until July 1997. They classified it as freely floating from August 1997 to 30 September 1998, when it became pegged to the dollar. |
| Mexico (independent float) | The peso was operated as a crawling band around the U.S. dollar until December 1994. Thereupon, it became de jure independently floating. RR noted that prior to 1994, the band was widening over time but the floor was fixed while the ceiling was crawling. RR classified the peso as freely falling/freely floating as of 22 December 1994. RR classified the peso as a managed float starting April 1996. |
| Morocco (conventional peg) | Morocco kept its currency in a moving band around the French franc from 1973 until 1 January 1999. Thereupon, it switched to a moving band around the euro. |
| Pakistan (conventional peg) | Pakistan switched from a managed floating regime to a conventional peg on 1 January 2005. In contrast, RR described the unit as having alternatively been a de facto crawling peg and crawling band in the prior times. |
| Peru (managed float) | The *AREAER* describes Peru as a managed float. RR showed the history of the currency to have been a de facto crawling band to the U.S. dollar and a de facto peg to the U.S. dollar at previous times. |
| Philippines (independent float) | The Philippine peso became an independent float in December 1997. RR reported that it was a banded peg around the U.S. dollar until August 1995. It was a de facto peg from September 1995 to June 1997 and freely floating from July 1997 to December 1997. |
| Poland (independent float) | The Polish zloty became an independent float in April 2000. RR listed it as a de facto crawling band around the euro in previous times. |

(continued)

**Exhibit 5.2. Emerging-Markets Nations: Reported and De Facto Exchange Rate Arrangements** (continued)

| Country (2006 *AREAER* classification) | De Facto Regime |
|---|---|
| Russia (managed float) | The *AREAER* lists the ruble as a managed float. Russia was forced to abandon its peg to the U.S. dollar in August 1998, when it defaulted on various maturing Treasury obligations. RR classified the ruble as a preannounced crawling band around the U.S. dollar starting in July 1995. RR classified it as a freely falling currency from 17 August 1998 to December 1999. They classified it as a de facto crawling band around the U.S. dollar from the period at least up to December 2001 (when their sample ends). |
| South Africa (independent float) | South Africa operated a dual rate/managed float against the U.S. dollar from September 1985 until 13 March 1995, whereupon it became freely floating. |
| Thailand (managed float) | Thailand operated the baht under a basket peg (predominantly U.S. dollars) from August 1978 until the crisis in May 1997. The baht was suspended from trading until July 1997, when it became a managed floating currency. RR described it as having been freely falling from July 1997 to January 1998, whereupon they declared it to be a managed float. |
| Turkey (independent float) | The *AREAER* describes the Turkish lira as an independent floater. RR described Turkey as having had a crawling band around the German mark until January 1999, when it became a crawling band around the euro. RR described it as a freely falling/freely floating exchange rate from February 2001 until October 2001. |

*Note*: RR = Reinhart and Rogoff (2003a).

*Sources*: Based on data from Reinhart and Rogoff (2003a), the International Monetary Fund (2006), Herault (2002), Al-Mashat and Billmeier (2007), Almekinders, Cebotari, and Billmeier (2007), and the website of the central bank of Hungary: http://english.mnb.hu/Engine.aspx?page=mnben_1_jegybankrol&ContentID=2326.

Finally, it is interesting to look at the record of how often countries elect to change their foreign exchange regimes. One indication comes from the 2006 *AREAER*. Data from this report are sorted in **Exhibit 5.3**. Twenty-five countries made sufficiently large changes in their exchange regimes to warrant reclassification. For that time period, there was a movement away from independent and managed floating exchange rates:

- Nine countries moved from independent floating to managed floating.
- Ten countries moved from managed floating to some form of soft peg.
- Four countries switched from one soft peg to another.
- Two countries moved from soft peg to managed floating.

# The Great Hollowing Out

The intermediate zone, or soft-pegged exchange rate regimes that were popular in the 1980s and early 1990s in the emerging markets, seemed to offer prosperity, low rates of inflation, and exchange rate stability. Almost all these regimes, however,

**Figure 5.1. Exchange Rates for Selected Emerging Markets against the U.S. Dollar**

### A. Argentine Peso

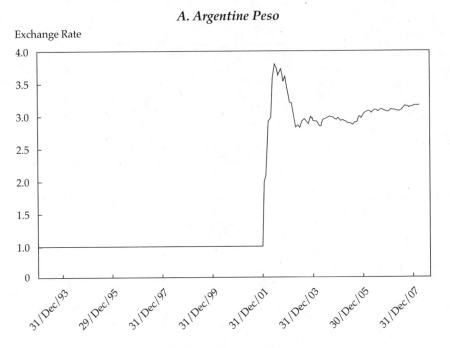

### B. Brazilian Real

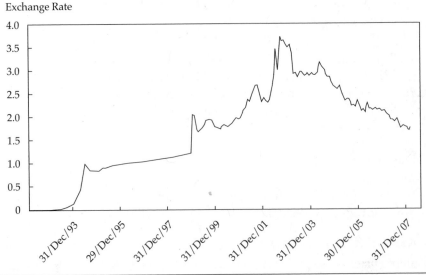

(continued)

**Figure 5.1.    Exchange Rates for Selected Emerging Markets against the U.S. Dollar** (continued)

### C. Mexican Peso

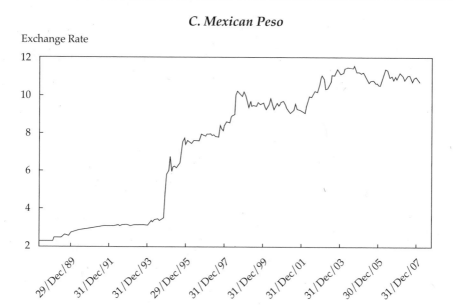

### D. Russian Ruble

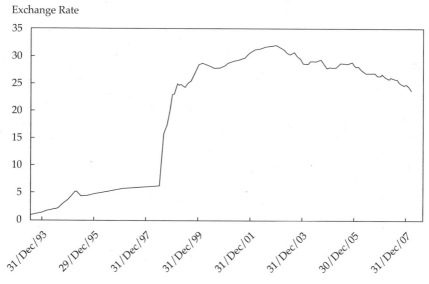

(continued)

**Figure 5.1.   Exchange Rates for Selected Emerging Markets against the U.S. Dollar** (continued)

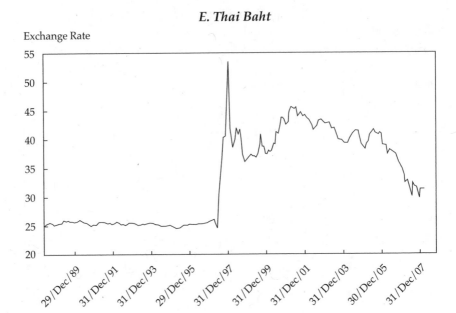

### E. Thai Baht

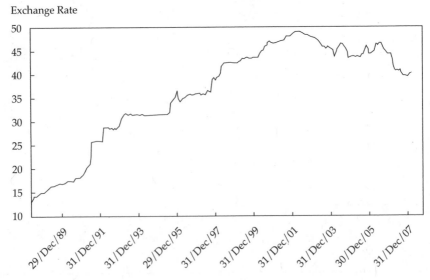

### F. Indian Rupee

*Source*: Based on data from Bloomberg.

**Exhibit 5.3. Reclassification of Exchange Rate Arrangements, 2005–06**

| Country | 2005 *AREAER* | 2006 *AREAER* Conventional Pegged | Peg with Horizontal Bands | Crawling Peg | Managed Float |
|---|---|---|---|---|---|
| Azerbaijan | Managed float | X | | | |
| Belarus | Crawling band | X | | | |
| Botswana | Conventional peg | | | X | |
| Colombia | Independently floating | | | | X |
| Dominican Republic | Independently floating | | | | X |
| Egypt | Managed float | X | | | |
| Guinea | Conventional peg | | | | X |
| Guyana | Managed float | X | | | |
| Honduras | Crawling peg | X | | | |
| Iran | Managed float | | | X | |
| Liberia | Independently floating | | | | X |
| Madagascar | Independently floating | | | | X |
| Malawi | Independently floating | | | | X |
| Malaysia | Conventional peg | | | | X |
| Mauritania | Managed float | X | | | |
| Papua New Guinea | Independently floating | | | | X |
| Pakistan | Managed float | X | | | |
| Slovak Republic | Managed float | | X | | |
| Solomon Islands | Crawling peg | X | | | |
| Sri Lanka | Independently floating | | | | X |
| Suriname | Managed float | X | | | |
| Uruguay | Independently floating | | | | X |
| Vietnam | Managed float | X | | | |
| Yemen, Republic of | Independently floating | | | | X |
| Zimbabwe | Managed float | X | | | |

*Source*: Based on data from the International Monetary Fund (2006a).

suffered sudden collapse. The first in a long series of dramatic currency crises was Mexico in December 1994. This crisis was followed by Thailand and Indonesia (the summer of 1997), South Korea (December 1997), Russia (August 1998), and Turkey (2001), to name a few. And before the emerging-markets crises, two currency crises occurred in the EMS fixed exchange rate ERM in 1992 and 1993. Earlier, still, were the collapses, first, of Bretton Woods and, second, of the follow-on Smithsonian target zone fixed exchange rate regimes in 1971 and 1973, respectively.

Exhibit 5.1 shows the spectrum of exchange rate regimes observed in the emerging markets in 1991—from Fischer (2001) and the International Monetary Fund (2006a). The center portion is what has been dubbed the "soft pegs." In the 1990s, this portion of the spectrum was eliminated by market forces—hence, the spectrum of foreign exchange regimes became "hollowed out." Target zones, crawling pegs, and basket pegs completely fell apart. The afflicted countries migrated to the extremes on the left, becoming floaters, or to the right, becoming hard pegs or currency zones. **Exhibit 5.4** shows a brief chronology of these crises.

**Exhibit 5.4. Selected Emerging-Markets Currency Crises, 1994–2002**

| Country | Date of Onset |
|---|---|
| Mexico | December 1994 |
| Thailand | July 1997 |
| Philippines | July 1997 |
| Malaysia | July 1997 |
| Indonesia | August 1997 |
| South Korea | December 1997 |
| Russia | August 1998 |
| Brazil | January 1999 |
| Turkey | January 2001 |
| Argentina | January 2002 |

DeRosa (2001a) analyzed these currency crises, including the two EMS crises, by examining the mechanics of the fixed exchange rate regimes and various other policies undertaken by the respective governments. A key finding was that all these crises were preceded by the accumulation of substantial at-risk positions that were short the U.S. dollar and long local currency. When the crises occurred, the entire market, not counting the central bank, had to buy dollars and sell the local currency immediately in order to hedge.

This position was exacerbated by the phenomenon of "original sin," a term that refers to cases where emerging-markets governments borrow in U.S. dollars or some other major currency. Greenspan (2003) wrote:

> Complicating the evaluation of the timing of a turnaround is that deficit countries, both developed and emerging, borrow in international markets largely in dollars, rather than in their domestic currency. (p. 6)

All governments borrow in their own capital markets, thereby creating debt denominated in their own currency. The size of the government's borrowing is constrained in part by the size of the local capital market. The trouble begins when the government makes a determination that it needs to supplement its local borrowing by issuing debt in the international capital market. Although the international capital market offers the advantage of being vastly larger than the local market, the former almost always requires the debt to be denominated in U.S. dollars, whereas the latter can be in local currency. The government's revenues are mainly, or exclusively, denominated in local currency. By borrowing in foreign currency, a government effectively creates a potentially huge foreign exchange risk for itself. Its position, seen from a trader's perspective, is short the dollar against its own local currency. The higher (lower) the dollar, the greater (smaller) the local currency value of the government's debt. This result is no different from what would occur if the government initiated a short dollar position in the foreign exchange market. As Calvo and Reinhart (2000) stated:

> In [emerging markets], devaluations (or large depreciations) tend to be associated with recessions—not the kind of benign outcome stressed in standard textbooks. This is hardly surprising in light of the fact that in [emerging markets] there is pervasive liability dollarization. (p. 8)

The case of Mexico is particularly instructive because that country reconstituted large portions of its international debt as dollar-linked bonds (tesobonos) before the December 1994 crisis. When Mexico was forced to float the peso, the peso plunged by approximately 40 percent of its starting value. As a consequence, the government's indebtedness in pesos for the tesobonos rose by about 75 percent.

Governments are not the only original sinners because businesses and individuals also borrow in "hard currency," which makes them short the dollar and long local currency. This phenomenon was present in all the fixed exchange rate crises in the 1990s and 2000s. What makes this position even more explosive is that when they engage in "carry trades" in foreign markets, most international investors are on the same side of the trade in terms of their foreign exchange risk. Carry trades are usually constructed by going long a high-interest-rate currency and simultaneously short a low-interest-rate currency.

If the exchange rate does not change, the investor profits by the difference in interest rates; investors typically use leverage to magnify this profit. Thus, when this trade can be initiated with a fixed exchange rate currency, the risk appears (incorrectly) to be nonexistent. This trade appears repeatedly in the foreign exchange market. One can do the trade through the bond market or simply by taking forward foreign positions or through any number of derivatives contracts, listed or over the counter. The problem is that all these carry trades make the investor short the dollar and long the local currency.

In sum, what happens as a fixed exchange rate explodes is that everyone, onshore and offshore, and even the government itself, finds themselves short dollars and long local currency. As the foreign exchange regime becomes insupportable, the entire market tries to sell the local currency to buy dollars; no one is on the other side of the trade to buy the local currency. This imbalance is what accounted for the severity of the problems in the 1990s and 2000s. DeRosa (2001a) stressed that this stacking up of short dollar positions would not have been likely to occur absent the fixed exchange rate regime. In this way, the existence of a fixed exchange rate regime was a precondition to the variety of currency crises that occurred in this era. The crises themselves were the phenomenon of foreign capital (and domestic capital alike) fleeing the emerging-markets nations to avoid the consequences of imminent devaluation of the local currency.

Frankel (1999) disagreed with assigning any causality for the emerging-markets crises to the fixed exchange rate regimes:

> What would have happened if the emerging-market currencies of East Asia had floated freely throughout the 1990s? Probably they would have appreciated strongly throughout 1996, producing even larger current account deficits than the countries in fact incurred. The crisis when it came would have taken a different form—a burst bubble—but arguably might have been even worse than it was, if larger international debts had been run up in the meantime. (p. 9)

Local conditions apart from the fixed exchange rate itself are indisputably important in understanding these crises. As a general rule, a government that defaults on its sovereign debt will find itself unable to maintain a fixed exchange rate regime, something that conforms to common sense. Some of the currency crises (defined here as the collapse of a fixed exchange rate regime) were simultaneously also fiscal debt crises. On a single day, 17 August 1998, Russia defaulted on certain maturing debt obligations, floated the ruble, and blocked the settlement of ruble forward foreign currency transactions. Russian debt had become one of the world's premier carry trades, riding on the assumption that Russia was "too big" and "too nuclear" to fail. More recently, Argentina defaulted on its foreign debt and dismantled its famous currency board in January 2002. In both Russia and Argentina, it could be argued that the fixed exchange rate regimes could have continued for some time had the debt crises not overtaken events. But one must also consider the reverse. Both countries had dollar-denominated debts. If the fixed peg regimes had failed, that, in and of itself, might have ignited a debt crisis because the governments might have become functionally insolvent.

One controversial theory of emerging-markets crises is that contagion has a role to play. During the Mexican crisis, this contagion got the nickname the "tequila effect"—meaning that investors would flee emerging markets as a group because Mexico had collapsed. DeRosa (2001a) asserted that contagion does not play a large role in spreading crisis. So did Schwartz (1998):

> The question is whether an individual country that has mismanaged its affairs will precipitate an international financial crisis. . . . One myth is that the individual country's loss of creditworthiness has a tequila effect. The supposed tequila effect is that other countries without the problems of the troubled country are unfairly tarnished as also subject to these problems. In this way, it is said contagion spreads the crisis from its initial source to other innocent victims. (p. 251)

Edwards (2005), in his study of sudden stops, found results that "do not provide strong support for the contagion hypothesis" (p. 18). All of this is very much in debate, and quite a few economists believe that contagion, properly defined, is a genuine risk to emerging markets.[63] Others disagree.

Less controversial is the proposition that policy makers often made things worse. Thailand and South Korea each had policies in place to discourage long-term borrowing before the crises. In other words, the official policy was to attempt to limit the private sector to short-term borrowings from foreign banks. When the crisis hit—especially in Korea—all debts came due almost at once, whereupon foreign banks were reluctant to roll over loans. Had the private sector been able to borrow longer term, the immediate needs for emergency refinancing during the crises would have been less intense.

Popular financial lore lays the blame for the crises on currency speculation. The analysis of the previous chapter, in terms of the properties of the forward exchange rate, shows that this explanation of currency crises is at best dubious. Take the example of the Mexican peso before the 1994 crisis. To have bet on the demise of the fixed exchange rate system would have required the short sale of the peso in the forward market. Interest parity indicates that the forward outright encapsulates the difference between the peso and U.S. dollar interest rates. Because peso interest rates were higher than dollar interest rates in the context of what was a fixed exchange rate regime, the short position would have been costly to the speculator.

Speculators shorting pesos incurred substantial risk. As the crisis built, the peso interest rate rose, sometimes to spectacular levels, elevating the cost of maintaining a short position in the currency. Speculating in fixed exchange rate currencies is never without risk. The size of the aggregate speculative position, although large at times, is likely to be relatively small compared with the hedging positions needed to immunize the carry trades and the government's foreign currency indebtedness. More to the point, timing is everything. The speculator needs to put on the short position as close as possible to the breakdown in the regime, and as time goes by, the risk and cost of a short position grow larger as the crisis approaches its crescendo. The point is that there are no "sure things" when speculating in fixed exchange rate currencies.

That said, governments have accidentally fueled a crisis by inept policy measures. The case of Thailand in 1997 stands out in this regard.[64] I discussed some of the risk to going short Thai bahts in the previous chapter, but there is more to the story. The crisis became manifest in the spring of 1997. The Thai baht was pegged to a basket of currencies consisting chiefly of the U.S. dollar but also containing the German mark and the Japanese yen. When selling pressure became severe, the central bank began to buy baht against the dollar forward. Ordinarily, central banks intervene in the spot market, but in this instance, the Bank of Thailand used forwards.

---

[63] See, for example, Rigobon (2002).
[64] See DeRosa (2001a).

The problem was not so much that the bank was buying baht forward but, rather, that it was doing so at an off-market rate. In effect, the bank was overpaying for baht (seen from the other perspective, the bank was selling forward dollars below market). The consequence was that speculators could sell forward baht short with substantially less risk than if they had to sell at the much lower true market price. This situation created a de facto subsidy for anyone wanting to go short the baht. In the end, the Bank of Thailand practically exhausted its foreign exchange reserves through forward transactions. Thereupon, it shut down onshore foreign exchange trading in May 1997. Finally, the bank reopened the market in early July 1997 when it depegged the baht. The Thai crisis was exacerbated—but not caused—by the bank's forward baht purchases.

The hollowing out of the intermediate zone of the foreign exchange spectrum in the 1990s and 2000s was largely a result of the currency crises that befell the emerging-markets countries. Whether these countries ever attempt to migrate back to intermediate zone exchange rate regimes remains to be seen. For now, the experience of crises appears to have scared the emerging-markets nations, and rightfully so, to the poles of floating or hard-pegged exchange rate regimes.

## The Classical Debate: Fixed vs. Floating

Emerging-markets nations look to their central banks to decide, or at least recommend, whether they should fix or float their exchange rate. The debate as to the relative merits of fixed versus floating exchange rates is an old topic in economics. This debate is unlikely to be resolved any time soon, but the issues and arguments that have been put forward are important to consider.

Some economists have argued an extreme view that there should be a single world currency and that the very existence of multiple currencies creates the need for unnecessary and costly transactions.[65] John Stuart Mill, who originally published *Principles of Political Economy* in 1848, was a supporter of the world currency concept:

> So much of barbarism, however, still remains in the transactions of most civilized nations, that almost all independent countries choose to assert their nationality by having, to their own inconvenience and that of their neighbors, a peculiar currency of their own. (Mill 2004, pp. 572–573)

One argument against having more than one currency is that an exchange rate is a superfluous "$N + 1$th" price in an otherwise system of $N$ prices and $N$ goods. With a world currency, there are only $N$ prices because foreign exchange does not exist—hence the argument that when countries have their own currencies, the world's economy is necessarily inefficient. But having a world currency is not without opportunity cost, the foremost being that individual countries are precluded from having their own independent monetary policy. No matter what the state of

---

[65]See Cooper (2006) and Bordo and James (2006) for dissenting views.

its economy, each country's interest rate would be permanently equal to whatever interest rate prevailed in every other country in the world, absent credit issues. Another variety of the single world currency idea is a return to gold as the basis for the world's monetary system. This idea, however, has the same drawbacks as a single world fiat currency: All countries would be constrained to having the same monetary policy. Moreover, at least one form of the gold standard, namely, the gold exchange standard (which existed between the first and second world wars), has been associated with the international spread of the Great Depression (see Bernanke 2004 and the discussion in Chapter 4).

More relevant to the topic here is fixed exchange rates between countries that each have their own currency. Mundell and Fleming have argued that fixed exchange rate regimes give more potency to fiscal policy. From an international perspective, a fixed exchange rate regime can serve as an anchor to constrain the policies of a potentially wayward central bank. As such, the "anchor" prevents policies that predictably result in the emergence of extreme inflation or even hyperinflation. One has to remember, however, that fixed exchange rate regimes are never permanent. They have been abandoned, and sometimes they have fallen apart. Their existence may ensure temporary monetary probity, but that happy state lasts only for as long as the central bank continues its support of the regime.

Frankel (2007) cited one advantage of having fixed exchange rates as the encouragement of investment because of the extraction of the "currency premium out of interest rates" (p. 16), by which he appears to mean that the interest rate will be lower with a fixed exchange rate than a floating one. He also includes as benefits the provision of a "nominal anchor for monetary policy," the prevention of "competitive depreciation," and the avoidance of "speculative bubbles that afflict floating" (p. 16).

Proponents of floating regimes argue that this regime affords the central bank maximum flexibility to implement monetary and fiscal policy. Aliber (1975) has stated:

> The fundamental argument for flexible exchange rates is that they allow countries autonomy with respect to their use of monetary, fiscal, and other policy instruments by automatically ensuring the preservation of external equilibrium. (p. 368)

Likewise, Frankel (1999) has written:

> The advantages of a flexible exchange rate can all be grouped under one major property: It allows the country to pursue independent monetary policy. When the economy is hit by a disturbance, such as a shift in worldwide demand away from the goods it produces, the government would like to be able to respond, so that the country does not go into recession. Under fixed exchange rates, monetary policy is always diverted, at least to some extent, to dealing with the balance of payments. (p. 12)

Frankel (2007) cited the following as advantages of floating exchange rates: monetary independence, "automatic adjustment to trade shocks," retention of seignorage, retention of the ability of the central bank to be the lender of last resort, and the avoidance of "crashes that hit pegged rates" (p. 17). The last point brings up one of the curious features of the debate: Fixed and floating regimes have both been accused of being prone to crises. Frankel (1999) has written about the danger of floating: "Large swings and speculative bubbles intrude on the nirvana of pure floating" (p. 9). And:

> [There is a] tendency toward volatility that does not always derive from macro-economic fundamentals, including occasional speculative bubbles (possibly rational, possibly not) and crashes. (p. 13)

Yet, as Fischer (2007) has said about the intermediate zone soft pegs: "Such regimes are crisis prone, in part because their policy dynamics are unstable" (p. 10). The irony is that two leading economists, who agree on many important issues, are describing essentially opposite currency regimes as inherently unstable or crisis prone.

On a more basic level, fixed exchange rates of any form can be criticized for creating economic distortions. The discussion in Chapter 3 describes the exchange rate as an equilibrating price, meaning that it, like interest rates and income, causes macroeconomic markets to clear. What happens when an equilibrating price is fixed? How economically efficient could that be? Three types of distortions are created when exchange rates are fixed:

- Exchange rates are prices—as are interest rates and stock prices and the prices of specific commodities, like energy and food. Prices bring about market-clearing conditions, in which the quantity supplied equals the quantity de-manded. Does it make any more sense to say exchange rates ought to be fixed than to say the price of bananas should be fixed? We also know that if one or more price is held constant by decree or by administrative action (such as a central bank fixing the exchange rate), the work done by the other equilibrating prices has to be greater than what would otherwise be the case. Moreover, it is true that economic outcomes will be different and perhaps less optimal if exchange rates, but not other variables, are frozen.

- Transactions in both the current and capital accounts are done at the wrong exchange rate; one country's goods are artificially expensive while the other country's goods are artificially cheap. As a consequence, the wrong quantities of goods and services are produced and consumed. The effects of the distortions carry all the way through the market for the factors of production. The extent of the misallocation of resources is proportional to the difference between the fixed exchange rate and what would be the correct market-clearing, floating exchange rate. The same is true of the capital account: Investment opportunities in one country are artificially cheap and opportunities in the other country are artificially expensive as a consequence of the misalignment in the exchange rate.

- Capital transactions are done in the expectation of an environment where exchange rates are artificially stabilized. The creation of artificial stability encourages transactors to attempt to take advantage of investment strategies that otherwise make no economic sense. An important example is the famous "carry trade" that is so popular in the foreign exchange market.

Many emerging-markets countries have what Calvo and Reinhart (2000) have described as a "fear of floating," as noted earlier. In particular, they have ascribed this fear to certain Latin American countries. Three reasons can be cited for a fear of floating: (1) the real and financial effects of excessive volatility in exchange rates, (2) balance sheet effects of sharp movements in the exchange rate (particularly a depreciation), and (3) a high pass-through from a depreciation of the local currency to inflation.

Whatever the reasons, emerging-markets central banks have at various times been reluctant to trust the foreign exchange market to set the value of their currencies. Ironically, today, very few emerging-markets nations have fixed exchange rate regimes. In effect, the 1990s crises forcibly converted them to floating or managed floating exchange rates—China, of course, being the exception. The capital market "voted with its feet" in the 1990s by leaving the soft pegs, and since that time, there have been few, if any, new currency crises.

## Currency Boards

A currency board's job is to fix the exchange rate. It may operate inside the central bank or as a stand-alone institution. The only asset that a currency board must hold is the reserve currency—such as dollars or euros. The essential feature of a currency board is that it must stand ready to buy or sell local currency for reserve currency at the established fixed exchange rate upon demand. When the currency board sells reserve currency, it buys domestic currency, thereby lowering the monetary base. When the currency board buys reserve currency, it sells domestic currency, thereby raising the monetary base. In a sense, a currency board is a central bank that does foreign exchange intervention on automatic pilot.

In an extreme situation, flight from the local currency would obligate the currency board to reabsorb much of, or even all of, the money supply in exchange for its hoard of reserve currency. By definition, the monetary base would shrink, and unless there were a change in the money expansion process, the broad monetary aggregates would also shrink.

At this point, currency board advocates usually invoke the quantity theory of money: As money supply shrinks, the domestic currency becomes more valuable but the exchange rate (between the local and the reserve currency) has not changed. An increase in demand for the domestic currency produces the opposite result. Either way, an expansion or contraction of the currency board's balance sheet is an unsterilized change in the nation's money supply. Monetary economics indicate that such a change in the money supply can have broad implications for the short-run functioning of the economy.

The advantage of a currency board over a conventional peg may be marginal credibility. It is hard to see how a currency board can ever run out of reserve currency. Put another way, advocates say no currency board can ever fail, unless its government decides it wants it to fail. In this regard, Frankel (1999) is critical: "The current fad [a currency board] is sometimes sold as credibility in a bottle" (p. 3). He explained his reservations in the following:

> Proclaiming a currency board does not automatically guarantee the credibility of the fixed rate peg. Little credibility is gained from putting an exchange rate peg into law, in a country where laws are not heeded or are changed at will. A currency board is unlikely to be successful without the solid fundamentals of adequate reserves, fiscal discipline, and a strong and well-supervised financial system, in addition to the rule of law. (p. 20)

Hanke obviously disagrees; he has been a vocal proponent of currency boards as solutions to exchange rate instability.[66]

The major disadvantages are, first, that the local currency interest rate will be determined by the reserve currency's central bank and, second, that the domestic money supply will be a pawn of the demand for the reserve currency, as has been mentioned. External considerations, meaning keeping the local currency pegged at a fixed rate, receive absolute preference over domestic economic stability. Bullet proof, perhaps, but at what cost?

The most famous currency board in operation today is run by the Hong Kong Monetary Authority. It has shown itself to be durable but not completely invulnerable to a crisis. In a crisis, what happens is that interest rates adjust upward, sometimes to astronomical levels, driving the forward exchange rate far away from the spot level (a currency board fixes the spot but not the forward exchange rate). In the process, the economy suffers the impact of high interest rates, which is what happened at least twice to Hong Kong—once in October 1997 and again in the summer of 1998. The peg held both times.

But then there is the case of Argentina, a country that had a currency board–like monetary regime that ended in total economic catastrophe in 2002. In 1991, Argentina adopted what came to be called the "convertibility law" to combat excessive inflation. Convertibility meant that the Argentine peso and the U.S. dollar were interchangeable at the rate of one for one. The dollar became the anchor for the Argentine central bank, and sure enough, Argentina's inflation problems virtually disappeared. Hanke (2008) has pointed out that the consumer price index at the end of 2001 was about where it was in 1994. The whole concept of convertibility appeared to be a tremendous success. Yet, by the late 1990s, strains on the Argentine Treasury began to appear.

---

[66]Steve Hanke has written extensively on currency boards (see his website www.jhu.edu/iaesbe/ Hankepublist.pdf). Some examples of his recent work on currency boards are Hanke (2002, 2003, 2005a, and 2005b).

Was the currency board responsible for the Argentine crisis? Many economists seemed to think so, at least at the time. If they are correct, then currency boards should never be used. Other economists, in particular Hanke (2008), who is well known for his advocacy of hard currency regimes such as currency boards and dollarization, has said: "The Argentine crisis was not caused by the failure of a currency board, but by its absence" (p. 56). He contended that Argentina never had a proper (or "orthodox") currency board:

> The [charter of] BCRA (Banco Central de la Republica Argentina, meaning the central bank) allowed it to behave more like a central bank than a currency board in many important respects. (2008, p. 48)

Hanke (2008) has claimed that the convertibility law created:

> . . . a central bank with a pegged exchange rate and a domestic monetary policy, distinguished by the unique feature of the convertibility of pesos to dollars on demand. And like most central banks employing a pegged exchange rate, the Argentine system proved vulnerable to conflicts between the peg (the exchange rate policy) and domestic monetary policy. (pp. 49–50)

Whatever the currency board was or was not, it is clear that Argentina created for itself a mammoth debt crisis. A simple explanation of what happened in Argentina is that, although the convertibility law prohibited the central bank from "printing money," meaning creating excessive amounts of money supply, no similar restraint was placed on the Treasury being able to "print bonds." Argentina borrowed until it went broke. Along the way, it played a great number of shenanigans involving debt swaps (some forced), multiple exchange rates, and other ruses. Finally, it defaulted on hundreds of millions of dollars of sovereign debt at more or less the same time it depegged the peso from the dollar.

## Dollarization

Dollarization is when a country adopts another country's currency, usually the U.S. dollar, to replace its own currency.[67] Typically, this decision is made when a country is very new or when it is in dire financial and monetary straits.

A classic example of the latter circumstance is the last days of the Argentine convertibility period before the default in 2002. One way out for Argentina was to dollarize, meaning to simultaneously abandon the currency board–like arrangement and announce that the peso, and all peso-denominated assets and liabilities, would be converted to U.S. dollars by law, which is what Hanke and others recommended. DeRosa (2001b), weeks before the default and depegging of the peso, wrote that dollarization might be preferable to floating the peso because "handcuffs would be

---

[67]It does not have to be U.S. dollars. For example, it could be "euro-ization" or "yen-ization" if the currency being adopted is the euro or the yen.

placed on the central bank so it could not engineer a Latin American–style hyperinflation" and because all currency risk would disappear. Instead, Argentina let the peso float; it dropped like a stone. Worse yet, the government set about forcing the conversion of bank accounts between dollars and pesos at nonmarket rates. One could say that there were four (at least) disasters happening at once: the government's default on its debt, the plunge in the peso, the crash of the local stock and bond markets, and the inept handling of the crisis by the government.

The main advantage, it would seem, to dollarizing is that the central bank ceases having to worry about its own exchange rate. It does, however, have to start worrying about the exchange rate for the U.S. dollar against other major currencies. If the dollar rises in value, the dollarized country's exports may suffer. If the dollar falls, then imports become expensive. What dollarization does achieve, at least in principle, is monetary stability and a potentially substantial reduction in the cost of its borrowing in international markets. A more subtle, yet important, point is that dollarizing eliminates the risk of borrowing internationally in dollars (i.e., no "original sin").

The most serious drawback is that there is no a priori reason to think that U.S. monetary policy would be appropriate for the country that dollarizes. Moreover, the central bank of the United States—or of Europe or Australia—cannot be expected to conduct monetary policy with consideration for the economic circumstances in other countries. Greenspan (1999) affirmed this stance in Senate testimony:

> Our basic monetary policy does take into consideration what is going on in the rest of the world largely because the rest of the world does affect us. But what we do not do is focus on the well-being of the rest of the world as distinct from the well-being of the United States. (p. 13)

A second problem with dollarization is that the dollarized country loses its rights to seignorage revenue because it no longer has its own currency. Bordo (1981) has defined seignorage as:

> . . . the return earned by the U.S. monetary authorities of the issue of outstanding paper money liabilities. It is measured by the interest forgone by foreign holders of U.S. money balances. (p. 7)

Bordo (1981) has pointed out that seignorage is to be distinguished from the "inflation tax," the latter referring to the depreciation in real purchasing power of outstanding money balances.

Two operational issues must also be solved before a country can dollarize. First, an appropriate exchange rate of the domestic currency for dollars must be decided on. This rate covers the conversion of all prices for goods, services, assets, and liabilities. Obviously, a mistake here could have enormous consequences. The devil in this detail is that a country tends to think of dollarizing when its exchange rate is in crisis. As such, this is likely to be a shotgun wedding, with the marriage to dollars taking place when the exchange value of the currency is extremely cheap. The same problem exists when setting up a currency board.[68]

Second, it is true that any country can dollarize with or without the permission of the reserve currency country (such as the United States).[69] Yet, there is a very practical problem: Where will the dollarizing country obtain the large number of physical reserve currency banknotes (e.g., dollars) it will need to initiate the exchange for domestic currency? Some cooperation with the reserve country's central bank is needed if for no other reason than to obtain the necessary banknotes.

These problems notwithstanding, the idea of dollarization for an emerging-markets nation is worthy of serious consideration, at least when the alternative is to attempt to operate some sort of fixed exchange rate regime.

## Currency Zones

The custom in international finance has always favored every country having its own currency, the euro notwithstanding. Is this practice optimal? Can a small economy justify the expense of creating its own currency and maintaining a central bank? Does it make sense for small, geographically proximate countries to force their citizens to conduct foreign exchange transactions every time they travel short distances or engage in regional trade? In these cases, the potential cost savings from having a common currency and a common central bank carries the day. In fact, this is certainly the reality behind such currency zones as the Eastern Caribbean Currency Union and the Central African franc zones.

In what is perhaps his most famous work, Mundell (1961) theorized that degrees of mobility of factors of production, notably, labor supply, define optimal currency areas. Each optimal currency area ought to have its own monetary policy. Labor is supposed to be highly mobile inside an optimal currency area but relatively less so across such zones. Krugman and Obstfeld (1997) agreed:

> Optimum currency areas are groups of regions with economies closely linked by trade in goods and services and by factor mobility. (p. 630)

The concept can be explained with a highly stylized example based on Mundell's article. The United States and Canada share a border that in very rough terms cuts the top half of North America by latitude from east to west. Each country is made

---

[68]Indeed, this was one of the problems that faced Hanke when he tried, unsuccessfully, to establish a currency board in Indonesia during the last days of President Suharto. News sources claimed Suharto wanted to establish the currency board at an exchange rate wildly off market for that time, something that Hanke convincingly refutes. See Hanke (1998) for an interesting account of this bizarre episode in emerging-markets monetary history.

[69]Deputy Treasury Secretary Lawrence Summers (1999) expressed this sentiment in testimony before the Senate: "If a country says that as of now, the dollar is legal tender in our country, that is not something that requires any U.S. government action or requires any congressional authorization" (p. 9).

up of a farming and natural resources economy in the west and an industrial economy in the east. Yet each country has a central bank that makes monetary policy for the whole of each country. This arrangement is a purely political result. The economic reality is different. Farming and natural resource labor is mobile from north to south; the same could be said of industrial labor. The optimal currency zone argument would say there should be two currencies, two monetary policies, and two central banks—one of each for the combined eastern Canada and eastern United States and one of each for the combined western Canada and western United States. This, of course, is a highly abstract explanation, but it gets us to Mundell's point.

As an aside, Mundell's insight on optimal currency zones seems to have gotten mixed up with his advocacy for the creation of the euro (it was one of the contributions mentioned in his Nobel Prize award). The curious point is that Europe is not an optimal currency zone, not by any stretch.[70] Krugman and Obstfeld (1997) wrote: "On balance, there is little evidence that Europe's product and factor markets are sufficiently unified to make it an optimum currency area" (p. 633).

Moreover, the more the European Union expands to the east, the less of an optimal currency zone it becomes. You might see German factory workers driving taxis in Paris, but you are less likely to see them behind the wheel in Bulgaria, the latter a planned entry to the euro zone.

So, why have the euro if not for optimal currency area reasons? Basically, the euro is a political phenomenon. It was conceived during the post–World War II wave of European federalism that created the European Union. The argument put forward by the statesmen of the time for the euro can be paraphrased as follows: The chances of future wars in Europe, meaning between European nations, is diminished by making the political and economic affairs of the member nations sufficiently intertwined, which includes having a single currency and a single central bank. Never mind that familiarity, it is said, breeds contempt.

Despite there being economic reservations, some of the smaller European countries have arguably drawn economic benefits from the single currency project, notably, a reduction in the cost of their foreign debt service. Without a doubt, the entire euro zone benefits from having eliminated tariffs between the member nations, something that came as part and parcel of the European Union. The deadweight costs of maintaining foreign exchange inventories for travelers have also been eliminated.

The drawbacks with the euro currency zone are the same as those that go with a currency board or dollarization. Having the euro means that a one-size-fits-all monetary policy is adopted. What are the chances that the monetary policy appropriate for Germany will always be right for Spain or Portugal? Furthermore,

---

[70]The Nobel Prize committee apparently disagreed. The press release announcing Mundell's award lauds him for his work on optimum currency areas with application to the euro. See press release dated 13 October 1999 (http://nobelprize.org/nobel_prizes/economics/laureates/1999/press.html).

after the establishment of a currency zone, instead of having, say, 12 competing exchange rates, each capable of making independent equilibrating adjustments to macroeconomic markets (had they been floating inside the EMS), there now is 1. Seen this way, the euro is an extreme repudiation of the concept of floating exchange rates inside Europe (although the euro itself is independently floating against the U.S. dollar and other currencies).

What value do currency zones have for emerging-markets countries? In the developing world—but not usually the part of the developing world that is considered to be the emerging markets—countries have sometimes formed currency zones for the simple cost saving of each country not having to operate its own central bank with its own currency. Does that rationale make sense for the emerging markets? What are the marginal advantages of a currency zone over dollarization? To use an analogy, with dollarization, monetary policy is controlled by a foreign landlord; with a currency zone, monetary policy is controlled by a condominium association. If the zone is dominated by one or two large, wealthy countries, the difference between monetary policy in a currency zone and dollarization might not be significant. If power is decentralized, however, all the members of a currency zone will have a voice in monetary policy.

Perhaps the greater value to joining a currency zone comes not from the exchange rate regime itself but from the fact that such arrangements are "tie-in sales" with becoming a member of a free trade region; the decision to join may bring with it the important bonus of low, or even no, tariffs or import/export quotas. Yet, a country could have all these advantages without having a common currency.

## Bipolarity Hypothesis

The term "bipolarity," or the "bipolar view," was popularized by Fischer in a celebrated paper he published in 2001. The bipolar view is that the intermediate zone of exchange rate arrangements (see Exhibit 5.1) will gradually disappear as countries migrate toward either floating rate regimes or hard pegs and currency zones. Fischer (2007), in answering critics of his 2001 paper, reasserted that "I will argue that the bipolar view is fundamentally correct for emerging market and industrialized countries with open capital accounts" (p. 2) and:

> For countries with international capital flows, [the bipolar view] includes as sustainable regimes both very hard pegs, and a variety of floating rate arrangements, including managed floats. For countries not yet open to international capital flows, it includes a full gamut of exchange rate arrangements. (p. 3)

In the 2001 paper, Fischer explained that the bipolar hypothesis is an application of the impossible trinity theorem:

> The impossible trinity—of a fixed exchange rate, capital mobility, and a monetary policy dedicated to domestic goals—is surely the major part of the explanation for the non-viability of the soft pegs. (p. 8)

Fischer's evidence in the 2007 paper consists of demonstrating that the migration of emerging-markets countries to the poles was indeed a matter of historical fact, as **Figure 5.2** shows for the emerging-markets countries, the developed countries, and all other countries as observed in 1991, 1999, and 2006. The bipolar view works well for the emerging markets, although the process of movement to the poles has slowed down somewhat in recent years, as he has noted.

In contrast, Frankel (1999) vigorously asserted in the title to his article that "no single currency regime is right for all countries or at all times."[71] This article and subsequent works attack the bipolar view, starting with the way Fischer used the impossible trinity. Frankel (1999) wrote:

> Whence the hypothesis of the disappearing intermediate regime (or the "missing middle"), to begin with? At first glance it appears to be a corollary to the principle of the impossible trinity. That principle says that a country must give up one of three goals: exchange rate stability, monetary independence, and financial market integration. It cannot have all three simultaneously. If one adds the observation that financial markets are steadily becoming more and more integrated internationally, that forces the choice down to giving up on exchange rate stability or giving up on monetary independence. But this is not the same thing as saying one cannot give up on both, that one cannot have half-stability and half-independence. There is nothing in existing theory, for example, that prevents a country from pursuing a managed float in which half of every fluctuation in the demand of its currency is accommodated by intervention and half is allowed to be reflected in the exchange rate. (p. 7)

Fischer (2007) responded:

> The usual justification is the impossible trinity, but Frankel suggests that a variety of managed floats are fully consistent with the impossible trinity—that one can have half-stability and half-independence. (p. 3)

> While the impossible trinity is usually stated in terms of an independent *monetary* policy, it should more accurately be stated in terms of independent *macroeconomic* policy, for when a currency comes under serious pressure, typically both monetary and fiscal policy have to adjust if the exchange rate is to be maintained. . . .

> Second, an "independent" monetary policy in this context is one that is targeted at something other than at the exchange rate. For many countries that have given up exchange rate pegging, the monetary regime switches to inflation targeting, in practice typically flexible inflation targeting. For others, the monetary policy

---

[71]Similarly, consider what Obstfeld and Taylor (2002) wrote: "The choice between fixed and floating exchange rates should not be viewed as dichotomous; nor should it be assumed that the choice of a floating-rate regime necessarily leads to a useful degree of monetary-policy flexibility. In reality, the degree of exchange-rate flexibility lies on a continuum, with exchange-rate target zones, crawling pegs, crawling zones, and managed floats of various other kinds residing between the extremes of irrevocably fixed and floating" (p. 8 footnote 12).

**Figure 5.2. Emerging-Markets Exchange Rate Regimes**

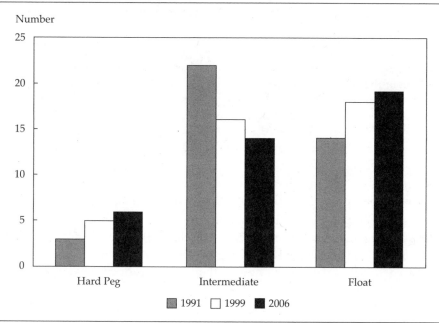

*Source*: Based on Fischer (2007).

is directed to a range of targets, including inflation and growth, sometimes also the real exchange rate, with tradeoffs among them to be determined by the policymakers. Once the goals of monetary policy have been specified, monetary policy is no longer independent of the factors that move the economic variables that it is targeting. . . .

Thus in practice by giving up exchange rate pegging and shifting to inflation targeting, a central bank does not gain monetary independence in the sense that its monetary policy becomes independent of monetary policy—more generally of economic developments—in other countries. Rather it has switched from targeting one economic variable—the exchange rate—to another, namely the inflation rate, both of which depend on differing extents on economic developments abroad and at home. This may be the meaning of Jeffrey Frankel's statement that a country can have half stability and half monetary policy independence [of the exchange rate]. (pp. 7–8)

Of course, other views exist. For example, Calvo and Mishkin (2003) have put forth what some describe as an "exchange rate agnostic view." They have examined the possibility that financial institutions in the less developed emerging markets are not mature enough to allow monetary policy to be effective. Why have floating exchange rates if monetary policy cannot work because of institutional factors? A large part of the argument for flexible exchange rates is to allow for independent monetary policy. They concluded:

> Overall, we believe that the key to macroeconomic success in emerging market countries is not primarily their choice of exchange rate regime, but rather the health of the countries' fundamental macroeconomic institutions, including the institutions associated with fiscal stability, financial stability, and monetary stability. In general, we believe that less attention should be focused on the general question of whether a floating or a fixed exchange rate is preferable and more on these deeper institutional arrangements. (p. 101)

> When choosing between exchange rate regimes, one size does not fit all (or always). . . . Instead, an informed choice of exchange rate regime requires a deep understanding of a country's economy, institutions, and political culture. (p. 115)

But the weight of the evidence, as well as the substance of the argument, favors Fischer. Having answered his major critic, Fischer (2007) reaffirmed his belief in the bipolar view. He concluded by writing that as countries develop and open their capital accounts, they will move toward either hard pegs or currency zones, on the one hand, or flexible exchange rates, on the other hand. Fischer then quoted Rogoff, Husain, Mody, Brooks, and Oomes (2003) as saying that "free floats register faster growth than other regimes without incurring higher inflation" (p. 6).

This consideration may tip the bipolar scales toward freely floating at the expense of the hard pegs. Although hard pegs can work, full independence can come only from having a floating exchange rate. In Chapter 1, I endorsed the idea that emerging-markets nations (but not all developing countries) ought to have central banks. Being in the emerging class, I argued, is to have the wherewithal to operate an independent central bank successfully. The same line of thought could be extended to emerging-markets nations with respect to learning to live with floating exchange rates, but that is a big step that I would not advocate unless the central bank is committed to a monetary rule, such as inflation targeting or the Taylor rule.

# 6. The Paradox of International Capital

International capital flows present contentious issues for developing and emerging-markets countries and their central banks.[72] The topic has grown in importance because of the trend among emerging-markets nations to allow exchange rates to become largely market determined and capital accounts to gradually move in the direction of becoming freely convertible. Previous chapters discussed capital flows and the balance of payments from a conceptual vantage point. Economists, notably Robert Mundell, believe that the mobility of capital circumscribes the range of policy options available to a central bank with respect to monetary policy and the choice of exchange rate regime. This chapter continues the story, updating the discussion for what economists have learned about capital flows from the experiences, and one could say the surprises, of the 1990s and 2000s.

## Growth Paradox

For decades, development economists have espoused the notion that injections of foreign capital are highly beneficial for countries attempting to achieve sustainable economic growth.[73] Foreign investment capital is presumed to be a necessary supplement to domestic savings for funding economic development. Lucas (1990) noted that "the central idea of virtually all postwar development policies is to stimulate transfers of capital goods from rich to poor countries" (p. 96).

Gruber and Kamin (2006) paraphrased (but did not endorse) the elements of what could be called "basic growth theory" in expressing why capital should flow to developing countries:[74]

> Because developing countries have higher labor/capital ratios, they should in principle have higher marginal productivities of capital and thus attract capital from labor-poor economies. Moreover, if developing countries can expect faster income growth as they catch up to industrial countries, this provides an incentive for them to borrow against their higher future income, also leading to current account deficits. (p. 1)

[72]The terms "developing" and "emerging" become synonymous in some of the discussions in this chapter. As I discussed in Chapter 1, emerging-markets nations are developing economies but not all developing nations have achieved emerging-markets status.

[73]The story of economic growth does not start nor does it end with foreign capital infusions. See Easterly (2001) for more on this topic.

[74]See Koszner (2007).

This simple paradigm establishes the basic conditions for supply and demand in developing economies for foreign investment.

Therefore, the broad advice that economists should give to emerging markets is to open their capital markets to foreign investment. Investment capital should move from developed countries to developing economies on a continual basis, absent impediments to the operation of capital markets. The argument does not consider risk, of course, but by this simple account, the process of capital flowing to the developing world ought to continue at least until rates of return are equalized around the world.

If the world worked according to this paradigm, there would be nothing more to discuss on the matter. The problem is that it does not even remotely mesh with economic reality. Some prominent episodes in economic history demonstrate this fact:

- After World War I, capital flows to developing countries were at first abundant but then all but halted during the Great Depression. Capital flows to the developing world did not resume in large volume until the early 1970s, when much of the flows to and from emerging markets were founded in the surge of oil revenues to exporters following the first oil crisis (1973). In that period, some capital, above and beyond the part representing the recycling of oil money, did move into the non-oil-exporting countries.

- Capital flows came to a screeching halt in mid-1982 when it became apparent that many highly indebted developing-markets nations were straining to service their external debt, which became known in the popular press as the "Latin American debt bomb." A variety of debt restructuring and refinancing plans ensued, known collectively as the "Brady Plan."

- After a time, capital resumed flowing to the emerging markets, aided in no small part by the dismantling of capital controls in these countries.[75] Capital flows in the early 1990s to these countries were large by historical standards. In the 1990s, capital surged into emerging markets—especially Mexico, Southeast Asia, and Russia. Investors displayed what could be described as unfounded optimism for these countries. But not for long. When they lost enthusiasm, capital flows abruptly reversed direction. The stampede of money out of these former favorite nations ignited a series of spectacular currency crises. The hemorrhaging of capital induced violent fluctuations in interest rates, asset prices, and exchange rates. The aftereffects are still with these countries; even a decade later, capital is still flowing out of many of these emerging-markets nations.[76]

---

[75] See Obstfeld and Taylor (2002) and Calvo et al. (1994).

[76] As I will discuss later, private capital flows are directed toward many of these nations at the same time that total capital flows are in the opposite direction.

This brief history alone illustrates the fact that capital does not always flow as is predicted by basic growth theory. Capital flows to emerging markets have been episodic; they have been nothing like a steady one-way flow from the developed to the developing economies. A logical follow-on question is whether capital flows are a benefit to the developing world. Some question whether international capital flows actually damage recipient economies. In due course, one will see that large capital flows can complicate monetary policy, cause overheating, or lead to unwarranted exchange rate appreciation. Worst of all, when foreign investors take their leave of an emerging-markets country, they have been known to do so en masse, staging a hasty exit—what is called a "sudden stop"—and in the process laying waste the host country.

## Water Running Uphill

Tables **6.1** and **6.2** and **Figures 6.1, 6.2,** and **6.3** show current account balances in billions of U.S. dollars and current accounts by percentage of GDP for selected countries and categories of countries from 1985 to 2006. (Note that the complete 1985–2007 data for Tables 6.1–6.5 can be found in the online supplemental materials at www.cfapubs.org.) One category that is of special interest is what the IMF calls "other emerging market and developing countries."

The data reveal the following:

- The current account balance for the IMF category "other emerging market and developing countries" was in deficit in the 1985–99 period. Thereafter, this group experienced current account surpluses (see Figure 6.1 and Tables 6.1 and 6.2).

  — Current account deficits crested in 1998, plunged in 1999, and turned into surpluses thereafter.

- The emerging and developing group accumulated foreign exchange reserves in large size for the whole 1989–2006 period but especially in the 2003–06 period (see **Table 6.3**).

- Private capital flowed into the region during the 1986–2006 period.

The current account data for selected Asian and Latin American countries are shown in **Table 6.4** and **Table 6.5**. The fact that capital has been flowing out of emerging markets toward the developed countries has attracted much attention, so much that it has earned itself the nickname "water running uphill." That phrase reflects the near astonishment in some circles that capital could be flowing out of the emerging markets, especially at the current time when their economies are doing rather well. The other part of the mystery is that capital during this period is flowing into the United States; this topic is the subject of the next section on global imbalances.

For some economists, this entire picture with its mysteries is not entirely surprising. It is no secret that capital flows do not always conform to what simple growth models predict. The profession became aware of this no later than with the publication of Lucas's seminal paper in 1990 that questioned why it is that capital

**Table 6.1. Summary of Current Account Balances by Country Groups in U.S. Dollars, 1985–2007** (billions)

| Country Group Name | 1985 | 1990 | 1995 | 2000 | 2001 | 2002 | 2003 | 2004 | 2005 | 2006 | 2007 |
|---|---|---|---|---|---|---|---|---|---|---|---|
| Advanced economies | –$51.24 | –$93.94 | $32.66 | –$263.30 | –$204.97 | –$208.80 | –$207.04 | –$224.18 | –$438.66 | –$525.21 | –$463.28 |
| Euro area | n/a | n/a | n/a | –35.08 | 8.41 | 50.11 | 45.20 | 108.21 | 23.59 | –6.38 | –30.02 |
| Major advanced economies (G–7) | –62.41 | –80.87 | –19.07 | –332.21 | –286.38 | –308.31 | –358.36 | –368.78 | –542.83 | –641.45 | –544.36 |
| Newly industrialized Asian economies | 11.08 | 16.80 | 2.14 | 38.86 | 46.80 | 54.56 | 79.24 | 80.61 | 73.51 | 82.75 | 102.27 |
| Other advanced economies (advanced economies excluding G–7 and euro area) | 4.61 | 5.15 | 11.63 | 87.54 | 98.83 | 100.30 | 147.54 | 148.74 | 160.25 | 193.99 | 215.50 |
| European Union | 7.45 | –53.29 | 33.13 | –81.37 | –26.39 | 22.23 | 23.62 | 63.00 | –32.43 | –113.05 | –202.75 |
| Emerging and developing economies | –30.11 | –35.05 | –90.99 | 86.90 | 41.13 | 76.65 | 144.28 | 213.64 | 439.53 | 606.71 | 630.88 |
| Africa | –2.12 | –5.13 | –14.66 | 8.30 | 1.31 | –8.59 | –3.88 | 2.04 | 15.81 | 29.60 | 1.60 |
| Africa: Sub-Sahara | –1.28 | –5.09 | –10.46 | 0.46 | –6.34 | –13.68 | –13.54 | –9.49 | –6.20 | –0.57 | –28.05 |
| Central and Eastern Europe | –5.60 | –4.90 | –6.47 | –31.34 | –15.85 | –24.04 | –37.25 | –59.30 | –61.28 | –90.95 | –121.47 |
| Commonwealth of Independent States and Mongolia | 3.10 | –16.69 | 3.30 | 48.25 | 33.10 | 30.21 | 36.01 | 63.79 | 88.27 | 97.79 | 76.15 |
| Developing Asia | –23.44 | –13.80 | –40.88 | 38.52 | 36.67 | 64.77 | 82.62 | 89.19 | 161.43 | 277.50 | 383.54 |
| ASEAN-5 | –4.67 | –14.20 | –33.29 | 24.67 | 18.24 | 19.66 | 24.45 | 19.24 | 14.03 | 43.43 | 51.61 |
| Middle East | –0.36 | 5.61 | 4.47 | 71.47 | 39.89 | 30.30 | 59.06 | 97.09 | 200.34 | 247.33 | 274.61 |
| Western Hemisphere | –1.69 | –0.13 | –36.76 | –48.30 | –53.98 | –16.00 | 7.71 | 20.83 | 34.97 | 45.43 | 16.45 |

*Note:* See Appendix A for definitions of the country group names.
*Source:* Based on data from the International Monetary Fund, World Economic Outlook Database (April 2008).

**Table 6.2. Summary of Current Account Balances by Country Groups as a Percentage of GDP, 1985–2007**

| Country Group Name | 1985 | 1990 | 1995 | 2000 | 2001 | 2002 | 2003 | 2004 | 2005 | 2006 | 2007 |
|---|---|---|---|---|---|---|---|---|---|---|---|
| Advanced economies | -0.544% | -0.532% | 0.135% | -1.036% | -0.817% | -0.797% | -0.705% | -0.688% | -1.283% | -1.463% | -1.184% |
| Euro area | na | na | na | -0.561 | 0.133 | 0.727 | 0.532 | 1.113 | 0.234 | -0.06 | -0.246 |
| Major advanced economies (G–7) | -0.777 | -0.563 | -0.097 | -1.582 | -1.381 | -1.439 | -1.515 | -1.419 | -2.004 | -2.269 | -1.79 |
| Newly industrialized Asian economies | 5.206 | 3.097 | 0.21 | 3.548 | 4.561 | 4.971 | 6.799 | 6.262 | 5.086 | 5.235 | 5.986 |
| Other advanced economies (advanced economies excluding G–7 and euro area) | 0.598 | 0.303 | 0.474 | 3.511 | 4.144 | 3.88 | 4.959 | 4.39 | 4.312 | 4.855 | 4.778 |
| European Union | 0.236 | -0.742 | 0.362 | -0.959 | -0.308 | 0.237 | 0.207 | 0.479 | -0.236 | -0.775 | -1.205 |
| Emerging and developing economies | -0.862 | -0.669 | -1.677 | 1.355 | 0.634 | 1.151 | 1.908 | 2.379 | 4.107 | 4.838 | 4.156 |
| Africa | -0.759 | -1.232 | -3.467 | 1.866 | 0.302 | -1.875 | -0.67 | 0.286 | 1.906 | 3.113 | 0.146 |
| Africa: Sub–Sahara | -0.657 | -1.624 | -3.21 | 0.136 | -1.982 | -4.025 | -3.106 | -1.749 | -0.971 | -0.077 | -3.291 |
| Central and Eastern Europe | -1.432 | -0.889 | -1.131 | -4.737 | -2.526 | -3.343 | -4.189 | -5.408 | -4.697 | -6.223 | -6.621 |
| Commonwealth of Independent States and Mongolia | 0.35 | -1.057 | 0.816 | 13.655 | 7.997 | 6.522 | 6.287 | 8.231 | 8.793 | 7.527 | 4.497 |
| Developing Asia | -2.855 | -1.244 | -2.258 | 1.664 | 1.509 | 2.445 | 2.746 | 2.556 | 4.023 | 5.916 | 6.7 |
| ASEAN–5 | -2.147 | -4.641 | -5.762 | 5.044 | 3.859 | 3.672 | 4.029 | 2.847 | 1.867 | 4.795 | 4.782 |
| Middle East | -0.1 | 1.299 | 0.957 | 11.366 | 6.308 | 4.764 | 8.317 | 11.785 | 19.728 | 20.862 | 19.804 |
| Western Hemisphere | -0.224 | -0.012 | -2.103 | -2.401 | -2.762 | -0.924 | 0.428 | 1.001 | 1.379 | 1.538 | 0.477 |

*Notes:* See Appendix A for definitions of the country group names. na = not applicable.
*Source:* Based on data from the International Monetary Fund, World Economic Outlook Database (April 2008).

**Figure 6.1.  Other Emerging and Developing Countries: Current Account Balances as a Percentage of GDP, 1985–2006**

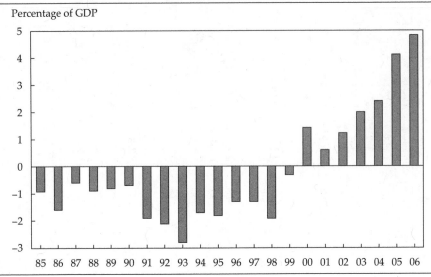

*Note*: The list of emerging and developing countries is in Appendix A.

*Source*: Based on data from the IMF World Economic Outlook Database.

**Figure 6.2.  U.S. Current Account Balance, 1980–2006**
            (US$ billions)

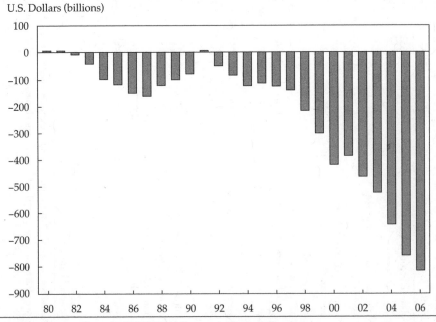

*Source*: Based on data from the IMF World Economic Outlook Database.

**Figure 6.3. U.S. Current Account Balance as a Percentage of GDP, 1985–2006**

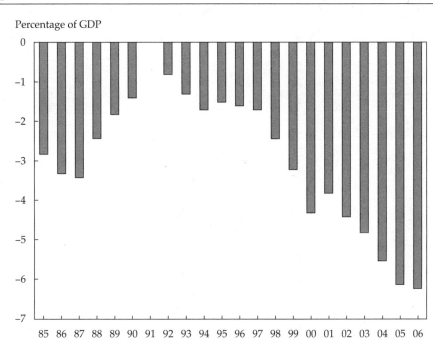

*Source*: Based on data from the IMF World Economic Outlook Database.

flows to poorer countries have been so meager compared with the much larger flows that simple growth models forecast. Since then, the general problem of explaining capital flows, or the absence thereof, has been called the Lucas paradox (see **Box 6.1**).

---

**Box 6.1. The Lucas Paradox**

Lucas (1990) produced a particularly striking result with relatively simple application of the Cobb–Douglas production function. He calculated that the marginal product of capital had to have been 58 times higher in India than it was in the United States (circa 1988) given a finding that production per person was 15 times higher in the United States than in India. Lucas asked:

> If this model were anywhere close to being accurate, and if world capital markets were anywhere close to being free and complete, it is clear that, in the face of return differentials of this magnitude, investment goods would flow rapidly from the United States and other wealthy countries to India and other poor countries. Indeed, one would expect no investment to occur in the wealthy countries in the face of return differentials of this magnitude. (p. 92)

The "Lucas paradox," as it has become known, is that capital flows do not conform to this simple paradigm.

---

**Table 6.3. Emerging and Developing Countries: Net Cash Flows and Changes in Official Reserves, 1985–2007**
(U.S. dollars billions)

| Item | 1985 | 1990 | 1995 | 2000 | 2001 | 2002 | 2003 | 2004 | 2005 | 2006 | 2007 |
|---|---|---|---|---|---|---|---|---|---|---|---|
| Private capital flows, net | –$0.68 | $38.03 | $165.22 | $74.78 | $79.55 | $89.84 | $168.60 | $241.90 | $251.84 | $231.94 | $604.96 |
| Change in reserves | 6.99 | –21.10 | –107.51 | –135.68 | –124.05 | –194.84 | –363.31 | –509.26 | –595.09 | –752.84 | –1,236.23 |
| *Memorandum* | | | | | | | | | | | |
| Current account | –30.11 | –35.05 | –90.99 | 86.90 | 41.13 | 76.65 | 144.28 | 213.64 | 439.53 | 606.71 | 630.88 |

*Note:* A minus sign indicates an increase.

*Source:* Based on data from the International Monetary Fund, World Economic Outlook Database (April 2008).

**Table 6.4. Current Account Balances of Selected Asian Countries, 1985–2007**
(U.S. dollars in billions and percentage of GDP)

| Country | 1985 | 1990 | 1995 | 2000 | 2001 | 2002 | 2003 | 2004 | 2005 | 2006 | 2007(e) |
|---|---|---|---|---|---|---|---|---|---|---|---|
| China | −$11.51 | $12.00 | $1.62 | $20.52 | $17.41 | $35.42 | $45.88 | $68.66 | $160.82 | $249.87 | $360.71 |
| | −3.8% | 3.1% | 0.2% | 1.7% | 1.3% | 2.4% | 2.8% | 3.6% | 7.2% | 9.4% | 11.1% |
| Indonesia | −$2.10 | −$3.20 | −$6.80 | $7.99 | $6.90 | $7.82 | $8.11 | $1.56 | $0.28 | $10.84 | $11.01 |
| | −2.1% | −2.5% | −3.0% | 4.8% | 4.3% | 4.0% | 3.5% | 0.6% | 0.1% | 3.0% | 2.5% |
| Korea | −$0.80 | −$2.01 | −$8.67 | $12.25 | $8.03 | $5.39 | $11.95 | $28.17 | $14.98 | $5.39 | $5.95 |
| | −0.8% | −0.8% | −1.7% | 2.4% | 1.7% | 1.0% | 2.0% | 4.1% | 1.9% | 0.6% | 0.6% |
| Malaysia | −$0.61 | −$0.92 | −$8.64 | $8.49 | $7.29 | $8.03 | $13.21 | $14.87 | $19.99 | $25.31 | $26.05 |
| | −1.9% | −2.1% | −9.6% | 9.0% | 7.9% | 8.0% | 12.0% | 11.9% | 14.6% | 16.2% | 14.0% |
| Philippines | $0.52 | −$2.69 | −$1.97 | −$2.23 | −$1.74 | −$0.28 | $0.29 | $1.63 | $1.98 | $5.35 | $6.35 |
| | 1.7% | −6.1% | −2.6% | −2.9% | −2.4% | −0.4% | 0.4% | 1.9% | 2.0% | 4.5% | 4.4% |
| Singapore | $0.06 | $3.12 | $14.39 | $10.72 | $10.73 | $11.12 | $21.59 | $18.24 | $22.28 | $29.77 | $39.16 |
| | 0.3% | 8.5% | 17.1% | 11.6% | 12.5% | 12.6% | 23.2% | 16.7% | 18.6% | 21.8% | 24.3% |
| Thailand | −$1.54 | −$7.14 | −$13.23 | $9.33 | $5.11 | $4.69 | $4.78 | $2.77 | −$7.64 | $2.17 | $14.92 |
| | −4.0% | −8.3% | −7.9% | 7.6% | 4.4% | 3.7% | 3.4% | 1.7% | −4.3% | 1.1% | 6.1% |

*Note:* (e) = estimate.

*Source:* Based on data from the International Monetary Fund, World Economic Outlook Database (April 2008).

**Table 6.5. Current Account Balances of Selected South American Countries and Mexico, 1985–2007**
(U.S. dollars in billions and percentage of GDP)

| Country | 1985 | 1990 | 1995 | 2000 | 2001 | 2002 | 2003 | 2004 | 2005 | 2006 | 2007(e) |
|---|---|---|---|---|---|---|---|---|---|---|---|
| Argentina | –$0.95 | $4.67 | –$5.10 | –$8.96 | –$3.78 | $8.72 | $8.07 | $3.16 | $3.69 | $5.41 | $2.81 |
| | –1.1% | 3.3% | –2.0% | –3.2% | –1.4% | 8.9% | 6.3% | 2.1% | 2.0% | 2.5% | 1.1% |
| Brazil | –$0.23 | –$3.79 | –$18.38 | –$24.23 | –$23.22 | –$7.64 | $4.18 | $11.68 | $14.19 | $13.62 | $3.56 |
| | –0.1% | –0.7% | –2.4% | –3.8% | –4.2% | –1.5% | 0.8% | 1.8% | 1.6% | 1.3% | 0.3% |
| Chile | –$1.41 | –$0.48 | –$1.35 | –$0.90 | –$1.10 | –$0.58 | –$0.78 | $2.08 | $1.32 | $5.26 | $6.05 |
| | –8.6% | –1.5% | –1.9% | –1.2% | –1.6% | –0.9% | –1.1% | 2.2% | 1.1% | 3.6% | 3.7% |
| Colombia | –$1.60 | $0.54 | –$4.60 | $0.76 | –$1.09 | –$1.36 | –$0.97 | –$0.91 | –$1.89 | –$2.91 | –$6.47 |
| | –3.9% | 1.2% | –5.0% | 0.9% | –1.3% | –1.7% | –1.2% | –0.9% | –1.5% | –2.1% | –3.8% |
| Mexico | $0.80 | –$7.45 | $1.58 | –$18.68 | –$17.70 | –$14.12 | –$8.57 | –$6.60 | –$5.22 | –$2.22 | –$7.37 |
| | 0.4% | –2.8% | –0.6% | –3.2% | –2.8% | –2.2% | –1.3% | –1.0% | –0.7% | –0.3% | –0.8% |
| Uruguay | –$0.11 | $0.19 | –$0.21 | –$0.57 | –$0.53 | $0.38 | –$0.06 | $0.04 | $0.00 | –$0.46 | –$0.18 |
| | –2.3% | 2.0% | –1.1% | –2.8% | –2.9% | 3.2% | –0.5% | 0.3% | 0.0% | –2.4% | –0.8% |
| Venezuela | $3.72 | $8.45 | $2.14 | $11.85 | $1.98 | $7.60 | $11.80 | $15.52 | $25.53 | $27.17 | $23.23 |
| | 6.0% | 17.5% | 2.8% | 10.1% | 1.6% | 8.2% | 14.1% | 13.8% | 17.7% | 14.7% | 9.8% |

*Note:* (e) = estimate.
*Source:* Based on data from the International Monetary Fund, World Economic Outlook Database (April 2008).

Gruber and Kamin (2006) addressed the flow of capital away from the emerging markets:

> The current account balances of major developing East Asian economies (China, Hong Kong, Indonesia, Korea, Malaysia, Philippines, Singapore, Taiwan, and Thailand) have moved from an aggregate deficit of $27 billion in 1995 to a surplus of $186 billion in 2004 or from negative 1.2 percent of GDP to positive 5.3 percent of GDP. More generally, the aggregate current account balance of the developing countries moved into surplus in 2000. (p. 1)

Gruber and Kamin's panel regression attempted to explain the current account/GDP ratios of 61 countries:

> We find that a model that includes as its explanatory variables the standard determinants of current accounts proposed in the literature—per capita income, relative growth rates, the fiscal balance, demographic variables, and economic openness—can account for neither the large U.S. deficit nor large Asian surpluses of the 1997–2003 period. However, when we include a variable representing financial crises, which might be expected to restrain domestic demand and boost the current account balance, the model explains much of developing Asia's swing into surplus since 1997. (p. 1)

Indeed, the crisis variable could be operating through suppression of aggregate demand. But it also could be an indicator that capital is leaving the emerging markets for fear of future crises. What investors might have taken from past crises is that policy initiatives are sometimes enacted that greatly compromise their interests. Experience may have soured the appetites of global investors for emerging markets.

But for this explanation to work, there also must be reason to believe that superior investment opportunities exist in the destination countries, such as the United States, as well as in other parts of the developed world. Capital flows are a "push–pull" phenomenon. What Gruber and Kamin have found is the "push" from the emerging-markets countries. They have not found the "pull" toward the United States. But other economists do make that exact case: They argue that rates of return in the United States are superior (an issue that I will discuss in the next section). From these two elements, push and pull, one can stitch together an explanation for the seeming enigma of capital flowing from developing nations to developed countries since the late 1990s. The result is satisfying because it consists of economic arguments about conditions both inside and outside the developing world.[77]

---

[77] Calvo, Leiderman, and Reinhart (1993) asserted that capital flows into Latin American countries in the 1990s were an "external shock" and referred to factors external to Latin America in this period as having been responsible for large components of the capital flows into the region.

The story gets even more complicated. Recent empirical studies reveal new puzzles that go beyond the Lucas paradox. Prasad, Rajan, and Subramanian, henceforth PRS (2007a and 2007b), uncovered a series of counterintuitive if not unsettling findings for the 1970–2005 period. First, they reported that "capital has been flowing from poor to rich countries" (2007b, p. 1). In addition, they stated:

> The average relative per capita income of countries running current account surpluses (weighted by their surpluses, with per capita income measured relative to the richest country in that year) has been trending downward. By contrast, there has been an upward trend in the relative income level of deficit countries. (PRS 2007a, p. 3)

Second, they found that capital sometimes perversely prefers low rate of return domiciles to those with high rates of return. Their third finding is the most interesting: Countries that are the fast growers fund not only their own development but other countries' growth as well. They stated that these findings "run counter to the predictions of standard theoretical models" (PRS 2007a, p. 6). They wrote of the contradiction:

> A large body of research has essentially reached the same conclusion: it is difficult, using macroeconomic data, to establish a robust causal relationship between private capital inflows and economic growth. But this does not mean that foreign capital does not matter. (2007b, p. 5)

The empirical findings in the PRS papers are likely to be discussed and tested for years to come. It would seem the Lucas paradox is merely the beginning of trouble for basic growth theory. What one learns is that not only do capital flows not go where they should; in terms of where they do go, they do not seem to make much of a difference.

Not to be overlooked is the composition of capital flows to developing countries. Private capital needs to be considered. Private capital flows are a component of total capital flows (total flows are the sum of official flows, such as when a central bank adds or subtracts foreign reserves, and private flows. Equation 3.1 makes this distinction. As it turns out, large private capital flows have been going in the direction of the emerging markets at the same time that total capital flows (the sum of official and private) have been moving in the opposite direction, away from emerging markets. Because the private flows are large, they themselves constitute a new set of worries. Could a sudden stop or reversal of private capital flows harm the emerging-markets nations? Even the very existence of private capital flows going into the emerging markets might be damaging if they produce what the IMF economists call "overheating," a term that is less than precise.[78] Can private capital flows overheat an emerging-markets country even when total flows are going the opposite direction?

---

[78] International Monetary Fund (2007, ch. 3, p. 1).

Although private flows seem to move more in line with what standard growth theory predicts, it is the total flow of capital that matters. As PRS (2007b) reported, foreign direct investment (a private flow) does "flow from richer to poorer countries, which is comforting," but "the pattern of overall flows is ultimately what is relevant in terms of resources available for financing investment in a country" (p. 2). Kroszner (2007) agreed that, although private capital in 2005 on net flowed from the industrial economies to the developing ones, "it is still true that, on the whole, net capital is flowing from the developing to the industrialized world" (p. 2). To understand these issues, one must apply a basic principle of economics, namely, that "money is money"—that is, money is fungible: Official flows are no less or no more important than private capital flows.

Official flows are, however, interesting. Table 6.3 shows that the developing and emerging-markets central banks have been accumulating foreign exchange reserves at a remarkable rate, especially starting in 2003. This accumulation is confirmed in the IMF's data for Currency Composition of Official Foreign Exchange Reserves (COFER) shown in **Table 6.6**, in which one can see that the reserves of the developing countries more than doubled in the period from 2003 to the third quarter of 2007.

## Global Imbalances

Global imbalances are another concern related to capital flows and emerging markets that receives considerable attention from economists. Although no precise definition exists of what constitutes an imbalance, or to be more precise, when it is that capital markets might reach a state of identifiable global imbalance, most discussions on this topic center on the U.S. current account deficit.

The U.S. current account deficit in 2005 and 2006 exceeded 6 percent of U.S. GDP, a number that is colossal by any historical measure. As seen in Tables 6.1 and 6.2 and Figures 6.2 and 6.3,

- The U.S. current account deficit has steadily increased in dollars and as a percentage of GDP since 1991. (The deficit had dropped as a percentage of GDP from 1987 to 1991).

  — The greatest increases occurred after 1999.

  — The current account deficit rose from roughly zero (actually a small surplus of $2.895 billion) in 1991 to $811.5 billion in 2006.

- As a percentage of GDP, the U.S. external deficit was less than 3 percent of GDP until 1999.

**Table 6.6.  Composition and Change in Official Foreign Exchange Reserves, 1995–2007**
(U.S. dollars in millions)

| | 1995 | 1996a | 1997 | 1998 | 1999 | 2000 | 2001 | 2002 | 2003 | 2004 | 2005 | 2006b | 2007c |
|---|---|---|---|---|---|---|---|---|---|---|---|---|---|
| *All countries* | | | | | | | | | | | | | |
| Total foreign exchange holdings | $1,389,639 | $1,566,151 | $1,616,167 | $1,643,867 | $1,781,466 | $1,936,570 | $2,050,064 | $2,408,619 | $3,025,701 | $3,748,730 | $4,174,991 | $5,037,088 | $6,037,142 |
| Allocated reserves | $1,034,175 | $1,224,464 | $1,271,982 | $1,282,406 | $1,378,620 | $1,517,374 | $1,568,849 | $1,795,447 | $2,221,773 | $2,651,031 | $2,838,019 | $3,309,851 | $3,834,501 |
| Growth in reserves | | 18% | 4% | 1% | 8% | 10% | 3% | 14% | 24% | 19% | 7% | 17% | 16% |
| Claims in U.S. dollars | $ 610,337 | $ 760,071 | $ 828,887 | $ 888,724 | $ 978,562 | $1,078,992 | $1,121,791 | $1,204,205 | $1,464,420 | $1,747,194 | $1,897,613 | $2,166,841 | $2,445,180 |
| % U.S. dollar claims | 59% | 62% | 65% | 69% | 71% | 71% | 72% | 67% | 66% | 66% | 67% | 65% | 64% |
| % U.S. dollar share of total growth | | 79% | 145% | 574% | 93% | 72% | 83% | 36% | 61% | 66% | 80% | 57% | 53% |
| *Industrial countries* | | | | | | | | | | | | | |
| Total foreign exchange holdings | $ 657,618 | $ 723,866 | $ 706,235 | $ 674,166 | $ 726,113 | $ 783,171 | $ 789,427 | $ 905,573 | $1,121,070 | $1,318,343 | $1,295,046 | $1,395,248 | $1,478,270 |
| Allocated reserves | $ 649,813 | $ 706,528 | $ 689,473 | $ 664,428 | $ 721,303 | $ 780,403 | $ 788,318 | $ 903,242 | $1,118,408 | $1,315,115 | $1,291,213 | $1,390,682 | $1,473,254 |
| Growth in reserves | | 9% | –2% | –4% | 9% | 8% | 1% | 15% | 24% | 18% | –2% | 8% | 6% |
| Claims in U.S. dollars | $ 340,337 | $ 405,453 | $ 407,620 | $ 449,378 | $ 528,404 | $ 565,639 | $ 570,976 | $ 618,223 | $ 783,799 | $ 935,234 | $ 946,133 | $ 995,748 | $1,028,855 |
| % U.S. dollar claims | 52% | 57% | 59% | 68% | 73% | 72% | 72% | 68% | 70% | 71% | 73% | 72% | 70% |
| % U.S. dollar share of total growth | | 115% | –13% | –167% | 139% | 63% | 67% | 41% | 77% | 77% | NA | 50% | 40% |
| *Developing countries* | | | | | | | | | | | | | |
| Total foreign exchange holdings | $ 732,022 | $ 842,286 | $ 909,932 | $ 969,702 | $1,055,353 | $1,153,399 | $1,260,637 | $1,503,046 | $1,904,631 | $2,430,387 | $2,879,946 | $3,641,840 | $4,558,872 |
| Allocated reserves | $ 384,361 | $ 517,935 | $ 582,509 | $ 617,978 | $ 657,317 | $ 736,971 | $ 780,531 | $ 892,206 | $1,103,365 | $1,335,916 | $1,546,806 | $1,919,170 | $2,361,247 |
| Growth in reserves | | 35% | 12% | 6% | 6% | 12% | 6% | 14% | 24% | 21% | 16% | 24% | 23% |
| Claims in U.S. dollars | 270,000 | 354,618 | 421,267 | 439,346 | 450,158 | 513,353 | 550,815 | 585,982 | 680,621 | 811,961 | 951,480 | 1,171,093 | 1,416,325 |
| % U.S. dollar claims | 70% | 68% | 72% | 71% | 68% | 70% | 71% | 66% | 62% | 61% | 62% | 61% | 60% |
| % U.S. dollar share of total growth | | 63% | 103% | 51% | 27% | 79% | 86% | 31% | 45% | 56% | 66% | 59% | 55% |

*Notes:* End of quarter data is voluntarily reported by 120 member countries of the IMF, comprising all 25 industrial countries and 95 out of 160 developing countries. Unallocated reserves capture the difference between the total reserves data reported to the IMF's International Financial Statistics and to COFER. p = preliminary.
aCountries with sizable reserves either joined (began reporting) the sample or left (stopped reporting) the sample.
bPreliminary.
cThrough the third quarter.
*Source:* Based on data from COFER (www.imf.org/external/np/sta/cofer/eng/index.htm).

These numbers are quite striking. Why did the U.S. current account deficit grow so large, and are such levels sustainable? (See **Box 6.2**.)

---

**Box 6.2.   Is There an Upper Limit to the U.S. Current Account?**

This is a very practical thing to wonder. Why would it be true? As it turns out, quite a few very good economists wonder whether there is a limit.

Bernanke wrote (2007b): "The large U.S. current account deficit cannot persist indefinitely because the ability of the United States to make debt service payments and the willingness of foreigners to hold U.S. assets in their portfolios are both limited" (p. 5).

This idea was echoed by Fischer (2006), who described the conventional wisdom about the current account as "the situation cannot go on forever, though it is very hard to know when it will stop" (p. 1) and that a "sustainable current account deficit for the U.S. is about 2.5%-3% of GDP" (p. 1). When these remarks were made, the then-current magnitude of the U.S. current account deficit was 6 percent of GDP.

Similarly, Mussa (2004) wrote: "There is probably a practical upper limit for the U.S. net external liabilities at something less than 100 percent of U.S. GDP and, accordingly…current account deficits of 5 percent or more of U.S. GDP are not indefinitely sustainable" (p. 114).

---

Does having so much capital flow to one country present a danger? Krugman seems to think it does (see **Box 6.3**). More to the point, what would be the impact on the emerging-markets nations if the flow of capital to the United States suddenly stopped or even reversed? In such a circumstance, the first question has to be, what would happen to the dollar and other exchange rates? Obstfeld and Rogoff (2005) set a pessimistic tone for the dollar:

> We show that when one takes into account the global equilibrium ramifications of an unwinding of the U.S. current account deficit, currently running at more than 6 percent of GDP, the potential collapse of the dollar becomes considerably larger than our previous estimates—as much as 30 percent or even higher. (p. 1)

This does not mean they are calling for a global meltdown, but they do say, "We argue that the current conjecture more closely parallels the early 1970s, when the Bretton Woods system collapsed" (p. 1).

Any collapse in the dollar could be trouble for the emerging markets. There are at least three channels through which a dollar plunge would harm them. The direct effect would be on emerging-markets industries that export to the United States. The cheaper dollar would make their exports more expensive for buyers in the United States, a development that could retard growth prospects. The same could be said of countries that export dollar-denominated commodities, such as oil or precious metals.

---

## Box 6.3.   The China Syndrome and Paul Krugman

If one believes in the predictions of a global financial meltdown, what is needed is a source of the interruption to capital flows—a precondition to the meltdown. The disturbance could come from policy changes inside a large accumulator of U.S. dollars, such as China. Krugman (2005) has mused on what might happen if China changes its pattern of buying U.S. dollars with its trade surpluses:

> Dollar purchases by China and other foreign governments have temporarily insulated the U.S. economy from the effects of huge budget deficits. This money flowing in from abroad has kept U.S. interest rates low despite the enormous borrowing required to cover the budget deficit. . . . When China changes its current policy and those cheap loans are no longer available, U.S. interest rates will rise; the housing bubble will probably burst; construction employment and consumer spending will both fall; falling home prices may lead to a wave of bankruptcies. . . . In other words, we have developed an addiction to Chinese dollar purchases, and will suffer painful withdrawal symptoms when they come to an end.

This is curious logic. As Calvo and Talvi (2006) pointed out: "The view that if Asian central banks stop buying U.S. public debt, hell breaks loose, has wide appeal" (p. 606). And "At first blush, losing this 'official' credit line should be a major blow to the U.S. economy, right? Wrong" (p. 608).

Krugman's argument is suspect because if China stops buying U.S. dollar bonds, it will presumably substitute bonds denominated in another currency, such as Japanese government bonds or euro-denominated sovereign debt of the larger European nations. As Calvo and Talvi indicated, this move amounts to a change only at the margin in the currency composition of world debt; the supply of bonds worldwide would be unaffected. Whereas changes in interest rates and exchange rates might ensue, it is hard to imagine a financial crash occurring.

Meanwhile, we have had a financial crash (in 2007–2008) for reasons that are completely unrelated to China's not buying U.S. dollar bonds. Although China has continued to buy such bonds and U.S interest rates remain low, subprime mortgage defaults and other factors have caused a credit crunch of unprecedented proportions as well as a sharp decline in the foreign exchange value of the dollar.

---

The second channel would be through wealth effects. This channel has to be looked at on a case-by-case basis by examining the balance sheet of the combined governments and central banks of particular emerging-markets nations. Many of these countries have accumulated substantial holdings of dollar-denominated bonds; these assets would depreciate in local currency terms if the dollar fell. Furthermore, many of the same countries have issued substantial dollar-denominated sovereign debt; a drop in the dollar would mean currency gains because their debts would have depreciated, again in local currency terms.

The third route would be through monetary policy. The effectiveness of this channel relies on the decline in the dollar being seen by the U.S. central bank as inflationary (only because the prices of imported goods would be rising). Suppose the Federal Reserve responded by tightening credit (raising the federal funds rate). All of the usual tight money things would happen, such as investment activity falling, income falling, and unemployment rising. So much of the world is interconnected with the U.S. economy, through goods markets and capital markets, that the downturn could spread to the emerging markets.

Possibly ambiguous wealth effects aside, the general presumption is that a sudden, large drop in the value of the dollar associated with a reversal of capital flows to the United States would be harmful to the emerging-markets nations.

How desperate is the situation? To assess the danger that the current account poses, one must first understand how it became so large. Clues to how it might unwind may be found in how it came into being in the first place. The U.S. Congressional Budget Office (2004) delineated three categories of reasons for the rise in the U.S. current account deficit since 1991:

> Relatively rapid growth in income in the United States compared with other major industrialized economies during the period. (p. 3)

> A surge in foreign demand for dollar assets in the late 1990s, which contributed to a higher dollar exchange rate and lower U.S. interest rates. (p. 3)

and

> A drop in the national savings rate owing to a rising federal deficit that has helped push the current-account balance lower since 2001. (p. 3)

The first argument about differential rates of income growth across countries is standard fare. Income is a determinant of domestic demand for foreign goods but not of foreign demand for domestic goods. Hence, a country that experiences a relatively fast rate of income growth, all other things being equal, will experience deterioration in its current account (this was part of the macroeconomic models discussed in Chapter 3). **Table 6.7** shows annual growth in real gross domestic product (i.e., using constant prices) for the United States, Germany, the European Union, and Japan. The data in the table confirm the Congressional Budget Office's hypothesis that growth rates in income for the United States have been generally higher than for other industrialized countries.

The Congressional Budget Office explains the second factor, the rise in the demand for dollar assets, as being the result of the rise in productivity growth in the United States, rapid growth in globalization that allowed more funds to move to the United States, a spate of financial crises that caused demand for a safe haven, and the emerging Asian countries (especially China) booking foreign exchange

**Table 6.7. Annual Growth Rates of Gross Domestic Product, Constant Prices: 1990–2007**
(annual percentages)

| Year | Germany | European Union | Japan | United States |
|------|---------|----------------|-------|---------------|
| 1990 | 5.7 | 2.3 | 5.2 | 1.9 |
| 1991 | 5.0 | 0.7 | 3.4 | −0.2 |
| 1992 | 2.3 | 0.7 | 1.0 | 3.3 |
| 1993 | −0.8 | −0.2 | 0.2 | 2.7 |
| 1994 | 2.6 | 2.9 | 1.1 | 4.0 |
| 1995 | 1.8 | 3.0 | 2.0 | 2.5 |
| 1996 | 1.0 | 2.0 | 2.7 | 3.7 |
| 1997 | 1.7 | 2.7 | 1.6 | 4.5 |
| 1998 | 2.0 | 2.9 | −2.0 | 4.2 |
| 1999 | 1.9 | 3.0 | −0.1 | 4.4 |
| 2000 | 3.1 | 3.9 | 2.9 | 3.7 |
| 2001 | 1.2 | 2.1 | 0.2 | 0.8 |
| 2002 | — | 1.4 | 0.3 | 1.6 |
| 2003 | −0.3 | 1.5 | 1.4 | 2.5 |
| 2004 | 1.1 | 2.7 | 2.7 | 3.6 |
| 2005 | 0.8 | 2.0 | 1.9 | 3.1 |
| 2006 | 2.9 | 3.2 | 2.6 | 2.9 |
| 2007 | 2.5 | 3.1 | 2.2 | 2.9 |

*Source*: Based on data from the IMF World Economic Outlook.

reserves. The rise in productivity is mentioned by Ferguson (2005); he explained the connection between productivity and the current account deficit as follows:

> . . .[L]abor productivity growth [surged] from about 1½ percent annually in the two decades preceding 1995 to roughly 3 percent in the period since then. This surge is viewed as having several important consequences. First, higher productivity growth boosted the perceived rate of return on U.S. investments, thereby generating capital inflows that boosted the dollar. Second, these higher rates of return also led to a rise in domestic investment. Finally, expectations of higher returns boosted equity prices, household wealth, and perceived long-run income, so consumption rose and savings rates declined. Under this explanation, all of these factors helped to widen the current account deficit. (pp. 4–5)

According to one theory, accumulation of reserves by central banks represents their building a "war chest" for future use in stabilizing possible future crises. Better to have their own reserves, over which they have full discretion in use, than, as Calvo and Talvi (2006) somewhat cynically said, "calling the IMF doctor, [which] might make things worse" (pp. 607–608).

The third issue is national savings in the United States. This is a factor in the current account, especially after 2000.[79] The Congressional Budget Office believes the drop in savings was attributable to the worsening federal budget deficit.

The Congressional Budget Office's analysis is fairly conventional economics. It can, however, be supplemented with what has become a celebrated explanation set forth in two papers by Bernanke (2005, 2007b), who introduced the term "global savings glut." Bernanke (2007b) stressed that the U.S. economy alone cannot explain the rise in the U.S. deficit. He also attempted to explain the contemporaneous phenomenon of relatively low real rates of interest around the world. Bernanke (2005) wrote:

> I will argue that over the past decade a combination of diverse forces has created a significant increase in the global supply of savings—a global saving glut—which helps explain both the increase in the U.S. current account deficit and the relatively low level of long-term real interest rates in the world today. (pp. 1–2)

He attributed the origin of the savings glut to:

> . . .the strong savings motive of rich countries with aging populations, which must make provision for an impending sharp increase in the number of retirees relative to the number of workers. With slowly growing or declining workforces, as well as high capital-labor ratios, many advanced economies outside the United States also face an apparent dearth of domestic investment opportunities. As a consequence of high desired savings and low prospective returns to domestic investment, the mature industrial economies as a group seek to run current account surpluses and thus to lend abroad. (p. 4)

Bernanke (2007b) argued that the current account may not be a "problem," in his terms, because it is a "market phenomenon" that reflects the attractiveness of the United States and the "depth, liquidity, and legal safeguards" of its capital markets (p. 4).

In other words, through a combination of factors, some internal and others external, the United States has become the capital magnet of the world. Will it ever reverse, and if so, when will that be? The correct answer, then, is that the current account deficit will begin to fade when the factors that created it reverse. The differential in income growth favoring the United States may continue indefinitely, but there is no reason to think that the elevation of productivity will remain the permanent province of one country. Most transitory of all has to be the need of central banks to accumulate dollar assets on the scale that has been witnessed in recent times. In addition, investment opportunities outside the United States, including in the emerging markets, might become viewed as relatively more attractive than those in the United States. When and if these factors materialize, the U.S. current account will diminish.

---

[79] See Bernanke (2007b).

Greenspan (2003) is among those who have argued for a benign adjustment in the current account:

> I conclude that spreading globalization has fostered a degree of international flexibility that has raised the probability of a benign resolution to the U.S. current account imbalance. Such a resolution has been the general experience of developed countries over the past two decades. Moreover, history suggests that greater flexibility allows economies to adjust more smoothly to changing economic circumstances and with less risk of destabilizing outcomes. (p. 1)

Even more to the point is recent writing by Cooper (2005), who, like Bernanke, believes that the current account deficit in the United States comes from an excess of savings abroad and a lack of investment opportunities outside the United States. He concluded:

> The startlingly large U.S. current account deficit is not only sustainable but a natural feature of today's highly globalized economy. (p. 1)

> A large U.S. current account deficit could continue for a long time, so long as the American economy is producing attractive financial assets. (p. 4).

> Why does this savings come to the United States rather than going to emerging markets, where returns should be expected to be higher? The answer is complex. Some of it of course does go to emerging markets, but those countries at present, as a group, also have excess saving. Since the financial crises of the 1990s, risk-averse investors, especially in Japan and Europe, have been reluctant to invest significantly in emerging markets outside central Europe, which has largely joined the European Union, plus China. Returns in emerging markets are not only volatile but on the basis of recent experience in Russia and Argentina, may be insecure from political or legal action as well. Also, some emerging markets, notably China, have high domestic savings rates themselves, more than enough to cover their requirements for domestic investment. The United States, in contrast, has investment opportunities that produce higher yields than Japan and Europe and that are less volatile and more secure than investments in many emerging markets. (p. 4)

I may be tempting fate to say so, but a response to the current account disaster theorists can be borrowed from T.S. Eliot (1925): It will end "not with a bang but a whimper." To continue on this theme, the term "imbalance" itself is loaded. "Imbalance" connotes something unsustainable; it is something that could only end badly because it is called an imbalance. Labeling it a global imbalance makes it seem larger in importance and ever more ominous.

But the so-called imbalance may reflect nothing more than unfamiliarity with the current environment compared with recent economic history. And the unfamiliarity is understandable because the signature financial development of the new millennium has been a great expansion in depth of the capital markets. This expansion was illustrated in Chapter 4, in which the data on the foreign exchange market showed a massive surge in currency trading in the past six years. The rapid development of new market economies (especially China), advances in trading technology, greater use of derivatives for risk taking and hedging, and lowering of barriers to the flow of capital—all worked to enlarge the size of the capital market. The fact that current accounts are now very large by historical standards may signify nothing more than that the new greater depth of capital markets can accommodate large surpluses and deficits.

The special situation of the United States also is worth examining. Indeed, a lot of the concern about the U.S. current account deficit reflects fears that something along the lines of the emerging-markets currency crises of the late 1990s could happen to the United States. By comparison, the financial crisis that gripped the world, and in particular the United States, in 2008 had to do with an acute revaluation of real estate–related loans and derivatives transactions. The type of crisis that I have primarily been considering in this book is one that might originate from the U.S. current account deficit. Could the U.S. financial system implode simply because the current account deficit is large? Such an outcome is extremely unlikely. The United States does not have a fixed exchange rate regime, something that almost all the afflicted emerging-markets countries tried to operate. The comparison then jumps to the current account, but this also is not a valid comparison because of the fact that the U.S. dollar is the primary reserve asset of the world. The data from Table 6.6 show that the dollar is the predominant reserve currency and that it continues to be the currency of choice when new international reserves are created. There may be a "slow drip" away from the dollar, as some observers write, but the fact remains that 9 out of 10 currency trades involve the dollar and two-thirds of the world's reserves are in dollars.[80] Moreover, major commodities, such as oil and precious metals, are traded in dollars everywhere in the world.

A more subtle point is the concept of "original sin," a term for countries borrowing in currencies other than their own. I discussed this topic in Chapter 5 when I reviewed the emerging-markets crises. Note that the United States, unlike most countries, can borrow in the international debt markets in its own currency. Greenspan (2003) has stated that "less than 10 percent of aggregate U.S. foreign liabilities are currently denominated in nondollar currencies" (footnote 12) and:

> Complicating the evaluation of the timing of the turnaround is that deficit countries, both developed and emerging, borrow in international markets largely in dollars rather than in their domestic currency. The United States has been rare in its ability to finance its external deficit in a reserve currency. (p. 6)

---

[80] As of 18 August 2008, the IMF's COFER listed total projected first quarter 2008 allocated reserves (all countries) as US$4.322 trillion, of which US$2.723 trillion were claims in U.S. dollars.

What is more, the unique currency composition of the liabilities of the United States makes its economy resilient to depreciation of the dollar. In other countries, the concept of original sin makes their external liabilities rise in local value when their currency depreciates. But this is not the case for the United States, as Edwards (2005) has noted:

> While more than 70 percent of gross foreign assets held by U.S. nationals are denominated in foreign currency, approximately 95 percent of gross U.S. liabilities in the hands of foreigners are denominated in U.S. dollars. This means that net liabilities as a percentage of GDP are subject to "valuation effects" stemming from changes in the value of the dollar. Dollar depreciation reduces the value of net liabilities; a dollar appreciation, on the other hand, increases the dollar value of U.S. net liabilities. (p. 6)

At least for now, the United States' "exorbitant privilege" (a famous phrase of Valéry Giscard d'Estaing that is usually, but erroneously, attributed to Charles de Gaulle[81])—that of being able to run large current account deficits—is intact. Today, the dollar is still king, and that fact has to figure in any evaluation of the prospects for the U.S. current account deficit's stability.

## Mixed Blessing

Professor Guillermo Calvo and fellow scholars are the source of a great deal of thought on the topic of capital flows and monetary policy in the emerging markets. Calvo, Leiderman, and Reinhart, hereafter CLR (1993), studied capital flows into 10 Latin American countries in the early 1990s. They raised the point that capital inflows in their sample produced a "marked appreciation in the real exchange rate in most of their sample countries" (p. 110). The relevance of this fact stems from the importance that development specialists see in export industries as mainsprings of growth. Indeed, many developing countries have improved their economic standards by creating export-oriented manufacturing sectors. Any such opportunity would be impeded if the exchange rate were unnecessarily—one could say unnaturally—higher than it would otherwise be. The concern is that upward movements in real exchange rates, induced by capital flows, could derail development by making newly formed export industries uncompetitive. This argument appears repeatedly throughout the literature on international finance in discussions of foreign capital flows. For example, a recent article by Prasad, Rajan, and Subramanian (2007a) stated:

> A more damaging view of foreign capital is that when it flows in, it leads to overvalued exchange rates, and further reduces the profitability of investment, beyond any constraints imposed by an inadequate financial system. Indeed, by stifling the growth of manufacturing exports that have proved so crucial to facilitating the escape of many countries from underdevelopment, the real exchange rate overvaluation induced by foreign inflows can be particularly pernicious. (p. 7)

[81]See Gourinchas and Rey (2005, footnote 4).

CLR wrote about substantial capital flows into many of the Latin American countries that began soon after the establishment of stabilization (anti-inflation) policies and general market-oriented reforms. Conditions for capital export in the developed countries were also ideal, in that their interest rates were low. Are we left to pity the stereotypical emerging-markets nation? First is hyperinflation, followed by stabilization. Next, capital flows arrive and pump up the exchange rate. In the process, the prospects for sustainable economic growth originating from development of export industries are quashed, or at least constrained, by the ensuing rise in the exchange rate. There is no winning, or so it might seem.

But how big a problem is it that exchange rates might rise when capital flows into emerging markets? Does it make sense to concentrate exclusively on exchange rates? Would it be a problem if capital flows caused interest rates to fall? What if foreign investment caused national income and employment to rise? These would not be bad. Moreover, the supposed rise in the exchange rate that is seen as malevolent to export industries might be a self-regulating phenomenon because it would reduce the incentives for still more capital to flow into the emerging-markets nation. The new constellation of macroeconomic prices, given the capital flows (meaning interest rates, exchange rates, income, and employment), might be Pareto optimal with respect to the alternative of no capital inflows.[82] In a larger sense, the rise in the exchange rates that Calvo and his co-authors noted demonstrates that macroeconomic processes that formulate new market-clearing equilibriums actually do work in the emerging markets.

Further discussion of the CLR paper, as well as of successor papers, is in Chapter 7 with respect to sterilized intervention programs. For now, my emphasis is on the tone set by Calvo and his co-authors: Capital inflows may be only a "mixed blessing," as Reinhart and Reinhart (1998) stated in their article title.

## Sudden Stops and Reversals

The currency crises of the late 1990s call attention to the fact that capital flows into emerging markets can reverse direction abruptly. These episodes have become known as "sudden stops and reversals," a topic that is very much on the minds of macroeconomists today.[83] The very idea that capital flows are capable of making either a sudden stop or a reversal, or both, is disquieting. Presumably, this is the

---

[82] An equilibrium is said to be Pareto optimal if none of the participants can be made better off (with a different equilibrium) without another participant being made worse off.

[83] Calvo (2003) noted that the term "sudden stop" was first suggested and the phenomenon highlighted in Dornbusch, Goldfajn, and Valdés (1995). Edwards (2004) distinguished between sudden stops and reversals.

effect that famed hedge fund manager George Soros (1998) meant when he once referred to capital flows as a "wrecking ball," rather than a gentle pendulum. Edwards (2004) defined the term "sudden stop" as follows:

> I define a "sudden stop" episode as an abrupt and major reduction in capital inflows to a country that up to that time had been receiving large volumes of foreign capital. (p. 15)

As it turns out, sudden stops and reversals are not rare events. Edwards (2004) grouped reversals into two categories: (1) reversal 4 percent, reduction in current account deficit of at least 4 percent of GDP in a one-year period and an accumulated reduction of at least 5 percent of GDP in three years, and (2) reversal 2 percent, reduction in current account deficit of at least 2 percent of GDP in one year with an accumulated reduction in three years of at least 5 percent. He found 9 instances of reversals greater than 4 percent of GDP and 26 instances of reversals greater than 2 percent of GDP in his 1976–94 sample period. Calvo (2003) counted 15 sudden stops in the 1981–97 period. Catão (2006) found much earlier sudden stops and reversals, occurring between the late 1880s and the advent of World War I.

What accounts for the existence of sudden stops and reversals? Calvo (2003) set forth a theory of the cause of sudden stops. A key feature of his model is that growth is a negative function of the fiscal burden of the state (hence his term "distortionary output taxes"). The larger the government expenditure, the lower the growth rate will be. He explains the phenomenon of sudden stops as manifestations of the existence of multiple equilibriums wherein "growth discontinuously switches from high to low as fiscal burden reaches a critical level" (p. 1). Importantly, he believes this kind of switch occurs when critically high levels of government debt exist. This observation leads Calvo to an admonition as to the level of government debt; he expressly advises the lowering of fiscal deficits as a "medium term" step to minimizing the chance of a sudden stop.

How or why does the economy switch from the high-growth state to the low-growth state? Something has to happen to disturb the system and flip the economy abruptly into the low-growth state. What sort of thing does Calvo believe is capable of tripping an economy from one state to the other? His model, in his words, is silent about the factors that "trigger" a sudden stop:

> Any shock that pushes the economy beyond the critical debt level would trigger a sudden stop. It could be an external factor as Calvo, Izquierdo, and Talvi (2002) claimed was the case recently in Argentina, but it also could be an internal factor like domestic or political or corporate governance scandal.[84] (p. 15)

---

[84]Calvo (2003) did not contain a citation to the Calvo, Izquierdo, and Talvi paper, although it probably is actually Calvo, Izquierdo, and Talvi (2003).

In another paper, Calvo (1998) argued that the composition of a country's debt also matters, with relative danger of sudden stops "the shorter the residual maturity structure of a country's debt" (p. 5). Calvo (1998) was so concerned about sudden stops that he recommended caution on opening developing countries suddenly to capital flows:

> Financially closed and underdeveloped systems (e.g., India's) should not be encouraged to liberalize the financial system in one fell swoop. (p. 14)

and

> Policymakers should get ready for the possibility of a sudden stop. They should go through sudden stop drills, much as well run buildings go through fire drills. Under normal circumstances, fires are low probability events. If not well managed, however, the resulting stampede may dramatically increase the number of casualties. (p. 15)

Empirical work on sudden stops and reversals has managed to isolate critical variables that seem to explain why sudden stops and reversals occur in some countries but not others. Milesi-Ferretti and Razin (1998b) analyzed capital flow reversals in a sample of 86 "low- and middle-income countries" over the 1971–92 period. They found that reversals are more likely to occur the higher the current account deficit and the smaller the central bank foreign reserves. Yet, a higher degree of openness predicts that an economy is less likely to experience a reversal. Edwards (2004) mapped capital flow reversals to a handful of macroeconomic variables that performed as expected:

> The probability of a country experiencing a reversal is captured by a small number of variables that include the (lagged) current account to GDP ratio, the external debt to GDP ratio, the level of international reserves, domestic credit creation, and debt services. . . . More open countries will suffer less—in terms of lower growth—than countries with a lower degree of openness. (p. 34)

No matter what the cause or trigger, it is hard to believe that sudden stops would ever be anything but trouble for any country. Some debate exists about the degree of damage they have caused. Calvo is convinced of their danger, as he says in numerous publications. Edwards, too, believes them to be dangerous: "Current account reversals have had a negative effect on real growth that goes beyond their direct effect on investments" (2004, p. 1).

But there is more to this question. Edwards (2004), citing the cross-sectional analysis of Milesi-Ferretti and Razin (1998a), noted that they "concluded . . . major current account reversals have not been costly. According to them, 'reversals . . . are not systematically associated with a growth slowdown'" (p. 303). And Talvi (2006), one of Calvo's frequent co-authors, wrote that "recoveries that follow collapses tend to be steep and apparently miraculous" (p. 1). Talvi (2006) is quite serious, however, about preventing future sudden stops because they produce, in his words, "long-lasting social consequences . . . and potentially large changes in political dynamics and the rules of the game" (p. 1).

If one supposes that Calvo and others are correct in that sudden stops and reversals are to be feared—and it is hard to imagine they would be welcomed—then one has to ask what it is a central bank can do to protect its country from this danger. By instinct, one might suppose that the antidote would be to keep capital accounts unconvertible, or no more than partially convertible. Empirical research shows just the opposite. Open economies and those with flexible exchange rates show up in testing as the ones best able to withstand the vicissitudes of capital flows—as Milesi-Ferretti and Razin (1998a) discovered. One of the most interesting findings of the sudden stops literature comes from Edwards (2004) concerning the choice of an exchange rate regime:

> The empirical evidence suggests that countries with more flexible exchange rate regimes are able to accommodate the shocks stemming from a reversal better than countries with more rigid exchange rate regimes. (p. 1)

In simple direct terms, having a flexible exchange rate appears to blunt some of the potential ravages associated with sudden stops and reversals.[85]

---

[85]Catão (2006) hinted at this finding but did not conduct a full analysis.

# 7. Intervention, Sterilization, and Capital Controls

This chapter deals with foreign exchange intervention, sterilization, and capital controls. These are some of the more familiar tools that central banks use when they attempt to regulate exchange rates and capital inflows.

Central banks in emerging-markets nations are more frequent users of foreign exchange intervention, sterilization, and capital controls than are the central banks of developed nations. The former see a greater risk from exchange rate fluctuations than do the latter. Also, emerging-markets central banks often regard capital flows into their countries as potentially damaging, especially in regard to their effect on the exchange rate. This mind-set motivates them to regularly conduct intervention, with and without sterilization, and in extreme cases, to install capital controls.

## Foreign Exchange Intervention

The term "intervention" refers to instances when a central bank buys or sells foreign currency in the open market as part of a policy to change the market for its exchange rate.

At the present time, the central banks of the developed nations have all but given up on using foreign exchange intervention, an exception being the Bank of Japan. The probable reason for their abandonment of intervention is dissatisfaction with its effectiveness. One can speculate that there is a simple reason for this lack of effectiveness. As described in Chapter 4, the size of the foreign exchange market has grown by leaps and bounds, now trading several trillions of U.S. dollars a day. Most of this trading is in the big currencies, meaning the U.S. dollar, euro, yen, sterling, and Swiss franc. Thus, at the current time, the size of an intervention would have to be truly colossal to make a difference, at least for the big currencies. Such large-scale intervention unquestionably would complicate a central bank's execution of monetary policy. Even then, recent increases in capital mobility bring into question whether an intervention of any size would make an impression on the foreign exchange market.

The emerging markets are different; their central banks frequently conduct foreign exchange intervention. When an emerging-markets central bank intervenes, it may trade a sizable portion of the overall market for its own currency, at least in some cases. Hence, size, which seems to thwart intervention by the large central banks, may actually assist the emerging markets.

The need to intervene obviously depends on the central bank's choice of exchange rate regime.

**Intervention with Fixed Exchange Rates.** In a fixed exchange rate regime, the central bank announces a peg for its currency at a level (or in a band) against a reserve currency, such as the U.S. dollar or the euro, or against a basket of currencies. The central bank enforces the fixed exchange rate arrangement by buying or selling whenever the market exchange rate deviates sufficiently from the targeted peg.

Whether the central bank must buy or sell depends on whether the peg represents an under- or overvaluation of what the market believes to be the correct value of the currency. If the peg is too high, the market will exert selling pressure. The central bank must then defend its peg by buying its currency, which means it is selling foreign reserves. This situation cannot last forever because the central bank's foreign reserves are finite. But absent the case of the central bank running out of foreign reserves, the process of propping up an overvalued peg—in and of itself—means that the monetary base contracts. Likewise, if the peg is too low, the market will exert buying pressure, which requires the central bank to sell its currency, acquire foreign reserves, and expand the monetary base.

**Intervention with Managed Floating Exchange Rates.** In a pure floating exchange rate arrangement, the central bank never conducts foreign exchange intervention to change the exchange rate level. But in a managed float, the central bank may decide to intervene because it is not satisfied with the level of its exchange rate or because it desires to change the volatility of exchange rate fluctuations. The Bank of Japan has become famous for this variety of intervention.

Ishii (2006, p. 1) identified four objectives for central bank intervention in developing countries:

- to accumulate foreign exchange reserves,
- to supply foreign exchange to the market,
- to calm disorderly markets, and
- to correct perceived misalignments in the relative value of currencies.

The first two are basically housekeeping operations. The third and fourth are policy initiatives.

The third objective, calming a disorderly market, sounds like a perfectly reasonable thing for a central bank to do. But there are reservations. It could prove to be a difficult, if not impossible, task, depending on the state of the market. On a higher level, a policy of regularly trying to cap exchange rate volatility involves the risk of modifying the price formation process and market structure. Fischer (2007) cautioned:

> *In extremis*, the central bank may have to intervene to stabilize a disorderly market, but it needs to be aware that the more frequently and easily it intervenes, the more it will impede the development of a deep and robust market, in which it is possible to hedge against exchange rate changes without having to rely on government intervention. (p. 10)

The fourth objective, aimed at correcting the level of the exchange rate, is the most difficult to achieve. All central banks at one time or another have been tempted to intervene to correct perceived temporary misalignments in exchange rates. Sustained intervention, however, is another matter. In the case of the emerging-markets central banks, protracted involvement in the currency markets can be associated with actions taken to forestall problems associated with capital inflows. Many bankers and economists are convinced that capital inflows are, at best, a mixed blessing—a topic I considered in the previous chapter. The specific problem is that capital inflows may cause overvaluation in exchange rates. Consider what the IMF wrote in its flagship *World Economic Outlook* in the October 2007 issue:

> The influx of large capital inflows has induced policymakers to adopt a variety of measures to prevent overheating and real currency appreciation, and reduce the economy's vulnerability to a sharp reversal of the capital inflows. A key policy decision for countries facing large capital inflows is to what extent to resist pressures for the currency to appreciate by intervening in the foreign exchange market. (p. 111)

These concerns are seen not just in the IMF's published research. For example, Reinhart and Reinhart (1998) wrote:

> Our first lesson is that attracting global investors' attention is a mixed blessing. Capital inflows provide important support for building infrastructure and harnessing natural and human resources. At the same time, surges in capital inflows may distort relative prices, exacerbate weakness in a nation's financial sector, and feed asset-price bubbles. (p. 93)

Spiegel (1995) worried about when capital inflows are short lived:

> In addition, the real exchange rate appreciations that often accompany these capital inflows can lead to undesirable resource reallocation, particularly if the reallocation of resources motivated by the capital inflow surge is likely to be temporary. (p. 17)

One can overdo the "mixed blessing" message about capital inflows. Capital flows can be stabilizing, as Bernanke (2007b) stated:

> [They] can help reduce tendencies toward recession, on the one hand, or overheating and inflation, on the other. During the late 1990s, for example, the developing Asian economies that had experienced financial crises and consequent collapses in domestic investment benefited from being able to run trade surpluses, which help strengthen aggregate demand and employment. During the same period, the trade deficits run by the United States allowed domestic demand to grow strongly without creating significant inflationary pressures. Until a few years ago, the euro area was growing slowly and thus also benefited from running trade surpluses; more recently, as domestic demand in Europe has recovered, the trade surplus has declined. (p. 4)

Another way to make this point is that current account balances and surpluses give countries the flexibility to spend more or less than their current output as dictated by economic conditions and needs. (footnote 11)

Although I side with Bernanke, the prevailing view among economists is that capital inflows may induce overheating and, especially, create overpriced currencies.[86] This view, in turn, leads to the question of what, if anything, a central bank can accomplish through intervention to protect its economy from the risks associated with capital flows.[87]

**How Does Intervention Work?** Suppose that intervention is the answer: That is, it affects the exchange rate in the way that it is intended to, as outlined previously. One might then ask, what are the mechanisms through which it works? Economists today think there are multiple channels through which intervention influences the exchange rate. Ishii (2006) and Archer (2005) identified four channels:

- monetary policy channel,
- signaling channel,
- portfolio balance channel, and
- microstructure channel.

The monetary policy channel refers to the potential for intervention to alter the relative spread between domestic and foreign interest rates. This channel will be closed if the central bank initiating the intervention chooses to sterilize the operation, which means that the intervention will not affect the monetary base. If the intervention is not sterilized, it will be similar in consequences to an open market operation, as discussed in Chapter 2.

The signaling channel operates through market expectations. This process occurs when an intervention is seen by market participants as hinting at the future direction of monetary policy.[88] It requires that the intervention alter the expectations of market participants as to future monetary and exchange rate policy. This channel can work against a central bank's interests. The potential danger comes in cases where intervention fails in its intended purpose; the signal to the market might be that the central bank is powerless to halt the move in the currency.

---

[86]The idea that capital inflows are debilitating dates back at least as far as the discussions of the so-called Dutch disease. This condition refers to the damage to the industrial sector a small open economy suffers from large-scale natural resource exports; see Corden and Neary (1982). Also, there are questions about whether capital flows can do damage to immature financial sectors in emerging markets; see Bercuson and Koenig (1993). From another viewpoint, Calvo (1991) wrote about capital inflows accompanying "the first stages of stabilization programs based on exchange rates" (p. 921).

[87]One report by the IMF makes the case for sterilizing foreign aid payments (see Prati, Sahay, and Tressel 2003).

[88]See Mussa (1981) and Dominguez and Frankel (1993).

The portfolio balance channel works if the central bank is large enough relative to the overall size of the market to be able to meaningfully change the relative scarcity of foreign and domestic assets, which, in turn, influences the exchange rate. This channel is not thought to be substantial for the larger central banks, but it might work for the emerging-markets central banks.

The microstructure channel refers to the theoretical possibility that a central bank can out-trade the foreign exchange traders, perhaps by "catching the market on the wrong footing," as financial journalists write. To the extent this actually happens, the effects are likely to be small and short lived.

**Intervention Mechanics.** The instrument of choice for foreign exchange intervention is spot foreign exchange. Archer (2005) reported that emerging-markets central banks make little use of forward, derivative, and cross-currency debt instruments (with important exceptions) to implement foreign exchange intervention.[89] The use of forwards for intervention is discussed in **Box 7.1**.

More subtle is the effect of forward intervention on interest rates when the spot exchange rate is pegged. If the action of the central bank is to sell the reserve currency forward (buy local currency), then the transaction will exert downward pressure on the domestic interest rate because the spot exchange rate is fixed and, from the central bank's point of view, so is the reserve currency interest rate. In this case, pushing down the forward outright is the same as pushing down the domestic interest rate. The problem to think about is that this operation will reduce both the cost and risk to speculators from selling the local currency forward.

In classical (unsterilized) foreign exchange intervention, the central bank expands or shrinks both sides of its balance sheet. The balance sheet of a prototypical central bank (as I first noted in Chapter 2) is as follows:

| Assets | Liabilities |
| --- | --- |
| Domestic assets (DA) | Currency (C) |
| Foreign assets of the central bank (FACB) | Commercial bank reserves (R) |

Suppose a central bank wishes to lower its exchange rate by conducting foreign exchange intervention. It goes about doing so by selling its own currency against another country's currency, the latter usually being the U.S. dollar, the yen, or the euro. The central bank will credit local currency to the reserve account of the dealing bank from whom it bought the foreign currency. The foreign currency then becomes part of the foreign reserves (FACB) of the central bank. A second transaction may take place in which the bank uses the foreign exchange it has acquired to buy foreign assets, which are usually the other country's government bonds.

---

[89] See Archer (2005, p. 48 and Graph 1).

---

## Box 7.1.  Using Forwards for Intervention?

Archer (2005) reported that the instrument of choice for intervention in emerging-markets foreign exchange is the spot transaction. Why not expand the toolkit to include forward foreign exchange transactions in intervention?

First, when a central bank conducts a spot transaction, it receives a credit or debit in two bank business days' time to the reserve account of the counterparty foreign exchange dealing bank. If the central bank, instead, conducts a forward transaction, a like credit or debit will be charged to the reserve account at a future date corresponding to the forward value date (i.e., settlement date). Thus, any change to the monetary base will not occur until the forward value date.

Many times an intervention to buy or sell foreign exchange is accompanied by a like purchase or sale of foreign government bonds. Hence, if the central bank uses intervention in an attempt to push down the value of its currency, it buys spot foreign currency (i.e., sells local currency) and then uses these proceeds to buy foreign government bonds. The change in the central bank's position in foreign bonds is what causes the change in its balance sheet—an increase in the FACB (foreign assets of the central bank) term.

What if the government intervenes in the forward market instead of the spot market? In this case, the transaction will be to buy foreign currency forward. But now there are no immediate proceeds in foreign currency that can be used to purchase foreign bonds; the second transaction cannot occur, at least not immediately. Moreover, the balance sheet of the central bank will not expand in the conventional way; there will be no immediate change in the FACB term and hence no change in the monetary base.

The forwards, however, will accrue mark-to-market changes in their value as changes in the spot exchange rate occur and as time passes. If, after the central bank has bought foreign currency forward, the value of the domestic currency climbs, there will be a negative mark. The opposite is true if the value of the domestic currency falls. This is one of the problems that the Bank of Thailand had in 1997 after it massively sold U.S. dollars forward against the baht. When the baht plunged in July 1997, the central bank was left with a massive speculative loss on its forwards book.

Hence, both the asset and liability sides of the balance sheet rise. Said another way, the sum of currency (C) plus commercial bank deposits at the central bank (R) must rise; this sum is the monetary base. This result is not different from what one gets when a central bank embarks on a program of buying domestic assets in open market operations (see the discussion of Mundell in Chapter 3).

On these grounds alone, and all other things being equal, intervention to lower the value of the home country currency is inflationary. This operation can theoretically be done in unlimited size because the central bank has the power to create money. Yet, if the central bank performs this operation in sufficient volume, the value of the currency will sink under the weight of the inflation produced by the intervention. Thus, there is a practical limit to the size of the operation.

Likewise, intervention (unsterilized) to raise the value of the home country currency is deflationary. But there is an asymmetric difference from the previous example, in which the central bank was buying foreign exchange. When the central bank is selling foreign exchange, a physical limit is imposed on the size of the operation because the central bank can run out of foreign reserves.

The visibility of the central bank's intervention operations also needs mention. For some reason, many central banks prefer to conduct intervention practically on the sly, as a survey done by the Bank for International Settlements (2005) revealed:

> A curious feature brought to light by surveys of different approaches to foreign exchange intervention is the sharp difference of views on the extent to which visibility of intervention is desirable. Part of this question related to issues of governance and accountability. Part is also tactical in nature. Some central banks believe that visibility brings greater effectiveness; some the opposite. (p. 45)

That lack of visibility would improve the effectiveness of intervention is a dubious proposition. I believe the best policies for a central bank are transparent ones. What is more, given time, there is no true hiding of mistakes or ineptitude where central banks are concerned; in the end, the results—exchange rates, inflation rates, real economic performance, and so forth—become known to all, indeed to the general public.

## Sterilization

The problem with intervention is that it requires a central bank to relinquish some degree of freedom with respect to its conduct of monetary policy. Aliber (1975) discussed the compromises associated with foreign exchange intervention policy: "If intervention is extensive, the monetary independence advantage of a floating exchange rate is compromised; for intervention leads to changes in the reserve base" (p. 366).[90]

Is there a way for a central bank to intervene in the foreign exchange market without changing its monetary base? The solution might be to conduct sterilization operations in concert with the intervention. Sterilization is an open market operation or a change in reserve requirements designed to reverse or suppress changes in the money supply caused by an intervention. If sterilized intervention is successful, a central bank will be able to manage its exchange rate without having to reconfigure its monetary policy.

Can it work? The Mundellian answer is that the effectiveness of sterilization requires that the bonds the bank buys (as new foreign reserves) *not* be perfect substitutes for the bonds it sells (the domestic bonds). If the two categories of bonds are not perfect substitutes, sterilized intervention may actually change the exchange rate.

---

[90]Aliber (1975) also observed that "a floating system does have the advantage that the authorities are not committed to a particular parity, as under a pegged rate system. The question is whether the floating exchange rate system would be superior to a pegged rate system, where the authorities change the peg whenever such changes are necessary" (p. 366).

In reality, local bonds are never perfect substitutes for international bonds. The question then becomes how imperfect a substitute they are (see Obstefeld 1982). A conference on intervention at the Bank for International Settlements (2005) concluded:

> Emerging market economies tend to have less substitutability of assets across currency boundaries, and the authorities tend to have greater financial—and certainly regulatory—weight relative to private markets. (p. 8)

In the imperfect substitutability case, after sterilized intervention intended to lower the value of the local currency, the value of foreign bonds in the hands of the investing public will be relatively smaller and the value of domestic bonds relatively larger. This transformation requires the local currency to be less valuable. Although this exercise might be potent in the short run, it is hard to see how a money-supply-neutral change in the composition of the central bank's balance sheet could have a permanent effect on the exchange rate.

Sometimes sterilization is popular only because of the institutional arrangement of power sharing within governments. In many countries, the decision to intervene in the foreign exchange market is not made by the central bank. For example, in the United States, foreign exchange policy is set by the Department of the Treasury, although the Federal Reserve carries out the actual interventions. The central bank, in this case the Federal Reserve, is responsible for monetary policy. The problem that arises is that unsterilized foreign exchange intervention changes the money supply. Hence, the Treasury, in ordering an intervention, is at risk of having contravened the Federal Reserve's authority with respect to monetary policy. The Federal Reserve Bank of New York (2007) stated:

> The Federal Reserve routinely "sterilizes" intervention in the [foreign exchange] market, which prevents the intervention from changing the amount of bank reserves from levels consistent with established monetary policy goals. For instance, if the New York Fed sells dollars to buy a foreign currency, the sale adds reserves to the banking system. In order to sterilize the transaction, the Fed, in its domestic open market transactions, may remove reserves through the sale of government securities. (p. 2)

In this way, the dichotomy of authority is respected. But my interest in sterilization is more a result of its role as a policy instrument, which I will discuss later.

**Sterilization Mechanics.** The most basic form of sterilized intervention consists of an exchange of foreign reserves and domestic assets. In the intervention, suppose that a central bank sells its own currency and buys foreign currency. The central bank can either keep the foreign currency as an asset or exchange it for foreign-currency-denominated bonds. Referring to the prototypical balance sheet, one can see that the monetary base $(C + R)$ must expand by an amount equal in size to the growth in foreign assets (FACB). If the central bank elects to sterilize, it performs a second operation, that being selling domestic assets (DA) equal in size to the amount of foreign assets it purchased during the intervention. The net effect leaves the monetary base unchanged. I can write this relationship as

$$\Delta FACB = -\Delta DA. \tag{7.1}$$

The combination of these two steps is fully sterilized intervention. Kept constant are the central bank's total assets and total liabilities. Hypothetically, the central bank can keep this activity up until it has pushed down the exchange rate to whatever level it originally desired. Foreign assets on the central bank's balance sheet grow as domestic assets shrink. Sterilization appears to allow the central bank to separate its exchange rate policy from its money supply policy. Of course, this is too good to be true.

Canales-Kriljenko (2006) stated that for the largest central banks, meaning the U.S. Federal Reserve, the European Central Bank, and the Bank of Japan, normal policy is to fully sterilize intervention, although as I have noted, intervention is more a thing of the past for these banks. He reported that, according to a survey of central banks of developing countries:

> About 10 percent of the survey respondents reported that foreign exchange intervention is never sterilized; about half indicated that it is sometimes sterilized; about 20 percent said it is always sterilized. About 25 percent of the survey respondents did not answer the corresponding section of the survey. (p. 19)

The paradigm can easily be modified for partial sterilization. The change in the central bank's holding of foreign assets ($\Delta FACB$) would not be evenly matched by the change in domestic assets. I can write

$$k\Delta FACB = -\Delta DA, \tag{7.2}$$

where $k$ is the fraction of the intervention that is sterilized. If $k$ is unity, the sterilization is full; if $k$ is less than unity, the sterilization is partial. The portion that is not sterilized $(1 - k)$ is effectively an open market operation using foreign assets. The monetary base is expanded in proportion to the unsterilized expansion in the central bank's foreign assets.

A second type of sterilization occurs when a central bank itself issues bonds for the sole purpose of the sterilization operation. Let the central bank issue bonds, sometimes called "sterilization bonds" (SB), in the amount of the increase in foreign assets. These bonds appear as a liability on the prototypical central bank balance sheet:

| Assets | Liabilities |
|--------|-------------|
| DA | C |
| FACB | R |
| | SB |

If the quantity of new sterilization bonds issued equals the change in foreign reserve,

$$\Delta FACB = \Delta SB, \tag{7.3}$$

the monetary base will be unchanged. The central bank, however, might decide to sterilize some but not all of the intervention. If I use $k$ to represent the sterilization coefficient, as I did earlier, I get

$$k\Delta FACB = \Delta SB. \tag{7.4}$$

Here, too, there is an expansion in the monetary base resulting from the portion of the intervention that is not sterilized.

A third method in the sterilization toolkit is for the central bank to allow the monetary base to expand but to choke off the resultant increase in the broad-based aggregates, like M2, by raising the deposit reserve requirement. "Sterilization by reserve requirement," as it is sometimes called, allows the monetary base to rise but not the broad-based aggregates. The composition of the aggregate balance sheet of the banking system (the central bank plus the commercial banks) changes, but its size does not change. Of course, the change in the reserve requirement might not be large enough to completely prevent the broad-based aggregates from expanding; in this case, the reserve requirement would achieve a partial sterilization of the intervention.

Other tools are available for central banks to use in sterilization. Some are in the category of supplemental tools, meaning they are used in conjunction with open market operations or the sale of sterilization bonds. Lee (1997) considered a number of these measures aimed at mopping up capital inflows, including

- discount policy and direct lending.
- switching government deposits: In many emerging-markets countries, the government sector deposits are a great fraction of the deposit base of the banking system. Lee (1997) stated that Malaysia and Thailand were effective in controlling money supply expansion by moving government deposits out of commercial banks to the central bank.
- foreign exchange swaps: The mechanics of this transaction greatly resemble a purchase/repurchase transaction in the bond market. In a foreign exchange swap, the central bank sells spot foreign currency against local currency and simultaneously buys foreign currency for forward value against domestic currency (presumably transacting at the forward outright). The immediate effect is to reduce the domestic monetary base. When the transaction comes to value, the central bank may decide to roll it forward by doing another swap.
- other transactions that are forms of capital controls, to be discussed later in this chapter.

I will now consider three episodes of sterilization in emerging-markets history.

**Latin American Sterilization: The 1990s.** Parts of Latin America began to experience a renewal of capital inflows in the early 1990s. This inflow represented a dramatic turnaround from the 1980s, as Calvo et al. (1993) wrote:

> The revival of substantial international capital inflows to Latin America is perhaps the most visible economic change in the region during the past two years. Capital flows to Latin America, which averaged about $8 billion a year in the second half of the 1980s, surged to $24 billion in 1990 and $40 billion in 1991. Of the latter amount, 45 percent went to Mexico, and most of the remainder went to Argentina, Brazil, Chile, Colombia, and Venezuela. (p. 108)

Examination of these episodes is what caused economists to begin to wonder if the arrival of foreign capital is uniformly good news. Calvo et al. (1993) indicated:

> In most countries the capital inflows have been accompanied by an appreciation in the real exchange rate, booming stock and real estate markets, faster economic growth, an accumulation of international reserves, and a strong recovery of secondary-market prices for foreign loans. (p. 109)

These concerns are the root of much of the attention given by economists and central bankers to such policy measures as intervention, sterilization, and even capital controls, as Calvo, Leiderman, and Reinhart (1996) stated:

> Sterilization has been, by far, the most popular policy response to capital inflows in both Latin America and Asia. This policy aims at insulating the money supply and/or exchange rate from the effect of capital inflows; the intent is to mitigate inflationary pressures, [avoid] real exchange rate appreciation, and avoid . . . loss of control over the domestic money stock. (pp. 133–134)

**East Asian Sterilization: 1987–1997.** Takagi and Esaka (1999) investigated sterilization policies in East Asia that predate the 1997 currency crises. The East Asian countries of Indonesia, Korea, Malaysia, the Philippines, and Thailand received large volumes of capital flows from the end of the 1980s through early 1997.[91] The cumulative inflows, as reported in Takagi and Esaka, were massive: 45.8 percent of GDP in Malaysia, 51.5 percent in Thailand, 23.1 percent in the Philippines, 8.3 percent in Indonesia, and 9.3 percent in Korea.[92] The pattern of flows into these countries, however, was irregular across the region over time. Central banks in the region accumulated intervention-related reserves amounting to 25–35 percent of the net capital inflows. Takagi and Esaka reported:

> Short of allowing the exchange rate to appreciate, the East Asian monetary authorities responded decisively to the massive reserve inflows, first by the conventional form of sterilization and then by taking a wide range of measures to limit the effect of the reserve inflows on the growth of the monetary aggregates. (p. 16)

---

[91]In the early years, the capital flows were composed principally of foreign direct investment. The composition then shifted to short-term borrowing with a prominent role by offshore banks and private corporations. See Takagi and Esaka (1999, p. 1).

[92]Takagi and Esaka (1999, p. 2).

Capital was flooding into the region throughout the precrisis period. It is worthy of note that all the countries, except Malaysia, had declared some form of fixed exchange rate. The common enemy before the beginning of the crises in 1997 was the pressure on the local exchange rates to rise above their pegs, or creeping peg in the case of Indonesia. Thus, the respective central banks were in constant need to buy foreign reserves. How much they needed to buy was a function of the excess demand for their currency at the pegged exchange rate. According to Takagi and Esaka, sterilized intervention was:

> common and extensive, at least initially. . . . Often lacking the depth of markets in government securities, the East Asian central banks supplemented operations in government securities by issuing their own debt instruments.[93] (p. 6)

The phrase "their own debt" refers to what I have been calling sterilization bonds.[94] Also, sterilization by reserve requirement was used extensively by all the East Asian central banks.

Spiegel (1995), working with data on the Asian countries that included part but not all of the precrisis period (the crisis began when Thailand depegged the baht in July 1997), found that these central banks used all three of the sterilization methods discussed here: selling domestic assets, issuing sterilization bonds, and moderating the reserve requirement. He concluded that no one single sterilization method is dominant in its effectiveness.

How successful was the East Asian sterilization? The money supply measures were growing during the period of sterilization in all these countries. Of course, some increase in money supply was needed because income was rising during this period; this is a basic application of the demand for money function discussed in Chapter 2. The East Asian sterilization program did not stop money supply from growing; rather, it appears to have kept monetary growth within an acceptable range. And for a long time, the fixed exchange rate pegs held. During the precrisis period, the growth of money, narrow and broad (M1 and M2, respectively), was

---

[93] According to Takagi and Esaka (1999), Villanueva and Seng (1999) reported the periods of active sterilized intervention as 1988–1995 for Thailand, 1989 and 1992–1993 for Korea, 1990–1993 and 1996 for Indonesia, 1990–1993 for the Philippines, and 1992–1993 for Malaysia. Only Thailand seems to have sterilized throughout the entire period, which is consistent with the finding that capital flows came into Thailand uniformly throughout. Malaysia, by comparison, received the majority of its capital flows in the period from 1989 to 1993. In 1993, Malaysia became aggressive about suppressing what it regarded as dangerous speculation in the ringgit and installed temporary capital controls. For a time afterward, capital flowed out of Malaysia, but inflows resumed in 1996.

[94] Takagi and Esaka (1999) stated that Thailand began to issue short-term Bank of Thailand bonds with maturities of six months to one year. The Korean central bank and the Indonesian central bank issued what they called "monetary stabilization bonds" and Bank Indonesia Certificates, respectively. The central bank of the Philippines and Bank Negara, the central bank of Malaysia, also issued debt to conduct sterilization operations.

not terribly different from the accumulation of foreign reserves. However, Takagi and Esaka's (1999) sophisticated time-series analysis and regression tests were unable to establish a causal relationship between the surge in foreign reserves and the growth in money supply. Hence, they concluded that the sterilization policies of the East Asian central banks were effective in controlling the growth in the narrow- and broad-based monetary aggregates, meaning M1 and M2, respectively.

But they reported at least one important complication: "The capital inflow problem of East Asia leading up to the crises of 1997 was made more serious by the active and persistent policy of sterilization" (p. 18). They asserted that sterilization kept domestic interest rates higher than they would otherwise have been. Sterilization exacerbated the problem of surging capital inflows.

If one believes that capital surging into East Asia was the precondition for the crises that followed, then one can hardly conclude that central bank policies, including sterilization, were successful. The opposite conclusion is hard to ignore given the magnitude of the crises that nearly destroyed these economies in 1997 and 1998. The answer to the question posed earlier about whether the East Asian sterilization programs were successful has to consider the totality of the program, and the conclusion has to be that the entire program, consisting of fixed exchange rates with support from sterilized intervention, was a colossal failure.

**Sterilization in China: 1995–Present.** The most ambitious sterilization project ever attempted began in China in 2002 and continues to this day.[95] The size of these operations alone shows that this program is something out of the ordinary.

The origin of this colossal effort comes from the fact that China is operating a fixed exchange rate at the same time that it is running a massive current account surplus. This configuration requires the central bank to absorb vast amounts of foreign currency onto its balance sheet, much of which it attempts to sterilize to prevent an explosion of its money supply. Even then, the Chinese are watching the domestic price index creep up despite these heroic sterilization measures. The effort to constrain the money supply and the probable effects of its expansion are taking the form of internal capital controls, meaning that officials, including those at the central bank, are telling the banks which companies and industries they may grant loans to. As a consequence, what started out as a fixed exchange rate regime—in the context of a nonconvertible capital account—has become a massive sterilization effort with supplemental measures to suppress price inflation. Those measures include steps that are tantamount to central planning.[96]

---

[95] See Greenwood (2008).
[96] See DeRosa (2005).

China's monetary statistics for 2002 and 2007 are summarized in **Table 7.1**. Several points are striking:

- The central bank accumulated more than 10 trillion yuan in foreign reserves in the course of five years—an increase of 437 percent. This amount derives from innovation to suppress the incipient rise in the yuan.
- The monetary base rose by 5.6 trillion yuan (an increase of 125 percent).
- The central bank issued 3.3 trillion yuan of bonds.
- The broad-based aggregates, M1 and M2, slightly more than doubled over the period.
- The ratios of the broad-based aggregates to the monetary base fell somewhat over the five years covered in the table.

That China has accumulated so vast a hoard of foreign reserves is well known. The less-well-recognized fact is that the sterilization operations included the central bank's issuing debt (what I have termed "sterilization bonds"). The bond issuance began in August 2002. The amount of debt outstanding is not trivial; by 2007, it had grown to about 35 percent of the monetary base. Said another way, the issuance of debt has mopped up about 33 percent of the total increase in foreign reserves from sterilization efforts.

Another feature of the Chinese experience is that the central bank has used the reserve requirement as part of the sterilization. Starting with a reserve requirement of 6 percent in 1999, the central bank raised the ratio to 7 percent and 7.5 percent in 2003 and 2004, respectively. The ratio was raised three times in 2006 and again in January 2007 to 9.5 percent, which might account for the drop in the ratio of the aggregates to the monetary base. Studies by Green and Chang (2006) and Laurens and Maino (2007), however, reported that the money multiplier itself appeared to be both unstable and unreliable in its ability to control the broad-based aggregates.

**Table 7.1. Key Monetary Statistics for China, 2002 and 2007**
(yuan in billions; U.S. dollars in billions)

| Item | 31 Dec. 2002 | 31 Dec. 2007 | Change | Percentage Change |
|---|---|---|---|---|
| Foreign reserves (yuan) | 2,324 | 12,482 | 10,158 | 437% |
| Foreign reserves (dollars) | $   286 | $ 1,528 | $ 1,242 | 434 |
| Total assets (yuan) | 5,110 | 16,914 | 11,804 | |
| Bond issues (liabilities in yuan) | 148 | 3,446 | 3,298 | |
| Monetary base (yuan) | 4,513 | 10,154 | 5,641 | 125 |
| M1 (yuan) | 7,088 | 15,251 | 8,163 | 115 |
| Ratio of M1/Base | 1.57 | 1.45 | | |
| M2 (yuan) | 18,500 | 40,340 | 21,840 | 118 |
| Ratio of M2/Base | 4.10 | 3.87 | | |

*Source*: Based on data from the People's Bank of China.

All of this activity is designed to preclude foreign exchange intervention from becoming excess money supply (which, in turn, could generate inflation). What about moving the peg itself to relieve some of the need for intervention? The yuan had been pegged at 8.27 to the U.S. dollar since 1995. A great deal of political tension between the United States and China may have helped China decide to begin a gradual revaluation of the yuan in July 2005; see **Figure 7.1**. At the time of writing, the yuan is 6.9725, meaning it has revalued by approximately 18 percent. Still, the central bank finds it necessary to continue sterilized intervention operations.

**Figure 7.1. Exchange Rate for the Chinese Yuan against the U.S. Dollar, June 1988–May 2008**

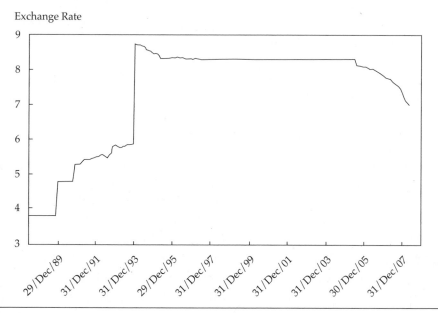

*Source*: Based on data from Bloomberg.

Political motives aside, the policy of pegging the yuan has resulted in the central bank's having to issue a massive amount of sterilization bonds and also deal in other ways with the consequences of near fourfold expansion in its foreign reserves. In 2008, another complication of the sterilization program became evident. The bank had accumulated a massive portfolio of U.S. dollar-denominated assets. As it so happened, the U.S. dollar was falling. Then, in September and October 2008, U.S. mortgage-related securities and other assets suffered sharp declines in value. These market movements adversely affected the bank's portfolio and, as a consequence, diminished its net capital (i.e., its "owner's equity").

Normally, one does not spend a lot of time worrying about the net capital of a central bank, but in this case, questions about the sustainability of the bank's balance sheet began to circulate. No obvious solution, however, was at hand. Further enlargement of the balance sheet risked setbacks to the anti-inflation policy. Obtaining fresh capital from the ministry of finance put the independence of the central bank at issue.

One fine point to consider is that the central bank did not always sterilize interventions. In fact, the sterilization did not begin until 2002, eight years after the yuan was pegged. Why was sterilization not needed earlier? In the first place, the yuan originally might not have been so severely undervalued by reference to the rate at which it was pegged; therefore, the size of the intervention needed to hold the peg might have been far less substantial than in more recent times.

A second reason was voiced by Harberger (2008), who described the earlier period as the "people's sterilization":

> Between 1995 and 2006 the real exchange rate depreciated by 4 percent, the money supply (M2) increased by over 400 percent while real GDP grew by some 150 percent. It is clear that the big change was in people's holdings of real monetary balances ("sterilization by the people"). Part of this came simply as a consequence of the rise in real income, with the income elasticity of demand for real monetary balances probably greater than unity. But it is likely that forces other than the increase in real incomes were also at work—namely, the absence (for most of the period) of alternative financial assets (or markets) where people could place their savings, a greater desire to save so as to provide for a better standard of living during one's retirement years, and a weak social security system. (p. 235).

This is a lesson in monetary economics. In his use of the term "people's sterilization," Harberger is suggesting that for a time, rising demand for real balances, triggered by rising income, was sufficient to mop up the excess supply of money created by the intervention needed to support the exchange rate peg. More subtle is his observation that in these early days of the peg, meaning 1994–2002, Chinese citizens had very few places to invest their savings. "Money"—that is, bank balances or cash on hand—was one of the few such places (hence the observed high income elasticity). Gradually, as China became more open, alternative investment vehicles, such as equities, bonds, and real estate, began to appear. Money became less important as a form of savings, and as that happened, the need for sterilization arose, seemingly since 2002.

In abstract, this scenario is very Mundellian: Harberger's insights demonstrate that as China became more open to capital markets, the problems of its maintaining a fixed exchange rate peg became ever so much more complex, as evidenced by its present needs to conduct massive intervention and sterilization.

**Problems with Sterilization.** Anyone who has studied modern finance knows to be aware of sleight-of-hand balance sheet tricks. Finance teaches one to question such things as whether a company can be worth more in aggregate simply because it substitutes some equity financing for debt financing, or vice versa. Similarly, it leads one to ask whether a business project is more acceptable only because it is financed with debt rather than equity. The indifference propositions of Modigliani and Miller (1958) say clearly that, except in unusual circumstances, such balance sheet decoration does not affect real economic value. In the same way, one has to wonder whether it matters if a central bank rearranges its balance sheet, tipping the composition more toward foreign bonds than domestic bonds, which is what basic sterilized intervention accomplishes. Consider that the central bank, like everyone else, must buy and sell bonds at market prices. Why would such an operation make any difference at all to an economy? Although it may be hard to see what positive impact sterilized intervention conveys at this high level, there are some concerns that harmful side effects might occur in practice.

▨ *Spread cost.* Consider the two most popular forms of sterilization for intervention to lower the value of the domestic currency. In the first, the net result is the central bank buys foreign assets and sells domestic assets. For simplicity, one can assume that those assets are government bonds. For the sterilization to be perfect, the value of the debt purchased (foreign) must be equal to the value of the debt sold (domestic). A problem surfaces immediately because the yields on the foreign debt are likely to be lower than the yields on the domestic debt. In effect, the sterilized intervention is a "negative" carry trade because its cost of funds will be larger than the yield it receives.

Similarly, in the second method of sterilization, the central bank itself issues sterilization bonds and acquires foreign assets, presumed to be foreign bonds. The problem here is similar because the yield on the sterilization bonds is likely to be higher than the yield of the purchased foreign bonds they finance. The spread problem is reported in Takagi and Esaka (1999):

> After the initial period, however, most of the central banks began to rely much less on conventional sterilized intervention, in part owing to the quasi-fiscal costs of such operations. The quasi-fiscal cost arises because, in sterilized intervention, the central bank typically exchanges high-yielding domestic assets for low-yielding foreign assets. In the consolidated government and central bank portfolio, the public sector ends up paying more on its liabilities than it receives on its assets, as more government debt is held outside the central bank. (p. 7)

A central bank is supposed to have the appearance of a cash-flow-bulletproof institution. Central banks issue money and require that reserves be deposited. These functions provide the central bank with two sources of capital, neither of which carries interest charges. On the asset side, the bank invests in interest-bearing bonds. Absent fraud, the prototypical central bank cannot help but sustain an operating profit, abstracting from the normal operating costs of such an institution. But sterilization can change that picture because the central bank may invest in assets whose returns are less than their funding costs. Sterilization can create a leak in the central bank's financial structure. If sterilization is sufficiently large, the cost of the interest rate spread will indicate a lack of sustainability of the sterilization program, and at the limit, of the central bank itself.

■ *Appearance of greater indebtedness.* Some are wary about the appearance of an excessive amount of sterilization bonds. Calvo et al. (1996) stated:

> Eventually this policy could result in a rise in public debt so large as to undermine the credibility of policymakers, especially if the public begins expecting a partial repudiation of the debt—expectations that may well halt the inflows altogether. (p. 134)

Calvo (1991), in the aptly titled paper "The Perils of Sterilization," wrote:

> If the associated open market operation is carried out by expanding the stock of nominal domestic debt, forces may be set in motion that could also jeopardize the credibility—and, hence, sustainability—of the anti-inflationary effort. (p. 921)

Here, again, is a way that a sterilization program of sufficient size can call into question the credibility of the central bank.

■ *Attraction of still more foreign capital.* As I have discussed, sterilized intervention is often undertaken to blunt the effects of capital inflows. Ironically, sterilization can make the capital inflow worse. Calvo et al. (1996) wrote:

> It is not clear that this policy can provide a lasting solution, and it can be costly. Presumably, funds are being attracted into the country by the promise of higher expected interest rates. But if the capital inflow is sterilized, this will prevent the interest rate differential from narrowing and may thus induce further capital inflows. (p. 136)

The logic is that, were there no sterilization, the differential between the domestic and foreign interest rates would shrink with the inflow of foreign capital. This narrowing of the spread will not happen to the same degree, or at all, if the central bank sterilizes intervention. To the extent this is true, sterilization will have an effect opposite from that desired in the first place.

■ *Sterilization by reserve requirement.* Lee (1997) noted that some countries, notably Colombia in 1991, have raised the reserve requirement sharply in an attempt to sterilize inflows.[97] The practical limit, however, is that raising the reserve requirement, in effect, levies a tax on banks, and as such, it is an incentive for the economy to disintermediate financial activity away from the banking system, thereby diminishing the monetary control of the central bank. Folkerts-Landau, Schinasi, Cassard, Ng, Reinhart, and Spencer (1995) pointed to two drawbacks of

---

[97]See also Lee (1996).

reserve requirement sterilization. The first is that increasing reserve requirements is not costless because reserves do not earn market rates of return; this is a distortion to the banking system. Second, it encourages disintermediation.[98]

■ *Inflation postponed?* The economist John Greenwood, speaking at the 2008 Cato Monetarist Conference, referred to sterilization as "inflation postponed." The question he asked was: What will happen in the future when the central bank, perhaps responding to negative carry on its sterilization position, decides to unwind its position?

No better example can be found than that of China (whose central bank has made extensive use of the issuance of sterilization bonds) for examining the challenges involved in sterilization. The unwind of that position would consist of the central bank letting the bonds mature or buying back the sterilization bonds. In the process, either currency in the hands of the public or commercial bank reserves held at the central bank would have to rise. And either way, the monetary base must rise. All other things being equal, this situation poses a risk of inflation. Greenwood raised an interesting point for central bankers: When considering sterilization, one had better build into one's plans that someday the sterilization operation will have to be dismantled.

## Capital Controls

Capital controls are policies undertaken by central banks to restrict capital movements across their borders or to add special costs to such movements in an attempt to discourage them. They are often applied in conjunction with intervention and sterilization. Yet, capital controls are clearly in a different category from these other central bank policies. The main controversies about intervention and sterilization are concerned with whether they work and if so, how effectively and with what side effects. Although capital controls have similar issues, they are unorthodox by comparison. Central banks are less likely to use capital controls because they are designed to actually restrict the flow of capital into or out of a country and, as such, are distinctly antithetical to the concepts of openness and free markets. For these reasons alone, many economists who nonetheless worry about the adverse consequences of capital flows remain hesitant about recommending capital controls. Others think controls can be beneficial but recommend using them only sparingly and evaluating each case on its peculiar merits. Still others believe capital controls are never good policy.

For a time in the early 1990s, it looked as if capital controls might vanish altogether. Emerging-markets nations were gradually removing capital controls throughout the 1980s and early 1990s.[99] Indeed, some portion of the capital inflow problems analyzed by Calvo and his associates was a by-product of this process of removal of capital controls.

---

[98]See the discussion in Spiegel (1995).
[99]See International Monetary Fund (1997, p. 242).

Thus, the trend before roughly 1997 was away from capital controls. And this point is no better illustrated than by the fact that at one time, the IMF was debating about becoming the advocate of capital account convertibility. Current account convertibility is a fundamental objective of the IMF. It is also a precondition for membership in the organization. Capital account convertibility is another matter. Cooper (1999) wrote of the ebb and flow of the popularity of capital account convertibility:

> At its semiannual meeting in April 1997 the Interim Committee of the International Monetary Fund (IMF) proposed that the organization's Articles of Agreement (the basic "constitution" of international financial relations among its 182 member countries) be amended to include currency convertibility for capital transactions among its fundamental objectives. . . . Shortly after the Interim Committee's meeting the Asian financial crises erupted. Some observers attributed the crises in part to unwise or excessive capital liberalization. (pp. 89–90)

**Varieties of Capital Controls.** The variety of capital controls is limited only by the imagination of central bankers.[100] Their ability to work as advertised is limited by the ingenuity of market participants who seek to render them ineffective. Capital controls can be put into two main categories: administrative and market based. Administrative controls are any measure that imposes administrative requirements on the banking system to control capital inflows. Market-based capital controls depend on making capital transactions more costly. Ariyoshi, Habermeier, Laurens, Ötker-Robe, Canales-Kriljenko, and Kirilenko (2000) listed three categories of market-based controls:

- dual or multiple exchange rate systems: The concept here is to allow trade flows, foreign direct investment, and equity investment to use one exchange rate but to confine speculative use of currencies to a second, harder-to-borrow, exchange rate.
- explicit taxation: This approach is a direct tax on capital flows. The tax rate can differ according to the type of transaction.
- indirect taxation: The usual form is a compulsory non-interest-bearing reserve/deposit requirement. This approach is sometimes called an "unremunerated reserve requirement." Examples are Thailand in 1996, Colombia in 2007, and Chile throughout the 1990s.

Other forms of capital controls mix administrative and market-based incentives (see Ariyoshi et al. 2000). Lee (1997) enumerated several forms of capital controls that are supplemental measures taken as part of sterilization policies, including variable deposit requirements and interest equalization taxes. Practitioners will realize at once that all the items on the list of capital control measures compiled by

---

[100]The IMF's *AREAER* is a rich source of information about capital controls as practiced by member nations.

Ariyoshi et al. are vulnerable to evasion. As Edwards (1999) described: "The simplest mechanisms are the over-invoicing of imports, the under-invoicing of exports, and the mislabeling of the nature of the capital movement" (p. 67).

Practically speaking, there is no such thing as a government or central bank that can literally control capital flows. Black and gray markets always exist.[101] And a way can always be found to get around the regulations if enough effort is applied and cost incurred. Certainly, one of the principal faults of capital controls is that they are always porous. As Callen (2007) has written:

> Even in cases in which a narrow range of objectives [was] met, controls had only temporary effects as market participants eventually found ways to circumvent them. (p. 114)

**Why Have Capital Controls?** The literature on capital controls refers to at least five reasons why such controls are sometimes necessary. None of these is without counterargument.

The first supposed reason is that international capital is capricious or, worse, the raw material of future financial crises. In other words, capital is subject to fits and starts, or in Kindleberger's (1996) terms, might be the fuel of manias, panics, and crashes. Better to get control of capital coming into one's country before it gets control of the country. This argument presumes that capital is irrational, a conclusion that I could not broadly accept in Chapter 6. Still, even if the hypothesis of capital as a malevolent agent were correct, it is a broad reach to conclude that capital controls can control the beast. And if controls are effective, what is to say that the policy makers have the wisdom and experience to use them correctly?

A second reason is that countries that have been closed or restricted to international capital markets are apt to have less than fully developed financial sectors. And their central banks might not be up to the daunting tasks of dealing with capital flows. The counterargument is that the financial sector of an emerging-markets nation might be immature, but how does that make capital inflows bad? Do not cases exist in which it would be better for a country to receive the benefits of capital inflows even if there is a price to pay in terms of inflation or other side effects?

Third, a crash or crisis is likely to affect an emerging-markets nation far worse than it would a developed country because the response from policy makers is likely to make things even worse. My response is that emerging-markets central banks would do well to learn better skills for dealing with crises and, more to the point, preventing them.

Fourth, it is said that capital must be restricted from freely entering an emerging-markets country to preclude it from causing the exchange rate to rise, which is the side effect that concerns Calvo and others. Moreover, Calvo is correct that

---

[101] See Edwards (1999) and Garber (1998).

sterilization, meaning sterilized intervention, has its limits, if not its "perils," to use his term. These issues were discussed at length earlier in this chapter; intervention with and without sterilization does indeed have its limits. So do capital controls.

Fifth, the trinity (see Chapter 3) indicates that by restricting the flow of capital, a central bank regains control of its monetary policy in the context of fixed exchange rates, which may be true in theory but it ignores some important lessons learned from the 1990s, as discussed in Chapter 6. In particular, market participants remember that capital controls were widely introduced as part of the dreadful policy response to the crises of the 1990s, and they may fear a repeat performance. To avoid this risk, participants shun the markets where they think such crises are likely to occur. This is one explanation for the "water running uphill" phenomenon (capital flowing out of the emerging markets) and suggests that capital controls will hurt (by repelling capital) more than they will help (by returning control of monetary policy to the central bank).

**Chile as a Counterexample?** Chile stands in stark contrast to the anti-capital-control movement. It seemed to prosper in spite of the fact that it relied on capital controls to produce a moderating effect on inflows of capital throughout the 1990s. Nadal-De Simone and Sorsa (1999) wrote in their comprehensive paper on capital controls in Chile:

> Like other countries in Latin American and Asia, Chile faced a surge in capital inflows at the beginning of the 1990s. . . . The authorities favored the introduction of controls on capital inflows to offset, or at least moderate, the appreciation of the currency while keeping the interest rate differential required for reducing excess of desired expenditure of output. . . . Chilean controls on capital flows in the 1990s were unrelated to the central issue in the on-going debate of whether controls would allow countries to forestall crises. (p. 4)

The principal form of capital control was the *encaje* (1991–1998), which Nadal-De Simone and Sorsa (1999) referred to as an "asymmetric Tobin tax amounting to a one-year unremunerated reserve requirement" (p. 4). Forbes (2005) wrote: "The exact terms of the *encaje* were frequently modified, but was basically a tax on capital inflows with a higher effective tax rate for shorter-term investments" (p. 156).

Chile's experiment with capital controls has been the subject of a great deal of economic analysis. For a while it seemed as though the Chileans had something to teach the world regarding how to manage foreign capital flows. Then, with the passage of time, doubts began to spring up as to just how successful capital controls were for Chile, especially considering costs associated with the controls.

Nadal-De Simone and Sorsa (1999) found, after noting significant econometric and methodological problems:

> Controls on Chile's inflows had only a temporary impact in reducing specific inflows because they were affected by avoidance. There is some evidence that controls increased interest rates and altered the composition of capital inflows. . . . It seems premature to view the Chilean experience as supportive of controls on capital inflows. (p. 1)

Likewise, Edwards (1999) wrote:

> The effectiveness of Chile's controls on capital inflows has often been exaggerated. . . . Moreover, Chile's capital controls have also had costs. The most important one is that they have increased the cost of capital significantly, especially for those small- and medium-sized Chilean firms that find it difficult or impossible to evade the controls on capital inflows. (p. 82)

Forbes (2005) is also skeptical of the value of capital controls in Chile:

> There is no conclusive evidence that the *encaje* reduced Chile's vulnerability to crises or increased its growth rate. Although the period from 1991 to 1998 was a period of strong economic performance in Chile, this undoubtedly resulted from the package of sound economic policies enacted by the Chilean government—such as strengthening its banking system, liberalizing trade, supporting privatization, increasing exchange rate flexibility, maintaining low inflation, and running sensible fiscal policy. It was this package of sound market-oriented policies that drove Chile's strong economic performance during the 1990s. There is no compelling evidence that the Chilean capital controls significantly contributed to this impressive economic performance. (p. 157)

**Sand in the Gears.** The argument against full capital account convertibility picked up a powerful and influential supporter in the person of Nobel Prize-winning economist James Tobin in the late 1970s. Tobin (1978) was an early advocate of a form of capital controls that bears his name. In this famous paper, Tobin proposed instating a tax on foreign exchange transactions.[102] The concept has become known as putting some "sand in the well-greased wheels" of the international capital markets. Tobin was indifferent between fixed and floating exchange rates. He enumerated reasons why his tax should be enacted, including his belief that it would restore some autonomy to national economic policy makers. Furthermore, he asserted that his tax would increase the potency of monetary policy relative to fiscal policy. He wrote that "after all, monetary policy is the more flexible and responsive instrument of domestic stabilization" (p. 155).

---

[102]Tobin's recommendation was for the proceeds of his tax to be paid to the IMF or the World Bank.

Tobin's tax has never become a reality, but it moved the debate toward the possibility that absolute convertibility might not always be best. Edwards (1999) wrote that in contrast to Tobin-like alterations of the global capital market:

> Recent discussions on the future of the international monetary system have tended to shy away from grand and universal schemes, focusing instead on the merits of more modest proposals aimed at restricting capital mobility in (some of) the emerging markets. (p. 66)

Following the eruption of the 1997 currency crises, the focus of analysis grew to include cases where a central bank might install out-going capital controls to prevent funds from leaving its country.

**Malaysia as a Counterexample?** The concept of using capital controls to restrict the flow of outbound capital picked up adherents after the Southeast Asian crisis. Malaysia stands out in this regard. Malaysian Prime Minister Mahathir did a considerable amount of grandstanding, introduced capital controls, and boasted he had found a "kinder and gentler" way through the hard times.

Thailand devalued its currency in July 1997. Malaysia's ringgit came under severe selling pressure almost immediately. At that time, Malaysia did not have capital controls (although it did have restrictions earlier). The ringgit plunged in value. Conventional stabilization policies (spending cuts and interest rate hikes) did not succeed in bringing the Malaysian economy any relief. In early 1998, Malaysia imposed capital controls and pegged the ringgit to the U.S. dollar. Details of this period are to be found in Johnson, Kochhar, Mitton, and Tamirisa (2006).

The idea of imposing capital controls was bolstered by Krugman (1998), who famously wrote:

> In short, Asia is stuck: Its economies are dead in the water, but trying to do anything major to get them moving risks provoking another wave of capital flight and a worse crisis. In effect, the regions' economic policy has become hostage to skittish investors. Is there any way out? Yes, there is, but it is a solution so unfashionable, so stigmatized, that hardly anyone . . . has dared suggest it. The unsayable words are "exchange controls."

Several points have to be understood about the Malaysian situation before concluding that capital controls were successful. The first is that Malaysia did not install its capital controls until a full 14 months into the crisis. Capital that wanted to leave Malaysia had already left when the controls were applied. Moreover, capital controls are notoriously porous. In effect, Malaysia locked the barn door after the horse had fled. Second, as noted, Malaysia simultaneously imposed a fixed exchange rate regime. This action happened almost exactly at a time when the currencies in the region hit rock bottom and began to recover upward against the U.S. dollar, the German mark, and the yen. In effect, therefore, Malaysia engineered a competitive devaluation against its neighbors. So, there is no reason to think the controls did much good or harm if for no other reason than they were too late and too ineffective to have mattered. Johnson et al. (2006) concluded: "In macroeconomic terms, these controls neither yielded major benefits nor were costly" (p. 1).

Yet the Malaysian controls did do one thing. They created an economic environment that greatly advantaged those firms that were politically close to Mahathir and his ruling party (and disadvantaged firms affiliated with Mahathir's political enemies). This situation was shown convincingly in Johnson et al. (2006) and Johnson and Mitton (2003). I quote from the latter:

> The evidence from Malaysia strongly supports the idea that firms with political connections were expected to lose subsidies in the first phase of the Asian crisis. Conversely, firms connected to the Prime Minister were expected to gain subsidies when capital controls were imposed in September 1998. (pp. 379–380)

**What Cost Capital Controls?** The sudden enthusiasm for the use of capital controls (applied selectively) following the Southeast Asian crises was not necessarily supported by an objective analysis of the costs associated with such policy initiatives. Forbes (2005) wrote:

> Just as surprising as this sea-change in views on the benefits of capital controls is the lack of rigorous economic analysis supporting this reversal. One of the most basic concepts underlying economics is that any policy measure should be assessed based on whether its benefits outweigh its costs. (p. 154)

At least three types of costs are associated with capital controls identified in the economic literature, according to the International Monetary Fund *World Economic Outlook* (2007). All of these are microeconomic costs.

The first is the cost of capital. Forbes (2007) estimated that small companies in Chile experienced higher costs of capital during, as opposed to before and after, the period of capital controls. In Forbes (2005), she elaborated:

> Many firms chose to list abroad through American Depository Receipts (ADRs) in order to avoid the tax. This may have hindered the development of the Chilean stock market. (p. 160)

The second cost refers to distortions and reduced market discipline. Malaysia, in 1998–1999, was a towering example of these distortions. The third cost is the reduced amount of international trade. Trade is reduced because capital controls raise the cost of doing foreign business.

No true consensus can be said to exist within the economic community as to whether capital controls should be adopted, if ever, by emerging-markets countries. Early on, economists were impressed by the cases of Chile and Malaysia. Now it would seem the bloom has come off the rose, as evidence in favor of controls seems ever harder to substantiate while the associated costs grow more apparent the more the issues are studied. The weight of the evidence and logic favors caution with respect to capital controls. The International Monetary Fund's 2007 *World Economic Outlook* may have the last word:

> In sum, although the macroeconomic impact of capital controls has been temporary at best, evidence suggests [the controls] have been associated with substantial microeconomic costs. While capital controls might have a certain role in certain cases, they should not be seen as a substitute for sound macroeconomic policies that include a prudential fiscal stance and a supporting exchange rate and monetary policy framework. (p. 12)

I have considered three types of central bank operations apart from the traditional application of monetary theory: intervention, sterilization, and capital controls. None of these appear to be particularly potent for sustained periods of time. The lessons are accurately summarized in the same IMF publication (*World Economic Outlook*, 2007):

> Resisting nominal exchange rate appreciation through sterilized intervention is likely to be ineffective when the influx of capital is persistent. Tightening capital controls does not appear to deliver better outcomes. (p. 105)

# 8. The Minimalist Emerging-Markets Central Bank

The final topic of my study is to resolve what issues *ought* to concern an emerging-markets central bank and what tools are at its disposal. The review undertaken in this book suggests these monetary authorities have the potential to confer great benefits—but also to do enormous harm. The central banks of emerging-markets nations can play large roles in the development and growth of these nations. But a large role does not necessarily mean a large degree of intervention. I believe that "minimalist" central banks are best for the emerging markets. Heroic central bank efforts, especially those that require elaborate market judgments and brinksmanship, are rarely advisable.

One of the most important decisions for a central bank to make is the choice of a foreign exchange arrangement. The record speaks in favor of the bipolar view. A minimalist central bank ought to peg hard (with a currency board or dollarization) or float or, alternatively, enter into a currency zone, effectively pegging hard to the other countries in the zone and floating with the rest of the world. The lessons of the 1990s tell central bankers of the dangers of intermediate exchange rate regimes, such as soft pegs of any variety and target zones. Although floating exchange rates have downsides, they appear to be relatively crisis free, something that fixed exchange rates arrangements cannot claim. In the long run, emerging-markets nations should gravitate toward floating or managed floating exchange rate arrangements.

Monetary policy is the other big decision for a central bank to make. My recommendation is to be conservative in applying discretion in the operation of monetary policy. Rules do better than authority. John Adams' principle that "a government of laws and not of men" is preferable applies here.[103] A fair number of economists recommend that a floating exchange rate central bank adopt inflation targeting as monetary policy. I concur, but I note that inflation targeting has the drawback that desirable auxiliary targets and goals, such as low rates of unemployment, are not included as part of the formal decision-making process. Nevertheless, inflation targeting is a well-defined goal; it reduces the sphere of decision making to a reasonable framework, and it appears to serve as an anchor for the currency. A compromise position that allows both inflation targeting and other goals is for a floating exchange rate central bank to diligently use Taylor rules or some other monetary guideline framework. By doing so, it will still be considered a minimalist central bank.

---

[103]Constitution of the Commonwealth of Massachusetts, Part the First, Article 30 (1780), accessed at www.mass.gov/legis/const.htm on 16 August 2008. The Massachusetts Constitution was principally authored by Adams.

If a central bank adopts inflation targeting, it implicitly decides to engage in open communication with the general public about its monetary policy decisions. That required degree of transparency may be beneficial in and of itself. Here, I think the debate has been won by economists who favor open communication with the general public.

My review of monetary policy measures indicates that some measures are far from satisfying. These include foreign exchange intervention, sterilization, and capital controls. The minimalist central bank regards these measures with a large degree of circumspection. In the first place, none of these measures appear terribly efficient, and in the second, they can have bad side effects.

Capital controls are particularly objectionable. I prefer to see central banks use so-called indirect methods to regulate capital markets. The distinction here is that an indirect method works through market prices, examples being interest rates and exchange rates. Direct methods are blunter instruments in the central bank policy toolbox and restrict the flow of capital through nonmarket mechanisms, such as barriers or taxes.

In this book, I shared with readers a sense of puzzlement at some of the findings I have discussed concerning what I (and others) have called the "paradox of capital." I was able to account in general terms for some of the most surprising features of recent capital market history. The global savings glut hypothesis can explain such things as the U.S. current account deficit, parts of the "water running uphill" phenomenon, and other circumstances that are often described as imbalances. Still, the allocation of capital flows among emerging-markets nations is a mystery.

Notwithstanding these puzzles, I recommend that central banks everywhere maintain a healthy respect for financial markets and market prices, such as interest rates, domestic prices, and exchange rates. The function of a price, such as an exchange rate, is to help bring about market-clearing conditions. If such a price is frozen or suffers excessive interference, the economy will come to rest at a different and possibly inferior equilibrium. Interference in capital markets is apt to have consequences, direct and otherwise, that are hard to predict. Intervention of any kind is to be approached with extreme caution.

Finally, I close this book with some advice that Friedman (1972) gave to the economics profession. I redirect it to include central bankers. His words reflect a concern that the economics profession has exaggerated its ability to use monetary policy to fine-tune the U.S. economy:

> I believe that we economists in recent years have done vast harm—to society at large and to our profession in particular—by claiming more than we can deliver. We have thereby encouraged politicians to make extravagant promises, inculcate unrealistic expectations in the public at large, and promote discontent with reasonably satisfactory results because they fall short of the economist's promised land. (pp. 17–18)

# Appendix A.  IMF Definitions of Country Groups in the World Economic Outlook Database

## Advanced economies
Composed of 31 countries: Australia, Austria, Belgium, Canada, Cyprus, Denmark, Finland, France, Germany, Greece, Hong Kong SAR, Iceland, Ireland, Israel, Italy, Japan, Korea, Luxembourg, Malta, Netherlands, New Zealand, Norway, Portugal, Singapore, Slovenia, Spain, Sweden, Switzerland, Taiwan Province of China, United Kingdom, United States.

## Euro area
Composed of 15 countries: Austria, Belgium, Cyprus, Finland, France, Germany, Greece, Ireland, Italy, Luxembourg, Malta, Netherlands, Portugal, Slovenia, and Spain.

## Major advanced economies (G–7)
Composed of 7 countries: Canada, France, Germany, Italy, Japan, United Kingdom, and United States.

## Newly industrialized Asian economies
Composed of 4 countries: Hong Kong SAR, Korea, Singapore, and Taiwan Province of China.

## Other advanced economies (advanced economies excluding G–7 and euro area)
Composed of 12 countries: Australia, Denmark, Hong Kong SAR, Iceland, Israel, Korea, New Zealand, Norway, Singapore, Sweden, Switzerland, and Taiwan Province of China.

## European Union
Composed of 27 countries: Austria, Belgium, Bulgaria, Cyprus, Czech Republic, Denmark, Estonia, Finland, France, Germany, Greece, Hungary, Ireland, Italy, Latvia, Lithuania, Luxembourg, Malta, Netherlands, Poland, Portugal, Slovak Republic, Slovenia, Spain, Sweden, Romania, and United Kingdom.

# Emerging and developing economies

Composed of 142 countries: Albania, Algeria, Angola, Antigua and Barbuda, Argentina, Armenia, Azerbaijan, Bahamas, Bahrain, Bangladesh, Barbados, Belarus, Belize, Benin, Bhutan, Bolivia, Botswana, Brazil, Bulgaria, Burkina Faso, Burundi, Cambodia, Cameroon, Cape Verde, Central African Republic, Chad, Chile, China, Colombia, Comoros, Congo (Democratic Republic of), Congo (Republic of the), Costa Rica, Côte d'Ivoire, Croatia, Czech Republic, Djibouti, Dominica, Dominican Republic, Ecuador, Egypt, El Salvador, Equatorial Guinea, Estonia, Ethiopia, Fiji, Gabon, Gambia, Georgia, Ghana, Grenada, Guatemala, Guinea, Guinea-Bissau, Guyana, Haiti, Honduras, Hungary, India, Indonesia, Iran (Islamic Republic of), Jamaica, Jordan, Kazakhstan, Kenya, Kiribati, Kuwait, Kyrgyz Republic, Lao People's Democratic Republic, Latvia, Lebanon, Lesotho, Libya, Lithuania, Macedonia (Former Yugoslav Republic of), Madagascar, Malawi, Malaysia, Maldives, Mali, Mauritania, Mauritius, Mexico, Moldova, Mongolia, Morocco, Mozambique, Myanmar, Namibia, Nepal, Nicaragua, Niger, Nigeria, Oman, Pakistan, Panama, Papua New Guinea, Paraguay, Peru, Philippines, Poland, Qatar, Romania, Russia, Rwanda, Samoa, São Tomé and Príncipe, Saudi Arabia, Senegal, Seychelles, Sierra Leone, Slovak Republic, Solomon Islands, South Africa, Sri Lanka, St. Kitts and Nevis, St. Lucia, St. Vincent and the Grenadines, Sudan, Suriname, Swaziland, Syrian Arab Republic, Tajikistan, Tanzania, Thailand, Togo, Tonga, Trinidad and Tobago, Tunisia, Turkey, Turkmenistan, Uganda, Ukraine, United Arab Emirates, Uruguay, Uzbekistan, Vanuatu, Venezuela, Vietnam, Yemen (Republic of), Zambia, and Zimbabwe

# Africa

Composed of 48 countries: Algeria, Angola, Benin, Botswana, Burkina Faso, Burundi, Cameroon, Cape Verde, Central African Republic, Chad, Comoros, Congo (Democratic Republic of the), Côte d'Ivoire, Djibouti, Equatorial Guinea, Ethiopia, Gabon, Gambia, Ghana, Guinea, Guinea-Bissau, Kenya, Lesotho, Madagascar, Malawi, Mali, Mauritania, Mauritius, Morocco, Mozambique, Namibia, Niger, Nigeria, Rwanda, São Tomé and Príncipe, Senegal, Seychelles, Sierra Leone, South Africa, Sudan, Swaziland, Tanzania, Togo, Tunisia, Uganda, Zambia, and Zimbabwe.

# Africa: Sub-Sahara

Composed of 45 countries: Angola, Benin, Botswana, Burkina Faso, Burundi, Cameroon, Cape Verde, Central African Republic, Chad, Comoros, Congo (Democratic Republic of the), Côte d'Ivoire, Djibouti, Equatorial Guinea, Ethiopia, Gabon, Gambia, Ghana, Guinea, Guinea-Bissau, Kenya, Lesotho, Madagascar, Malawi, Mali, Mauritania, Mauritius, Mozambique, Namibia, Niger, Nigeria, Rwanda, São Tomé and Príncipe, Senegal, Seychelles, Sierra Leone, South Africa, Sudan, Swaziland, Tanzania, Togo, Uganda, Zambia, and Zimbabwe.

## Central and Eastern Europe

Composed of 14 countries: Albania, Bulgaria, Croatia, Czech Republic, Estonia, Hungary, Latvia, Lithuania, Macedonia (Former Yugoslav Republic of), Poland, Romania, Slovak Republic, and Turkey.

## Commonwealth of Independent States and Mongolia

Composed of 13 countries: Armenia, Azerbaijan, Belarus, Georgia, Kazakhstan, Kyrgyz Republic, Moldova, Mongolia, Russia, Tajikistan, Turkmenistan, Ukraine, and Uzbekistan. Note that Mongolia, which is not a member of the Commonwealth of Independent States, is included in this group for reasons of geography and similarities in economic structure.

## Developing Asia

Composed of 23 countries: Bangladesh, Bhutan, Cambodia, China, Fiji, India, Indonesia, Kiribati, Lao People's Democratic Republic, Malaysia, Maldives, Myanmar, Nepal, Pakistan, Papua New Guinea, Philippines, Samoa, Solomon Islands, Sri Lanka, Thailand, Tonga, Vanuatu, and Vietnam.

## ASEAN-5

Composed of 5 countries: Indonesia, Malaysia, Philippines, Thailand, and Vietnam.

## Middle East

Composed of 13 countries: Bahrain, Egypt, Iran (Islamic Republic of), Jordan, Kuwait, Lebanon, Libya, Oman, Qatar, Saudi Arabia, Syrian Arab Republic, United Arab Emirates, and Yemen (Republic of).

## Western Hemisphere

Composed of 32 countries: Antigua and Barbuda, Argentina, Bahamas, Barbados, Belize, Bolivia, Brazil, Chile, Colombia, Costa Rica, Dominica, Dominican Republic, Ecuador, El Salvador, Grenada, Guatemala, Guyana, Haiti, Honduras, Jamaica, Mexico, Nicaragua, Panama, Paraguay, Peru, St. Kitts and Nevis, St. Lucia, St. Vincent and the Grenadines, Suriname, Trinidad and Tobago, Uruguay, and Venezuela.

# References

Abel, Andrew B., and Ben S. Bernanke. 2001. *Macroeconomics*. 4th ed. Boston: Addison-Wesley.

Aliber, Robert Z. 1975. "Monetary Independence under Floating Exchange Rates." *Journal of Finance*, vol. 30, no. 2 (May):365–376.

Al-Mashat, Rania, and Andreas Billmeier. 2007. "The Monetary Transmission Mechanism in Egypt," IMF Working Paper WP/07/285 (December).

Almekinders, Geert, Aliona Cebotari, and Andreas Billmeier. 2007. "Arab Republic of Egypt: Selected Issues." IMF Country Report 07/381 (November).

Archer, David. 2005. "Foreign Exchange Market Intervention: Methods and Tactics." In "Foreign Exchange Market Intervention in Emerging Markets: Motives, Techniques, and Implications." *BIS Papers* 24, Bank for International Settlements (May):40–55 (www.bis.org/publ/bppdf/bispap24d.pdf).

Ariyoshi, Akira, Karl Habermeier, Bernard Laurens, Inci Ötker-Robe, Jorge Iván Canales-Kriljenko, and Andrei Kirilenko. 2000. "Capital Controls: Country Experiences with Their Use and Liberalization." IMF Occasional Paper 190 (17 May).

Asso, Pier Francesco, George A. Kahn, and Robert Leeson. 2007. "The Taylor Rule and the Transformation of Monetary Policy." Research Working Paper (RWP) 07-11, Federal Reserve Bank of Kansas City (December): http://econpapers.repec.org/paper/fipfedkrw/rwp07-11.htm.

Bank for International Settlements. 2005. "Foreign Exchange Market Intervention in Emerging Markets: Motives, Techniques, and Implications." *BIS Papers* 24 (May): www.bis.org/publ/bppdf/bispap24.htm.

———. 2007. "Triennial Central Bank Survey: Foreign Exchange and Derivatives Market Activity in 2007" (December): www.bis.org/publ/rpfxf07t.pdf.

Bank of England. 1999. "The Transmission Mechanism of Monetary Policy." The Monetary Policy Committee (May): www.bankofengland.co.uk/publications/other/monetary/montrans.pdf.

Barro, Robert J. 1974. "Are Government Bonds Net Wealth?" *Journal of Political Economy*, vol. 82, no. 6 (November/December):1095–1117.

Batini, Nicoletta, and Edward Nelson. 2001. "The Lag from Monetary Policy Actions to Inflation: Friedman Revisited." Monetary Policy Committee Unit Discussion Paper 6, Bank of England (January).

Bercuson, Kenneth B., and Linda M. Koenig. 1993. "The Recent Surge in Capital Inflows to Three ASEAN Countries: Causes and Macroeconomic Impact." South East Asian Central Banks Occasional Paper 15, Kuala Lumpur, Malaysia.

Bernanke, Ben S. 2002. "On Milton Friedman's Ninetieth Birthday." Remarks at conference to honor Milton Friedman, University of Chicago (8 November).

———. 2004. "Money, Gold, and the Great Depression." Remarks at H. Parker Willis Lecture in Economic Policy, Washington and Lee University, Lexington, VA (2 March).

———. 2005. "The Global Saving Glut and the U.S. Current Account Deficit." Remarks at Sandridge Lecture, Virginia Association of Economists, Richmond (10 March).

———. 2007a. "Federal Reserve Communications." Speech at Cato Institute 25th Annual Monetary Conference, Washington, DC (14 November): www.federalreserve.gov/newsevents/speech/bernanke20071114a.htm.

———. 2007b. "Global Imbalances: Recent Developments and Prospects." Speech at Bundesbank Lecture, Berlin (11 September): www.federalreserve.gov/newsevents/speech/bernanke20070911a.htm.

Bernanke, Ben S., and Alan S. Blinder. 1992. "The Federal Funds Rate and the Channels of Monetary Transmission." *American Economic Review*, vol. 82, no. 4 (September):901–921.

Bernanke, Ben S., Thomas Laubach, Frederic S. Mishkin, and Adam S. Posen. 1999. *Inflation Targeting: Lessons from the International Experience*. Princeton, NJ: Princeton University Press.

Blinder, Alan S., Michael Ehrmann, Marcel Fratzscher, Jakob De Haan, and David-Jan Jansen. 2008. "Central Bank Communication and Monetary Policy: A Survey of Theory and Evidence." NBER Working Paper 13932 (April).

Board of Governors of the Federal Reserve System. 2005. *The Federal Reserve System: Purposes and Functions*. 9th ed. Washington, DC (www.federalreserve.gov/pf/pdf/pf_complete.pdf).

Bordo, Michael David. 1981. "The Classical Gold Standard: Some Lessons for Today." Federal Reserve Bank of St. Louis. *Review* (May):2–17.

———. 1993. ""The Gold Standard, Bretton Woods, and Other Monetary Regimes: A Historical Appraisal." Federal Reserve Bank of St. Louis." *Review*, vol. 75, no. 2 (March/April):123–191.

Bordo, Michael, and Harold James. 2006. "One World Money, Then and Now." In "What about a World Currency?" Bank of Greece Working Paper 44 (June): www.bankofgreece.gr/publications/pdf/Paper200644.pdf.

Bordo, Michael. D., and Anna J. Schwartz. 1997. "Monetary Policy Regimes and Economic Performance: The Historical Record." NBER Working Paper 6201 (September).

Bubula, A., and I. Ötker-Robe. 2002. "The Evolution of Exchange Rate Regimes since 1990: Evidence from De Facto Policies." IMF Working Paper 02/155 (September).

Cagan, Phillip. 1956. "The Monetary Dynamics of Hyperinflation." In *Studies in the Quantity Theory of Money*. Edited by Milton Friedman. Chicago: University of Chicago Press.

Callen, Tim. 2007. "PPP versus the Market: Which Weight Matters?" *Finance & Development*, vol. 44, no. 1 (March):1–2.

Calvo, Guillermo A. 1991. "The Perils of Sterilization." *IMF Staff Papers*, vol. 38, no. 4 (December).

———. 1998. "Capital Flows and Capital-Market Crises: The Simple Economics of Sudden Stops." *Journal of Applied Econometrics*, vol. 1, no. 1 (November):35–54.

———. 2003. "Explaining Sudden Stop, Growth Collapse, and BOP Crisis: The Case of Distortionary Output Taxes." *IMF Staff Papers*, vol. 50 (Special Issue):1–20.

Calvo, Guillermo A., and Frederic S. Mishkin. 2003. "The Mirage of Exchange Rate Regimes for Emerging Market Countries." *Journal of Economic Perspectives*, vol. 17, no. 4 (Fall):99–118.

Calvo, Guillermo A., and Carmen M. Reinhart. 2000. "Fear of Floating." NBER Working Paper 7993 (November).

Calvo, Guillermo, and Ernesto Talvi. 2006. "The Resolution of Global Imbalances: Soft Landing in the North, Sudden Stop in Emerging Markets?" *Journal of Policy Modeling*, vol. 28, no. 6 (September):605–613.

Calvo, Guillermo A., Alejandro Izquierdo, and Ernesto Talvi. 2003. "Sudden Stops, the Real Exchange Rate, and Fiscal Sustainability: Argentina's Lessons." NBER Working Paper 9828 (July).

Calvo, Guillermo A., Leonardo Leiderman, and Carmen M. Reinhart. 1993. "Capital Inflows and Real Exchange Rate Appreciation in Latin America: The Role of External Factors." *IMF Staff Papers*, vol. 40, no. 1 (March):108–151.

———. 1994. "The Capital Inflows Problem: Concepts and Issues." *Contemporary Economic Policy*, vol. 12, no. 3 (July):54–66.

———. 1996. "Inflows of Capital to Developing Countries in the 1990s." *Journal of Economic Perspectives*, vol. 10, no. 2 (Spring):123–139.

Canales-Kriljenko, Jorge Iván. 2006. "Survey of Foreign Exchange Intervention in Developing Countries." In *Official Foreign Exchange Intervention: Occasional Paper 249*. Edited by Shogo Ishii, Jorge Iván Canales-Kriljenko, Roberto Guimarães, and Cem Karacadag. Washington, DC: International Monetary Fund.

Catão, Luis. 2006. "Sudden Stops and Currency Drops: A Historical Look." IMF Working Paper 06/133 (May).

Congressional Budget Office. 2004. "The Decline in the U.S. Current-Account Balance since 1991." Economic and Budget Issue Brief (6 August): http://cbo.gov/ftpdocs/57xx/doc5722/08-06-CurrentAccounts.pdf.

Cooper, Richard N. 1999. "Should Capital Controls Be Banished?" *Brookings Papers on Economic Activity*, vol. 30, no. 1:89–142.

———. 2005. "Living with Global Imbalances: A Contrarian View." Policy Briefs in International Economics PB05-3, Institute for International Economics, Washington, DC (November).

———. 2006. "Proposal for a Common Currency among Rich Democracies." In "What about a World Currency?" Bank of Greece Working Paper 44 (June).

Corden, W.M., and J.P. Neary. 1982. "Booming Sector and De-Industrialisation in a Small Open Economy." *Economic Journal*, vol. 92, no. December:825–848.

Debelle, Guy, Jacob Gyntelberg, and Michael Plumb. 2006. "Forward Currency Markets in Asia: Lessons from the Australian Experience." *BIS Quarterly Review* (September):53–64.

DeRosa, David F. 1978. "Rates of Return on Common Stocks and Inflation: Theories and Tests." Unpublished doctoral dissertation, University of Chicago Graduate School of Business.

———. 1996. *Managing Foreign Exchange Risk: Advanced Strategies for Global Investors, Corporations, and Financial Institutions*. Revised edition. Chicago: Irwin.

————. 2000. *Options on Foreign Exchange.* 2nd ed. New York: John Wiley & Sons, Inc.

————. 2001a. *In Defense of Free Capital Markets: The Case against a New International Financial Architecture.* Princeton, NJ: Bloomberg Press.

————. 2001b. "Memo to Argentina: Dollarize or Die." *Newsweek* (17 December).

————. 2005. "China's Defense of the Peg Perpetuates Central Planning." *Cato Journal*, vol. 25, no. 1 (Winter):49–54.

Dominguez, Kathryn Mary, and Jeffrey A. Frankel. 1993. *Does Foreign Exchange Intervention Work?* Washington, DC: Institute for International Economics.

Dornbusch, Rudiger, Stanley Fischer, and Richard Startz. 1997. *Macroeconomics.* 7th ed. Boston: McGraw-Hill.

Dornbusch, Rudiger, Ilan Goldfajn, and Rodrigo O. Valdés. 1995. "Currency Crises and Collapses." *Brookings Papers on Economic Activity*, vol. 26, no. 2:219–294.

Easterly, William. 2001. *The Elusive Quest for Growth: Economists' Adventures and Misadventures in the Tropics.* Cambridge: MIT Press.

Edwards, Sebastian. 1999. "How Effective Are Capital Controls?" *Journal of Economic Perspectives*, vol. 13, no. 4 (Fall):65–84.

————. 2004. "Thirty Years of Current Account Imbalances, Current Account Reversals, and Sudden Stops." NBER Working Paper 10276 (February).

————. 2005. "The End of Large Current Account Deficits, 1970–2002: Are There Lessons for the United States?" NBER Working Paper 11669 (October).

Eichengreen, Barry, and David Leblang. 2003. "Exchange Rates and Cohesion: Historical Perspectives and Political-Economy Considerations." *Journal of Common Market Studies*, vol. 41, no. 5 (December):797–822.

Eliot, T.S. 1925. "The Hollow Men." In T.S. Eliot's *Poems: 1909–1925.*

Federal Reserve Bank of New York. 2007. "Fedpoint: U.S. Foreign Exchange Intervention" (May).

Ferguson, Roger W. 2005. "U.S. Current Account Deficit: Causes and Consequences." Remarks at Economics Club of the University of North Carolina at Chapel Hill (20 April). *BIS Review* 27/2005 (www.bis.org/review/r050422b.pdf).

Fischer, Stanley. 2001. "Exchange Rate Regimes: Is the Bipolar View Correct?" *Journal of Economic Perspectives*, vol. 15, no. 2 (Spring):3–24.

————. 2006. "Summing Up." Presentation given at International Monetary Fund Conference on Global Imbalances, Washington, DC (21 April).

————. 2007. "Exchange Rate Systems, Surveillance, and Advice." Delivered as the Mundell-Fleming Lecture at the Eighth Annual Jacques Polak Research Conference at the International Monetary Fund (15 November).

Fischer, Stanley, Ratna Sahay, and Carlos A. Végh. 2002. "Modern Hyper- and High Inflations." *Journal of Economic Literature*, vol. 40, no. 3 (September):837–880.

Fisher, Irving. 2006. *The Purchasing Power of Money: Its Determination and Relation to Credit Interest and Crises*. New York: Cosimo. Originally published by the Macmillan Company in 1912.

Fleming, J. Marcus. 1961. "Internal Financial Policies under Fixed and Floating Exchange Rates," Departmental Memorandum 61/28 (November 8), IMF Central Files (S 430, "Exchange Rates 1950").

————. 1962. "Domestic Financial Policies under Fixed and under Floating Exchange Rates," *IMF Staff Papers*, vol. 9 (November):369–379.

————. 1978. *Essays on Economic Policy*. New York: Columbia University Press.

Folkerts-Landau, David, Garry Schinasi, Marcel Cassard, Victor Ng, Carmen Reinhart, and Michael Spencer. 1995. "Effect of Capital Flows on the Domestic Financial Sectors in APEC Developing Countries." In *Capital Flows in the APEC Region*. Edited by Mohsin S. Khan and Carmen Reinhart. Washington, DC: International Monetary Fund.

Forbes, Kristen J. 2005. "Capital Controls: Mud in the Wheels of Market Efficiency." *Cato Journal*, vol. 25, no. 1 (Winter):153–166.

————. 2007. "One Cost of the Chilean Capital Controls: Increased Financial Constraints for Smaller Traded Firms." *Journal of International Economics*, vol. 71, no. 2 (April):294–323.

Fraga, Arminio. 2000. "Monetary Policy during the Transition to a Floating Exchange Rate: Brazil's Recent Experience." *Finance & Development*, vol. 37, no. 1 (March).

Frankel, Jeffrey A. 1999. "No Single Currency Regime Is Right for All Countries or at All Times." NBER Working Paper 7338 (September).

Frankel, Jeffrey. 2007. "Exchange Rate Regimes: Current Issues in Research and Policy." IMF Institute (25 May): http://ksghome.harvard.edu/~jfrankel/ExRRegimes-IMF_Inst.pdf.

‎‎

‎‎‎Frankel, J.A., and E.A. Cavallo. 2004. "Does Openness to Trade Make Countries More Vulnerable to Sudden Stops, or Less? Using Gravity to Establish Causality." NBER Working Paper 10957 (December).

Friedman, Milton. 1956. "The Quantity Theory of Money—A Restatement." In *Studies in the Quantity Theory of Money*. Edited by Milton Friedman. Chicago: University of Chicago Press.

———. 1961. "The Lag in Effect of Monetary Policy." *Journal of Political Economy*, vol. 69, no. 5 (October):447–466.

———. 1968a. "Inflation: Causes and Consequences." In *Dollars and Deficits: Living with America's Economic Problems*. Englewood Cliffs, NJ: Prentice Hall.

———. 1968b. "The Role of Monetary Policy." *American Economic Review*, vol. 58, no. 1 (March):1–17.

———. 1972. "Have Monetary Policies Failed?" *American Economic Review*, vol. 62, no. 2 (May):11–18.

———. 1992. *Money Mischief: Episodes in Monetary History*. New York: Harcourt Brace & Company.

Friedman, Milton, and Anna J. Schwartz. 1963. *A Monetary History of the United States, 1867–1960*. Princeton, NJ: Princeton University Press.

Garber, Peter M. 1998. "Buttressing Capital Account Liberalization with Prudential Regulation and Foreign Entry." Essays in International Finance 207, Princeton University.

Geithner, Timothy F. 2006. "Policy Implications of Global Imbalances." Remarks at Global Financial Imbalances Conference at Chatham House, London (23 January): www.newyorkfed.org/newsevents/speeches/2006/gei060123.html.

Ghosh, Atish, Anne-Marie Gulde, Jonathan Ostry, and Holger Wolf. 1997. "Does the Nominal Exchange Rate Regime Matter?" NBER Working Paper 5874 (January).

Gourinchas, Pierre-Olivier, and Hélène Rey. 2005. "From World Banker to World Venture Capitalist: U.S. External Adjustment and the Exorbitant Privilege." CEPR Discussion Paper 5220 (September).

Green, Stephen, and Jason Chang. 2006. "On the Ground, Asia. Sterilization: The PBoC Finally Gets Serious." Standard Chartered (11 July).

Greenspan, Alan. 1999. Testimony before the Joint Hearing of the Subcommittee on Economic Policy and the Subcommittee on International Trade and Finance of the Senate Banking, Housing, and Urban Affairs Committee. Washington, DC (22 April).

———. 2003. "Remarks." Remarks at 21st Annual Monetary Conference, co-sponsored by the Cato Institute and the *Economist*, Washington, DC (20 November).

Greenwood, John. 2008. "The Costs and Implications of PBC Sterilization." *Cato Journal*, vol. 28, no. 2 (Spring/Summer):205–217.

Gruber, Joseph W., and Steven B. Kamin. 2006. "Explaining the Global Pattern of Current Account Imbalances." Washington, DC: Federal Reserve Board (June): www.ecb.int/events/pdf/conferences/fgi/GruberKamin.pdf.

Hakkio, Craig S. 1995. "The U.S. Current Account: The Other Deficit." Federal Reserve Bank of Kansas City *Economic Review*, vol. 3rd quarter:11–24.

Hanke, Steve H. 1998. "How I Spent My Spring Vacation." *The International Economy*, vol. 12, no. 4 (July/August).

———. 2000. "Reform of the International Monetary Fund." Testimony before the Subcommittee on International Trade and Finance of the Senate Banking, Housing, and Urban Affairs Committee. Washington, DC (27 April).

Hanke, Steve. 2002. "Currency Boards." *The Annals of the American Academy of Political and Social Science*, no. 579 (January–February):87–105.

———. 2003. "Argentine Straw Man: A Response to Currency Board Critics." *Cato Journal*, vol. 23, no. 1 (Spring/Summer):47–57.

———. 2005a. "Bulgaria's 'Currency Board'." In *Emerging Bulgaria 2005*. London: Oxford Business Group.

———. 2005b. "Dollarization and Currency Boards: Error and Deception." In *The Capitalist Perspective*. South Hamilton, MA: H.C. Wainwright & Co. Economics (22 December).

———. 2008. "Why Argentina Did Not Have a Currency Board." *Central Banking Journal*, vol. 18, no. 3 (February):56–58.

Harberger, Arnold C. 2008. "Lessons from Monetary and Real Exchange Rate Economics." *Cato Journal*, vol. 28, no. 2 (Spring/Summer):225–235 (www.cato.org/pubs/journal/cj28n2/cj28n2-6.pdf).

Herault, Alejandro Reveiz. 2002. "Evolution of the Colombian Peso within the Currency Bands, Nonlinearity Analysis and Stochastic Modeling." *Revista de Economia del Rosario*, vol. 5, no. 1 (June).

Houthakker, H.S., and Stephen P. Magee. 1969. "Income and Price Elasticities in World Trade." *Review of Economics and Statistics*, vol. 51, no. 2 (May):111–125.

Hume, David. 1752. "Of Money." Reprinted in *Cambridge Texts in the History of Political Thought*. Edited by Knud Haakonssen. Cambridge University Press, 1994.

International Monetary Fund. 1997. "Annex VI: Capital Flows to Emerging Markets—A Historical Perspective." In "International Capital Markets: Developments, Prospects, and Key Policy Issues" (November):234–251 (www.imf.org/external/pubs/ft/icm/97icm/icmcon.htm).

———. 2005. *World Economic Outlook* (September).

———. 2006a. *Annual Report on Exchange Arrangements and Exchange Restrictions.* Washington, DC.

———. 2006b. "People's Republic of China: 2006 Article IV Consultation—Staff Report; Staff Statement; and Public Information Notice on the Executive Board Discussion." IMF Country Report 06/394 (October).

———. 2007. *World Economic Outlook* (October).

Ishii, Shogo. 2006. "Introduction." In *Official Foreign Exchange Intervention*. Occasional Paper 249. Edited by Shogo Ishii, Jorge Iván Canales-Kriljenko, Roberto Guimarães, and Cem Karacadag. Washington, DC: International Monetary Fund.

Johnson, Simon, and Todd Mitton. 2003. "Cronyism and Capital Controls: Evidence from Malaysia." *Journal of Financial Economics*, vol. 67, no. 2 (February):351–382.

Johnson, Simon, Kalpana Kochhar, Todd Mitton, and Natalia Tamirisa. 2006. "Malaysian Capital Controls: Macroeconomics and Institutions." IMF Working Paper 06/51 (February).

Kamin, Steven, Philip Turner, and Jozef Van 't dack. 1998. "The Transmission Mechanism of Monetary Policy in Emerging Market Economies: An Overview." Overview paper for BIS Policy Paper No. 3. Bank for International Settlements, Basle, Switzerland (January).

Keynes, John Maynard. 1924. *A Tract on Monetary Reform*. New York: Harcourt, Brace & Co.

Kindleberger, Charles P. 1996. *Manias, Panics, and Crashes: A History of Financial Crises.* 3rd ed. New York: John Wiley & Sons.

Kroszner, Randall S. 2007. "International Capital Flows and the Emerging Market Economies." Speech given at Banco Central de la Republica Argentina (BCRA) seminar, Central Bank of Argentina, Buenos Aires, Argentina (15 May).

Krugman, Paul. 1998. "Saving Asia: It's Time to Get Radical." *Fortune* (7 September): www.geocities.com/Eureka/Concourse/8751/ft0901z.htm.

———. 2005. "The Chinese Connection." *New York Times* (20 May): www.nytimes.com/2005/05/20/opinion/20krugman.html.

Krugman, Paul R., and Maurice Obstfeld. 1997. *International Economics: Theory and Policy.* 4th ed. Boston: Addison-Wesley.

Laurens, Bernard J., and Rodolfo Maino. 2007. "China: Strengthening Monetary Policy Implementation." IMF Working Paper 07/14 (January).

Lee, Jang-Yung. 1996. "Implications of a Surge in Capital Inflows: Available Tools and Consequences for the Conduct of Monetary Policy." IMF Working Paper 96/53.

———. 1997. *Sterilizing Capital Inflows.* Washington, DC: International Monetary Fund.

Lipscomb, Laura. 2005. "An Overview of Non-Deliverable Foreign Exchange Forward Markets." Federal Reserve Bank of New York (May): www.bis.org/publ/cgfs22fedny5.pdf.

Lucas, Robert E., Jr. 1976. "Econometric Policy Evaluation: A Critique." *Carnegie-Rochester Conference Series on Public Policy*, no. 1:19–46.

———. 1990. "Why Doesn't Capital Flow from Rich to Poor Countries?" *American Economic Review*, vol. 80, no. 2 (May):92–96.

———. 1996. "Nobel Lecture: Monetary Neutrality." *Journal of Political Economy*, vol. 104, no. 4 (August):661–682.

Ma, Guonan, Corinne Ho, and Robert N. McCauley. 2004. "Characteristics of Asian NDFs." In "The Markets for Non-Deliverable Forwards in Asian Currencies." *BIS Quarterly Review* (June):81–94.

Maino, Rodolfo, and Inese Buzeneca. 2007. "Monetary Policy Implementation: Results from a Survey." IMF Working Paper 07/7 (January).

McCandless, George T., Jr., and Warren E. Weber. 1995. "Some Monetary Facts." *Federal Reserve Bank of Minneapolis Quarterly Review*, vol. 19, no. 3 (Summer):2–11.

Milesi-Ferretti, G.M., and A. Razin. 1998a. "Current Account Reversals and Currency Crises: Empirical Regularities." *European Economic Review*, vol. 42 (April):897–908.

Milesi-Ferretti, Gian Maria, and Assaf Razin. 1998b. "Sharp Reductions in Current Account Deficits: An Empirical Analysis." *European Economic Review*, vol. 42, no. 3–5 (May):897–908.

Mill, John Stuart. 2004. *Principles of Political Economy*. Amherst, NY: Prometheus Books. Originally published in 1848; seventh edition published in 1871.

Mishkin, Frederic S. 1996. "The Channels of Monetary Transmission: Lessons for Monetary Policy." *Banque de France Bulletin Digest*, vol. 27 (March):33–44.

———. 2000a. "Inflation Targeting in Emerging Market Countries." *American Economic Review*, vol. 90, no. 2 (May):105–109.

———. 2000b. "Issues in Inflation Targeting." Proceedings of "Price Stability and the Long-Run Target for Monetary Policy" seminar, Bank of Canada (June):203–222 (www.bank-banque-canada.ca/en/res/wp/2000/mishkin.pdf).

———. 2004. "Can Inflation Targeting Work in Emerging Market Countries?" Paper presented at conference in honor of Guillermo Calvo, International Monetary Fund, Washington, DC (15–16 April).

Modigliani, F., and M. Miller. 1958. "The Cost of Capital, Corporation Finance and the Theory of Investment." *American Economic Review*, vol. 48 (June):261–297.

Mundell, Robert A. 1961. "A Theory of Optimum Currency Areas." *American Economic Review*, vol. 51, no. 4 (September):657–665.

———. 1963. "Capital Mobility and Stabilization Policy under Fixed and Flexible Exchange Rates." *Canadian Journal of Economics and Political Science*, vol. 29, no. 4 (November):475–485.

Mussa, Michael L. 1981. "The Role of Official Intervention." Group of Thirty Occasional Paper 6 (January).

Mussa, Michael. 2004. "Exchange Rate Adjustments Needed to Reduce Global Payments Imbalances." In *Dollar Adjustment: How Far? Against What?* Edited by C. Fred Bergsten and John Williamson. Washington, DC: Institute for International Economics.

Nadal-De Simone, Francisco, and Piritta Sorsa. 1999. "A Review of Capital Account Restrictions in Chile in the 1990s." IMF Working Paper 99/52 (April).

Obstfeld, Maurice. 1982. "Can We Sterilize? Theory and Evidence." *American Economic Review*, vol. 72, no. 2, Papers and Proceedings of the 94th Annual Meeting of the American Economic Association (May):45–50.

Obstfeld, Maurice, and Kenneth Rogoff. 2005. "The Unsustainable U.S. Current Account Position Revisited." Center for International and Development Economics Research Paper C05-145, University of California, Berkeley (30 November): http://repositories.cdlib.org/iber/cider/C05-145.

Obstfeld, Maurice, and Alan M. Taylor. 2002. "Globalization and Capital Markets." NBER Working Paper 8846 (March).

Pazos, Felipe. 1972. *Chronic Inflation in Latin America*. New York: Praeger Publishers.

Pick, Franz. 1981. *Pick's Currency Yearbook 1977–1979*. New York: Pick Publishing Corporation.

Prasad, Eswar, Raghuram Rajan, and Arvind Subramanian. 2007a. "Foreign Capital and Economic Growth." IMF Research Department (April): www.iie.com/publications/papers/subramanian0407.pdf.

———. 2007b. "The Paradox of Capital." *Finance & Development*, vol. 44, no. 1 (March): www.imf.org/external/pubs/ft/fandd/2007/03/prasad.htm.

Prati, Alessandro, Ratna Sahay, and Thierry Tressel. 2003. "Is There a Case for Sterilizing Foreign Aid Inflows?" Paper presented at "Macroeconomic Challenges in Low Income Countries" IMF Research Workshop (14 July): www.imf.org/external/np/res/seminars/2003/lic/pdf/tt.pdf.

Reinhart, Carmen M., and Vincent Raymond Reinhart. 1998. "Some Lessons for Policy Makers Dealing with the Mixed Blessing of Capital Inflows." In *Capital Flows and Financial Crises*. Edited by M. Kahler. New York: Council on Foreign Relations.

Reinhart, Carmen M., and Kenneth S. Rogoff. 2003a. "The Modern History of Exchange Rate Arrangements: A Reinterpretation," International Monetary Fund (March).

———. 2003b. "Part I: The Country Chronologies and Chartbook Background Material to a Modern History of Exchange Rate Arrangements," International Monetary Fund.

Rigobon, Roberto. 2002. *International Financial Contagion: Theory and Evidence in Evolution*. Charlottesville, VA: CFA Institute (www.cfapubs.org/doi/pdf/10.2470/rf.v2002.n2.3918).

Rogoff, Kenneth, Aasim Husain, Ashoka Mody, Robin Brooks, and Nienke Oomes. 2003. "Evolution and Performance of Exchange Rate Regimes." IMF Working Paper 03/243.

Schuler, Kurt. 1996. *Should Developing Countries Have Central Banks? Currency Quality and Monetary Systems in 155 Countries*. London: Institute of Economic Affairs.

Schwartz, Anna. 1993. "Currency Boards: Their Past, Present, and Possible Future Role." *Carnegie-Rochester Conference Series on Public Policy*, vol. 39, no. 1:147–187.

Schwartz, Anna J. 1998. "International Financial Crises: Myths and Realities." *Cato Journal*, vol. 17, no. 3 (Winter):251–256.

Simons, Henry. 1948. *Economic Policy for a Free Society*. Chicago: University of Chicago Press.

Soros, George. 1998. *The Crisis of Global Capitalism: Open Society Endangered*. New York: Little, Brown, and Company.

Spiegel, Mark M. 1995. "Sterilization of Capital Inflows through the Banking Sector: Evidence from Asia." Federal Reserve Bank of San Francisco, *Economic Review*:17–34.

Stein, Herbert. 2008. "Balance of Payments." In the *Concise Encyclopedia of Economics*. 2nd ed. Edited by David R. Henderson. Library of Economics and Liberty (www.econlib.org/library/Enc/BalanceofPayments.html).

Summers, Lawrence. 1999. "Official Dollarization in Emerging-Market Countries." Testimony before the Joint Hearing of the Subcommittee on Economic Policy and the Subcommittee on International Trade and Finance of the Senate Banking, Housing, and Urban Affairs Committee. Washington, DC (22 April): http://banking.senate.gov/99_04hrg/042299/summers.htm.

Takagi, Shinji, and Taro Esaka. 1999. "Sterilization and the Capital Inflow Problem in East Asia, 1987–97." Economic Research Institute, Economic Planning Agency, Tokyo (August): www.esri.go.jp/jp/archive/dis/dis090/dis086a.pdf.

Talvi, Ernesto. 2006. "On Sudden Stops and Output Collapses." Presentation at International Congress: "Global Imbalances and Risk Management—Has the Center Become the Periphery?" Madrid, Spain (16 May): www.iadb.org/res/files/Imbalances/pp/TALVI-ERNESTO-PPT.pdf.

Taylor, John B. 1992. "Discretion versus Policy Rules in Practice." *Carnegie-Rochester Conference Series on Public Policy*, vol. 39 (Fall): 195-214.

————. 2000. "Using Monetary Policy Rules in Emerging Market Economies." Working paper, Stanford University (December).

Tobin, James. 1978. "A Proposal for Monetary Reform." *Eastern Economic Journal*, vol. 4, no. 3–4 (July/October):153–159.

Villanueva, Delano, and Lim Choon Seng. 1999. "Managing Capital Flows in SEACEN Countries: A Policy Agenda." Southeast Asian Central Banks Research and Training Centre (February).